U.S.S.R.
IN CRISIS

**The Failure of an
Economic System**

BY MARSHALL I. GOLDMAN

U.S.S.R. IN CRISIS

The Failure of an Economic System

MARSHALL I. GOLDMAN

W.W. NORTON & COMPANY

New York · London

The text of this book is composed in 10/12 Times Roman with display type set in Trump.
Composition and manufacturing by The Maple-Vail Book Manufacturing Group. Book
design by Nancy Dale Muldoon.

First Edition

Library of Congress Cataloging in Publication Data

Goldman, Marshall I.
    USSR in crisis.

    Includes index.
1. Soviet Union—Economic conditions—1976–
I. Title.   II. Title: U.S.S.R. in crisis.
HC336.25.G637   1983   330.947′0853   82–14278

ISBN 0-393-01715-X
ISBN 0-393-95336-X   {PBK.}

W. W. Norton & Company, Inc., 500 Fifth Avenue, New York, N.Y. 10110
W. W. Norton & Company Ltd., 37 Great Russell Street, London WC1B 3NU

2 3 4 5 6 7 8 9 0

To the U.S.S.R.
for making an economist's life so interesting.

Contents

List of Tables

Preface

After several decades of impressive economic growth and expanding political power, the Soviet Union faces a critical turning point. What seemed to work so well initially now seems to work poorly. Economic growth is negligible, if not negative. Citizens living within the Soviet bloc have grown increasingly restless, both in the Soviet Union and Eastern Europe. Soviet political institutions seem frozen, unyielding, and unresponsive to the needs of the society. Leonid Brezhnev has bequeathed an unenviable legacy to Yuri Andropov.

American observers of the Soviet Union have noted these difficulties for some time. How much longer can the Soviet Union pursue its ways without some radical surgery, particularly since the Soviet Union now seems to be moving further and further from the course taken by most of the other countries of the industrialized world? Thus the pressure on Soviet planners increases to alter the existing situation.

Strangely enough, the stimulus for this study of the problems confronting the Soviet Union arose from a meeting with some Chinese social scientists. While visiting the People's Republic of China in January, 1980, I was asked to deliver a series of lectures about how the Soviet Union was likely to develop in the next decade or so. The Chinese said they were anxious to know what might happen to the Soviet Union if it failed to break out of its Stalinist model of economic and political development and held to its existing course. It turned out, however, that what really interested the Chinese was not what was going to happen to the Soviet Union, but what would happen to China if it failed to alter its course and reform its economy. Taking their lead from the Soviet Union, the Chinese had adopted the Stalinist model soon after their revolution. Although they tried to reshape their economy in 1957, the basic features of the Chinese economy remained as before. In the late 1970's, the Chinese decided to try again. After thirty years of experimentation, the Chinese had concluded that the Stalinist model had lost whatever usefulness it might once have had. The hidden message was clearly that if the Chinese themselves did not undertake some substantial reforms, they too would end up like the Soviet Union.

This exercise led me to speculate about why the Chinese seemed to be having so much trouble finding a new course for themselves.[1] In turn, it also led me to realize that if the Chinese were having such difficulties breaking away from a system that was only thirty years old, it would probably be even more difficult for the Soviet Union to alter its ways after as much as sixty-five years of the same model. Yet given the increasing number of economic problems the Soviet Union was encountering, the pressure to find a new economic model was clearly growing daily. But so far Soviet leaders have not been able to find any easy solutions. Will Andropov be any more successful?

A few years ago, Soviet prospects looked far more promising to me. When American Sovietologists painted a picture of the Soviet Union showing it on the verge of doom, if not collapse, I invariably responded that they were viewing something radically different from what I knew. Now I am not so sure. Conditions in the Soviet Union have deteriorated significantly, and it will take some skill and wise leadership to find a safe course. In the pages ahead, we will examine how the Soviets worked their way into their present predicament, why the Stalinist model did make sense initially, why it became inappropriate, why it has become difficult to switch to a new model, and what the chances are that the Soviets can find a new way.

As always, there are many who should be thanked for their help in making this study possible. Since some of the analysis explores the political dimension, a new area for me, I have to acknowledge my appreciation for the insights of many of my colleagues at the Russian Research Center. I should also express my thanks to my Wellesley colleagues and students for their forbearance while I was so distracted by what has been happening in the U.S.S.R. and Eastern Europe. As usual, I must thank my wife who agonized over this manuscript probably more than over anything else I have written. Finally I want to thank Seth and Karla Goldman for their proofreading and Ellen Lapenson and Rose DiBenedetto for their typing.   December 1, 1982

[1] Marshall I. Goldman, "China Rethinks the Soviet Model," *International Security,* Fall, 1980, p. 49.

U.S.S.R. IN CRISIS

**The Failure of an
Economic System**

1. The Stalinist Model

The Soviet Union is facing a very serious crisis. This crisis is the result of the Soviet Union's failure to adapt its economic planning model to meet the country's radically changed economic needs. Until the 1960's, the Soviet economy grew rapidly, and some feared that the Soviet Union would overcome and surpass American economic production by 1980. Such fears were groundless. While the Soviet model performed well in the early years of the country's industrialization, it has proven to be unresponsive, if not inappropriate, to the needs of a more mature economy, and, in recent years, it has failed badly. This failure was all but inevitable, given the type of economic model that was chosen.

Soon after he took over from Lenin, Stalin decided to embark on a program of rapid industrialization. In selecting a development strategy, he faced several constraints. For ideological reasons, he decided to do away with the profit and the market system. He also reasoned that growth would come faster if he could dispense with the waste and frivolity that seemed to be an indispensable part of the market and private-enterprise system. Therefore he decided on a new approach. Rather than take the time that would be necessary first to build up light industry in order to stimulate heavy industry, Stalin concluded that if he first concentrated on heavy industry, in the long run he would be able to build up a much larger productive capacity. He could then take that heavy industry and convert it to the production of consumer goods at what he assumed would be a record rate. This, in turn, would bring unprecedented prosperity for the workers and peasants.

It was with such ends in mind, that Stalin sought to build up the country's heavy industry as quickly as possible. To do that, he increased capital investment to 30 per cent of the gross national product (GNP), and instituted central planning. But to obtain the capital he needed for the heavy industrial sector, he had to cut back sharply on the resources which had traditionally gone to agriculture, light industry, and the consumer. This type of economic approach has come to be called the Stalinist model.[1]

To its credit, the Stalinist model did what it was initially expected to do. It helped bring about the industrialization of a backward country in what was then record time. Soon, however, it became clear that the Stalinist model had limited usefulness. Yet the model began to take on a life of its own. It developed a momentum that seems to have prevented the system from evolving into an economy that is more responsive to popular wants and sophisticated industrial needs. This system keeps producing steel and basic machine tools, when what is wanted is food, consumer goods, and more modern technology. After a period of remarkable growth, there followed an era of stagnation, inflexibility, and even decline.

The inappropriateness of the Stalinist model is most dramatically illustrated by what has happened to Soviet agriculture. A country that once was the world's largest grain exporter has, under the Stalinist model, become the world's largest grain importer. Similarly, despite vast grazing lands, the Soviet Union has also found it necessary to become one of the world's largest meat importers. The failure of the Soviet agricultural system is not due simply to bad weather. While good weather would help, a change in the weather would not eliminate the Soviet practice of leaving up to 25 per cent of some crops in the field to rot. This enormous waste is a result of a perverted incentive system, as well as an immense (as much as 27 per cent of total Soviet investment goes to agriculture) but misguided Soviet investment policy that goes into the wrong kinds of facilities.

While not as dramatic, the situation in industry reflects the same kind of mismanagement and distortion. True to the Stalinist model, the Soviet Union focused disproportionate emphasis on heavy industrial sectors such as steel and machine tools. Thus the Soviets lead the world in steel production but they are far behind in the production of high-technology products like computers. As Khrushchev used to say, the planners are "steel-eaters" and no one in the civilian sector seems to know where the steel goes. While this policy may have worked well at an earlier stage of Soviet development, it now has become counterproductive. The continued emphasis on heavy industry and central planning has resulted in the neglect of consumer goods and this, in turn, has come to generate more and more skepticism and cynicism among Soviet consumers. Because there is relatively little to buy, the consumer ends up with very large savings and very little respect for money. Thus money is not much of an inducement to work. Not surprisingly, therefore, the shortcomings in consumer-goods production, magnified by serious food shortages, have had a serious effect on workers' incentives and, more important, worker discipline. Beginning in 1980, a series of strikes, demonstrations, and riots has taken place. There have even been some bombings. Some workers have created unofficial unions. While some of these demonstrations stem from nationality and racial conflict, most reflect deteriorating consumer supply conditions. Almost sixty-five years after the Revolution, the Soviet Union has found it necessary to reintroduce food rationing in many large cities. And steel production, the system's proudest achievement, has not been immune to these problems; in 1981, steel production actually fell below the level reached in 1978. Other industries have fared similarly. These problems are compounded by the fact that an earlier drop in population growth now means that there will be fewer workers entering the labor force in the years ahead. In addition, the capital stock of the country has aged significantly and Soviet planners indicate that additions to that capital will come more slowly than was the case previously.

The outlook would not be quite so bleak if there were much hope for reform and improvement. Unfortunately, neither economic nor political reform is likely. The worry is that any reform, even a modest one, could set off a torrent of expectations that could lead to uncontrollable pressures. Moreover, economic reform will necessitate a change in priorities, which in turn will require the abandonment of steel mills and other huge industrial enterprises for a crash program to build up consumer-goods industries. This will mean unemployment, inflation, and economic disruption—the evils heretofore associated with capitalism, not communism. Political reform would set in motion similar traumas. Given the power to change or even influence governments, no populace would tolerate such sacrifice for long. The fear of political reform is reflected by how little the political system has changed in the last decade. But the longer economic and political change is postponed, the more violent it is likely to be when it eventually comes.

On top of all the domestic problems, the Soviets are also discovering that an empire can be costly. This is reflected not only by their military expenditures, but by the $20 billion or so they have had to spend each year in Cuba, Cambodia, Vietnam, Afghanistan, and now Eastern Europe.

The extent of Soviet problems poses some daunting challenges for Soviet leaders. Recessions are only supposed to occur in the capitalist world. The Soviet people have tolerated the lack of political freedom, seemingly with the tacit understanding that economic conditions would continually improve, even if at a slow rate. Now this implicit social contract seems to be falling apart. Under the circumstances, Soviet leaders, present and future, will find themselves faced with considerable pressure to improve the economy. What options are open to them? In what follows we will seek to understand what has brought about the present deterioration so that we may be in a better position to anticipate what may happen in the years ahead.

Making predictions may be bold, but it is also foolhardy. Those who have forecast energy supply and demand trends or even the course of political events in the United States now know how risky such an undertaking can be. If it is difficult to make predictions about economics and politics in the West, it is even more dangerous to make predictions about the U.S.S.R. Just to decipher what has already or is now happening in the Soviet Union is enough of a challenge.

Even the best informed may be unable to anticipate key trends. In response to criticism that he failed to predict Khrushchev's overthrow in 1964, Adam Ulam, the director of the Russian Research Center at Harvard, defended himself by retorting that Khrushchev was similarly unperceptive. Certainly, Khrushchev was not the only one guilty of faulty foresight. Zbigniew Brzezinski, one of the most prominent observers of the Soviet system, published his doctoral dissertation, *The Permanent Purge,* just as the systematic purging process in the U.S.S.R. came to an end.[2] Similarly, since 1975, Soviet economic planners have been promising the imminent publication of a long-range fifteen-year economic plan that would project economic trends out to 1990.[3] For a country addicted to the regular issuance of yearly and five-year plans, that should not have posed any extraordinary challenge. Yet as of 1982, no such plan had been released. Soviet planners have apparently been unable to agree, even among themselves, about what Soviet economic prospects and possibilities might be more than five years ahead. If they are having trouble, why should an American set out to analyze how, if at all, the Soviet system will evolve in the years ahead?

Notwithstanding the pitfalls of an analysis such as this, the fact remains that over the next few years, the Soviet Union confronts some delicate if not insoluble dilemmas. While we may not be able to pinpoint precisely every specific problem or solution, it is nonetheless important that we on the outside seek to understand the difficulties and options Soviet leaders will have to deal with in the years and decades ahead. The underlying problems that face the Soviet leadership in trying to reform their economic and political system are so basic that they will not disappear in a year or two.

Most of the Soviet Union's problems stem in one way or another from the type of economic and political system that was developed during the Stalinist era. This system has been in place a long time and has created many disproportions. Thus change will not come easily. Moreover, if and when Soviet leaders decide a change is necessary, how they proceed to implement those changes will affect not only those inside the Soviet Union, but in many instances, those of us on the outside.

I.

To understand the challenges confronting Soviet leaders, it is not enough to focus only on the Bolshevik era. Although the most important features of the present Soviet system were determined during Stalin's lifetime, the origins of the Soviet Union's present problems date back to prerevolutionary days, and have to do in part with whether or not Russia was a suitable country for the first Marxist revolution. The question is an important one. Marx anticipated that the industrially developed countries of the world would be the first to undergo his communist revolution. As he saw it, the growing oppression of the industrial class would ultimately alienate those workers so much that they would rise up and throw off the ruling class, the bourgeoisie. Since the clear focus of this movement was to be the industrial proletariat, it would have to have a strong industrial base. Moreover, the country's industry would have to be highly developed and technologically advanced. The problem in such capitalistic societies was not that they were unable to produce, but that given the exploitation of workers and the inequality of incomes, these systems were unable to distribute the goods produced in a fair manner. The purpose of the revolution, therefore, would be to change the distribution process so as to introduce a more equitable distribution of goods, which in turn would also contribute to the elimination of worker alienation. It was intended, therefore, that the new revolutionary government would not have to concern itself with industrial development—the bourgeoisie had already seen to that.

According to Marx's blueprint, therefore, the first communist revolution was never intended for a country that was as backward as Russia was in 1917. Since Russia had barely begun to industrialize, there was only a small proletarian class. At the time of the revolution, over 80 per cent of the country's population was rural. At best, a rural population of this size meant that there would be little to work with in the way of an urban proletariat. Consequently, the Soviet dictatorship of the proletariat had to take on a form other than the one envisaged by Marx.

The process of industrialization, under the best and most benevolent humanistic circumstances, involves disruption, tension, and sacrifice. Cultures clash, families split, people are uprooted, and mores change. In addition, there is physical and mental sickness with which to contend, as well as poverty, and sometimes violence. In capitalist societies, the blame for all of this is usually directed at the bourgeoisie and capitalists. They are the driving force behind this uprooting of traditional values as well as the ultimate beneficiaries of the resulting change. But because so little of Russia had been industrialized before the revolution, it was the Soviet state that had to build up the country's wealth. Instead of merely having to divide the wealth of an already industrialized state as Marx had intended, the dictatorship of the proletariat in the U.S.S.R. had to become the economic accumulator, and thus the brutalizing force, the head-knocker of the workers, the source of alienation. Not surprisingly, the dictatorship of the proletariat in Stalin's model had to suppress the bourgeoisie, the peasants, and most disturbing of all, the proletariat itself. The dictatorship of the proletariat, therefore, became the instrument that was to create Soviet industry. However, once that industry had been created, the dictatorship of the proletariat also became the instrument for the proletariat's subjugation.

It was Stalin who, after Lenin's death in 1924, assumed the task of pushing through the industrialization of the Soviet state. In the process, Stalin turned the Marxist revolution on its head. Stalin was in a hurry. He was determined to complete the painful process of industrialization as quickly as possible. Unfortunately, his quest for speed guaranteed that the process would be all the more painful. As he saw it, only a limited amount of time remained before his enemies, both inside and outside, would attempt to destroy his regime. To speed up the industrialization effort, Stalin concluded that he had to have a centralized system of planning and a planning bureau (Gosplan). To make up for the time that had already been lost, Gosplan would place its prime emphasis on heavy industry. Reflecting the stress on speed, factory managers would be judged according to how much more they produced in the current year as compared to the year before. Inevitably, this focused the economy's attention on quantity rather than quality.

To accumulate the resources necessary for this growth in heavy industry, the planners found it necessary to set investment, and thus savings rates, as high as 30 per cent of the GNP. Much of this capital Stalin intended to extract from the agricultural sector by paying very little to the peasants for their efforts. Consequently, consumption and consumer goods would be given a low priority. Thus there would be little available in the way of either manufactured or agricultural products for consumption.

This quick march toward industrialization had implications that went beyond the economic sphere. Since there would be little in the way of immediate economic reward for the workers and peasants who were the bearers of most of this burden, there was little likelihood that such a program would be very popular. As a consequence, the instruments of power would have to be firmly controlled by the leaders of the state. There could be no such thing as democracy and only limited forms of dissent.

The pattern set in the first decade after the Soviet revolution has remained intact with some variations for more than six decades. Moreover, this Stalinist model has been duplicated by almost all those countries whose revolutions have come under the influence of the Soviet Union. The hope was that ultimately the workers would come to accept the decision to use the state as an industrializing force because, sooner or later, the proletariat would come to recognize that all of this was being done for their own good. However, most of the workers were unable to distinguish between the dictatorship of the bourgeoisie and the dictatorship of the proletariat. After all, Karl Marx criticized capitalists for deceiving their workers with promises of paradise in heaven in exchange for abstinence now; this turned out to be not much different from what Stalin gave them. Heavenly paradise may not have been their goal in the Soviet Union, but earthly paradise, promised for tomorrow, appeared almost as unattainable.

Before too long the same type of hostility engendered by workers in capitalist societies was directed by the Soviet proletariat against the Soviet dictatorship of the proletariat and its instrument, the state. Partly out of self-defense and partly out of conviction, the party apparatus found it necessary, in response, to institute a very strict, far-reaching, and generally repressive government regime. Consequently, even the most benevolent and ideologically pure Soviet Marxist now finds it hard to say when the Soviet state will wither away. Rather than withering away as Marx had promised, the state in the Stalinist model has expanded and become omnipresent.

Presumably, this reality is a source of embarrassment to those who still believe in the Soviet revolution, particularly when members of the Politburo elite decree, as they periodically do, that the Soviet government has brought an end to exploiter classes and thus an end to exploitation.[4] This brings to mind the cynics' response to those who in a more naive day used to claim that the Soviet Union had ended the capitalist practice of exploitation of man by man. "Yes, in the Soviet Union they have the reverse." Indeed, occasionally a candid Soviet writer will even admit that the Soviet Union still has a long way to go, even though it is almost sixty-five years since the Revolution. As one writer put it, "No less important is the overcoming of social distinctions which arise because we still have a large section of manual, low-skilled, and very difficult physical labor. . . . It is clear that those employed in such activities, where they have little sense of creativity, develop a certain sense of job dissatisfaction which impedes the development of a communist attitude towards labor."[5] A Marxist writer finding such conditions in a capitalist society would quickly conclude that such workers were "alienated."

The Soviets may be forgiven for the fact that alienation is still a part of their system—after all, what state has done away with it? However, the task of ameliorating such conditions is made more difficult by the Politburo's reluctance to concede the very existence of the problem. It is hard to find a cure as long as the doctor insists there is no disease. The adherence to such rigid dogmas makes evolutionary change difficult.

II.

In other societies, change is sometimes implemented in the course of the normal turnover of leadership. But because leadership changes come infrequently in the U.S.S.R., that avenue is not open. One of the reasons for the very low turnover is that there are no institutionalized procedures for changing leadership. Except for Yugoslavia, and its system has yet to be tested, not one of the world's communist countries has successfully designed a systematic or institutionalized process for transferring power.

More often than not, the leaders in a communist country hold their power until death. On occasion, as in the case of Khrushchev, a faction in the Politburo may try to gang up secretly on an existing leader. If given enough time, as Khrushchev was, at least the first time such an attempt is made, the leader can try to convene a meeting of the larger Central Committee and override the vote of the Politburo. Otherwise, it normally takes some major political or economic strife, or physical infirmity, to produce a change in a totalitarian government. Moreover, when a totalitarian government lives beyond its original leader, the leader's death or removal often sets off disruption, intrigue, unrest, and sometimes even collapse while the contenders maneuver for leadership during the transition period. As with Brezhnev, when a leader has been displaced, his successors temporarily tend to adopt a form of collective leadership. Basically, such conditions are designed to mark time until a new leader or team emerges. Not surprisingly, these interregnums have been usually marked by uncertainty and indecision.

Exceptions to this ad hoc pattern are rare. While the Poles theoretically took the first steps to impose restraints and institutionalize a more orderly process, their system seems to have failed. For a time, it looked like the Chinese had somehow worked out a more orderly system. Hua Guofeng found himself out of a job as Party Chairman of China in what seemed to be a relatively civil and unusual process. However, even then, the replacement of Hua Guofeng was an ad hoc rather than a routinized process and was preceded by some rather heated and improvised maneuvering. The North Koreans have apparently solved the problem of leadership transition by creating something which, to the uninitiated, could pass as a monarchy. Kim Il Sung has unilaterally decided just to turn over the keys of the ruler's office to his son.

By contrast, an institutionalized system for transferring and transmitting power is probably one of the highest achievements of a democracy. No one likes to yield power. Yet to avoid strife, if not bloodshed, some way must be found to establish commonly accepted procedures for changing leadership. This is the best way to insure an ongoing life for the state. Most states cannot survive periodic struggles for leadership. Even when rival factions agree on a format for changing leaders, there is no guarantee that the present leader will consent to a peaceful transfer. But once a pattern of peaceful institutional change in leadership is established, the chances that the process will be repeated increase with each such transfer.

There is no such regularized procedure in a totalitarian state, because by its very nature, a totalitarian regime implies that the leaders feel that the population lacks the judgment needed to decide whether a leader or leadership group is good or not. It also implies a lack of confidence among the populace about the government. The assumption is that, were it not for police rule, the populace would overthrow the existing totalitarian government. These implications, therefore, all but rule out change, except when voluntarily agreed to by the leader.

Based on recent history, most leaders in totalitarian states hardly ever decide to resign voluntarily from power. Tito, who died at 87, and Brezhnev, who died at 75, are good illustrations of this. In part such longevity in office reflects the leader's belief in his own infallibility, and in part it is a reflection of the violent or at least conspiratorial way in which power was seized initially. Inevitably, when power is taken in an arbitrary fashion, enemies are created, and they are viewed as a constant counterrevolutionary threat to the rulers in power. This certainly characterized Stalin's code of conduct.

Most communist regimes have dispensed with the violence that existed during Stalin's day. Then it was not only rivals who were imprisoned and often killed, but ordinary subordinates whose only misfortune was that they performed poorly or, on occasion, too well. In either case, they were considered a threat to the leader. Naturally that made for considerable anxiety on the job. Party purges in Eastern Europe were equally bloody. The violence continued for a time after Stalin's death but gradually his heirs both in the Soviet Union and to a lesser extent in Eastern Europe adopted a more restrained policy. Removal from the Politburo is now usually accompanied by a forced retirement or assignment to some remote foreign embassy, or to the Mongolian atomic energy commission. But there still is no systematic procedure; it took secret plotting to displace Khrushchev in 1964, factionalism to push out Hua Guofeng in 1981, and strikes and near anarchy to force out Gierek in 1980. None of these cases followed a routinized process. They were all ad hoc arrangements.

The clear presumption is that once a party chairman in a communist state takes power, he will be the leader for life. There are exceptions, but the more typical case is like that of Castro in Cuba, Ho Chi Minh in Viet Nam, Tito in Yugoslavia, Lenin, Stalin and Brezhnev in the Soviet Union, or Mao in China. Increasingly, the other senior members of the Politburo come to hold the same expectations. While they may not trust each other, there is usually more trust for each other than for those on the outside. This reluctance to disturb the status quo, plus the sense of mutual self-preservation, explains as well as anything can the infrequency of change at the top, even though it may be sorely needed.

What happened at the Twenty-sixth Communist Party Congress in February of 1981, typified this rigidity. The Soviet economy in 1980 reflected one of the most dismal performances in years. Not only was the harvest about 15 per cent below planned output, but production of such important items as steel, coal, meat, and potatoes was actually lower in 1980 than in 1979. There were, moreover, serious political problems in Poland and Afghanistan. If the Soviet Union had been a private corporation or a democratic state, there would have been some shakeup. If the replacement of the chairman or president did not occur, at least some senior executives would have been removed. In contrast, not one change was made in the makeup of the Soviet Politburo.

This hesitancy to rock the boat helps to explain the political longevity of ailing leaders in communist states. While Tito was quite vigorous until shortly before his death, Brezhnev, Mao, and Ho Chi Minh had slowed measurably, yet they remained in office. As early as 1977, there were reports that Brezhnev had been seriously incapacitated. Presiding over a formal dinner in December, 1978, he required assistance to insure that he would rise properly to make his toast. His speech was slurred, and it was clear to those of us in the room that he lacked command over all his faculties. It was astounding that such a man would be left to run a country, particularly one in which power is so narrowly centralized and where the leader has to play such an active role. Given the magnitude of its needs, the Soviet Union requires, more than most countries, a leader who is active, acute, and energetic. That hardly described Brezhnev. Nor does it describe those around him. The average age of the full members of the Politburo in 1964 was 61; in 1982, just before Brezhnev's death, it was 70.[6] (See Tables I-1, I-2, and I-3.) One pictures this geriatric cluster of men spending their twilight years together helping each other stand up and sit down.

Table I-1
AGE OF THE SOVIET OLIGARCHY IN 1952, 1964, AND 1980

Institution	1952	Average Age 1964	1980
Politburo: full members	55.4	61.0	70.1
Politburo: alternate members	50.9	52.8	62.5
Secretariat of the Central Committee	52.0	54.1	67.0
Presidium of the Council of Ministers	54.9	55.1	68.1
All institutions	54.1	56.0	66.8

SOURCE: Bialer, *Stalin's Successors*, p. 83.

When a government goes without a major change in leadership, as Brezhnev's did for eighteen years, particularly when that government is a conservative one, there is likely to be a pent-up need for far-ranging adjustments. Soviet policies, as we have observed, have not kept up with the times, particularly in the economic field. And the policy paralysis has undoubtedly bottled up and frustrated numerous power-seekers. With Brezhnev gone, there is likely to be a power and policy struggle.

Table I-2
MEMBERS OF THE POLITBURO

Name	Age as of April 1982
Yuri Y. Andropov	68
Konstantin U. Chernenko	71
Mikhail S. Gorbachev	51
Viktor V. Grishin	68
Andrei Gromyko	73
Andrei Kirilenko	76
Dinmukhamed A. Kunayev	70
Arvid Y. Pel'she	83
Grigoriy Romanov	59
Vladimir V. Shcherbitskiy	64
Nikolai A. Tikhonov	77
Dmitriy F. Ustinov	74
Leonid Brezhnev	75

Table I-3

AGE GROUPS OF THE SOVIET OLIGARCHY, 1980

Institution	70 Years Old and Older (%)	60 Years Old and Younger (%)
Politburo: full members	50.0	7.1
Politburo: alternate members	22.2	33.3
Secretariat of the CC	50.0	20.0
Presidium of the Council of Ministers	35.7	7.1
Presidium of the Supreme Soviet	26.6	33.3
All institutions	28.4	25.5

SOURCE: Bialer, p. 82.

Yet because Andropov and his comrades come out of somewhat similar molds, they will more likely try to maintain the status quo or form a collective type of leadership. Because of their ages, they cannot hold out forever. Moreover, their failure to act decisively will only sustain, if not increase, the pressure for radical action sometime in the more distant future. That change could be accompanied if not precipitated by violence, and it may also serve as an outlet for those who seek revenge and who have never come to terms with the revolution and its aftermath.

Given the past pattern of leadership tenure in both Russia and the Soviet Union, it is unlikely that Soviet leaders will readily see the need for shorter and more regular terms of office. Indeed, perhaps the most onerous legacy from both the prerevolutionary and communist eras is the idea that the ruler is entitled to a long, if not indefinite term of office. This holds for both Russia under the czars and Russia under the communists. Because change tends to be such a foreign and disruptive phenomenon, it is not welcome. One reflection of this is how long rulers in both Russia and the Soviet Union have held on to their power. Not surprisingly, recent leaders have had reigns that were as long as those of the czars, if not longer. Consider that with the exception of a short period after Stalin's death, there were only four leaders in the Soviet Union in over sixty-five years of power. That means that each leader had an average reign of approximately sixteen years. In a democracy, a tenure of sixteen years for one leader, much less four leaders, is a rarity. Unfortunately, the lack of frequent change creates its own lack of dynamic. Infrequent and long-delayed change often sets off an over-reaction. The more frequent and regular it is, the more likely it is that the disparity between the bulk of the ins and the bulk of the outs will be a small one. Of course there will always be those on the far extreme who will probably never be satisfied by any change that satisfies the middle. Nonetheless with more frequent change, there is a greater likelihood that the fringe groups will remain weak and inconsequential.

III.

The contrast between the pressure for change in the United States and the Soviet Union highlights the problems facing the Soviet Union. In part, change has come easier to the United States because luckily, it has never had to contend with the extremes usually engendered by the creation of a nobility or aristocratic class. Most aristocracies derive control from having title over a nation's land. That is also their source of power and wealth. In the case of the United States, initial land-grants to the first arrivals did not set the tone for rule and privilege, because at least until the late nineteenth century, there was always abundant and sometimes richer land available for anyone who wanted to seek his way farther west.[7] In addition, by the time there was no longer any free land, the industrial revolution was in full bloom and its impact on the American social structure was much more important than land ownership. The industrial revolution meant that money, not land, was likely to have a greater effect on social status. Similarly, success in the industrial revolution depended more on ability and drive than on birth and longevity. By its very nature, the industrial revolution generated an enormous need for talented people. This was important because it meant that those Americans with ambition and push could more often than not sublimate their aggressive tendencies into constructive channels. Of course, not everyone was so nicely accommodated. Some dissidents in the United States found their way into crime and radical political opposition. Nonetheless, because of the great opportunities open in the mainstream of American economic life, the dissidents tended to be a narrow fringe, and as a consequence, they were generally ignored by the larger and very dominant middle classes. At the same time, because it was very mobile, the middle class tended to accommodate itself to change. These changes came frequently and tended to co-opt new trends so that extremists found it difficult to gain a hearing for any prolonged period of time. Moreover, once they had a chance, the dissidents tended to adopt the conventional patterns of behavior and send their children to college, where more often than not, they quickly became absorbed into the mainstream. This is not to deny or excuse the fact that there are important racial and income differences in the United States which have at times generated riots and even a civil war. But over the years, at least a fraction of most minorities has been able to succeed economically.[8] Overall the United States continues to be remarkably mobile. Thus the support for revolutionary change is seldom significant.

IV.

The absence of extreme class differences in the United States stands in sharp contrast with Russia at the time of the revolution and the U.S.S.R. as it has subsequently evolved. Except for a brief interval immediately after the revolution, Russia has been a land of extremes. The aristocracy was as privileged as any comparable group in Europe. Their land holdings were more extensive and in many ways more important. Since there was comparatively little industry, land ownership offered virtually the only route up the economic and social ladder. Mobility, therefore, was very limited. Reflective of the power of the landed nobility, the landlords managed to hold on to their serfs until 1861. That may not seem too bad considering that the emancipation of the slaves in the United States was decreed only in 1863. Nonetheless, it must be remembered that private and state serfdom encompassed almost one-third of the entire Russian population, a much larger percentage of the country's population than was affected in the United States.[9] Moreover, serfdom existed throughout Russia, not just in one region. The consequences of the pervasive effect of serfdom in Russia were not easily digested. As hard as it was in the United States to erase the effects of slavery, it was equally hard if not more difficult in Russia. Only after peasant uprisings and the subsequent 1905 revolution did the state begin to do anything of consequence to bring the peasants into the economic mainstream of the country. Even then, the nobility continued to hold on to most of its power and thus sustained the country's old class distinctions.

Admittedly, some late nineteenth-century and early twentieth-century reforms had an impact on the basic class-stratification in Russian society. Not only did rudimentary forms of democracy and participation begin to develop at the local level of government, but important changes also took place in agriculture. Some land holdings were consolidated and an agricultural middle class started to form. Similar changes occurred in industry. Instead of being artificially imposed or guided from on high by the government, more and more growth evolved from within domestic industry and the banking community itself. According to the late Alexander Gerschenkron, that progress was aborted by the chaos of World War I.[10] The failure to complete such reforms plus the general exacerbation of tensions set off by the war tended to increase rather than to decrease the extremes that existed in the country. This led inevitably to the revolutions of 1917.

Given the absence of far-reaching evolutionary changes, it is not entirely surprising that the Soviet people should succumb to something as extreme and discontinuous as communism. The strains of World War I highlighted the backwardness and disproportion that had always characterized the country. This in turn gave rise to enormous pressures to catch up, to find short cuts. Periodic efforts to leapfrog forward have historically been a part of the Russian growth strategy.[11] When this happens the advocates of gradualism are swamped by those who feel that change has been too long in coming. In such a climate it is hard for a middle class to grow or build a base of support.

Since revolutionaries are usually impatient people, anxious to make up for lost years, invariably they seek far-reaching changes. The abruptness of their changes more often than not lead to excesses, and consequently to the belief that sooner or later other efforts, equally abrupt and revolutionary or counterrevolutionary, will be made to redress the balance. These discontinuities when they came, at least in the early exuberance and fervor of the Revolution, tended to be far-ranging. Indeed, in the decade following the revolution, the Soviet Union was truly a revolutionary society. Hardly any sector was unaffected. At one time or another the country saw an end to money, the legitimization of free love, the end of religion, the confiscation of private industry and agriculture, a leveling of ranks in the army, the advent of avant-garde art, music, architecture, and theatre, the renunciation of some important international treaties and customs, and the elimination of the more conventional forms of domestic government. In the 1930's, the government of the U.S.S.R. had the youngest leadership of any major country.[12] While most of these changes lasted for only a brief period, the economic and political impact has been long-lasting. However, in a short time, these radical changes served to form the core of a new orthodoxy and gave rise to an intolerance for experimentation. Indeed, by the 1930's, virtually all experimentation in all fields had come to an end. As the historian Edward L. Keenan has said, by the onset of the 1930's, the U.S.S.R. had flipped from being one of the most innovative and radical regimes into becoming one of the most orthodox, if not reactionary.[13] For the most part, all traces of the spirit of experimentation were eradicated and a new orthodoxy, often more reactionary than before, was instituted.

The return to the climate of orthodoxy was in part a response to what can be described as the traditional nature of the people in the U.S.S.R. After all, the very free-living ways of the few after the revolution upset the morals and traditions of the majority who had grown up in the prerevolutionary era. In any case, an extreme response almost always provokes a counterreaction. Anticipating such counterreactions, those newly entrenched in power usually seek to head off any move toward counterrevolution particularly if the changes being implemented are harsh and far-reaching. They normally institute a very strict set of controls and repressive measures to insure that they do not lose the power they have only recently acquired. Often this is all done in the guise of restoring order and stability, but clearly the intent is to insure that there will be no cause or opportunity for counterrevolution. A by-product of this renewed emphasis on law and order is the cessation of virtually all experimentation and the suppression of the unusual. Any change at all becomes a threat.

Sustaining a revolutionary spirit is a problem common to all revolutions, not just the Bolshevik revolution. After having been outcast or imprisoned for most of their lives, the one-time revolutionaries develop a taste for privilege. Not surprisingly, this desire for tranquility and privilege extends to their children. It is only human for a parent to seek to smooth the way for a child. Obviously this further militates against the continuation of flux.

This conservative emphasis on stability and order is enhanced by the enormity of the strain created by the forced industrialization process and by the nationalization of all the means of production. The dictatorship of the proletariat, originally intended to insure that the capitalist and bourgeoisie would not rise again, broadens so that not only are the capitalists and bourgeoisie held in check, but ultimately the proletariat and peasants as well.

There is little about this system that resembles the communism Marx had in mind except that private ownership of the means of production is prohibited. But that could as well fit the description of state capitalism—where the state is the main economic force and inequality and privilege is accepted as a necessity for growth and a reward for service. The Soviets are incensed when their state-owned system of central planning is referred to as a form of state capitalism, but basically that is what it is. Since state capitalism, at least as practiced in the U.S.S.R., tolerates no competition, there is an absence of pluralism. This means that usually there is no alternative but to do as the state prescribes. Inevitably this further limits experimentation and therefore further reduces the likelihood of evolutionary change.

V.

Will the Soviets be able to throw off their Stalinist model and do away with the extreme concentration of power in the hands of one person or narrow group? Stalin's power within the Soviet Union was enormous. When summoned to his office, no one knew whether they would emerge free or be sent to prison. At the same time, Stalin became the source of all knowledge and morality in the country. His picture was everywhere and no article could be written without some acknowledgment of Stalin's wisdom. The cult of personality is something that was roundly criticized in the Soviet Union in the late 1950's and early 1960's, but both Khrushchev and Brezhnev assumed supreme power anyway. They did not seem to abuse that power as much as Stalin did, nor did they appear to be as psychotic as Stalin was. Yet no institutional or constitutional changes have been adopted in the Soviet Union which would preclude a return to terror and the cult of personality in the future. Nor is there much indication that Andropov will soon set in place a more democratic mechanism. Protestations by Soviet intellectuals and leaders that "we have learned our lesson and will not let this happen again" are hardly guarantee enough. In the absence of something more definitive, a repeat of such extremism is a possibility. If such a cult is as far-reaching as it was under Stalin, this in turn could have disastrous consequences, both inside and outside the Soviet Union.

Stalin's cult of personality was so encompassing that it has shaped the nature of the Soviet Union for many years to come. Conceivably if someone other than Stalin had taken over control of the country, as Lenin reportedly wanted, or if Lenin had lived longer, or if Hitler had not invaded the Soviet Union, the Soviet Union might not have been so thoroughly ravaged both internally and externally. Admittedly it is hard to conceive of how the Soviet Union could have been subjected to more punishment. Nonetheless, the conditioning to, and even acceptance of authoritarian rule which was so much a part of czarist life outlived the czars and made Stalin less of an anomaly than he would have been in other societies. For that matter, Lenin himself was not exactly a model democrat. He moved vigorously to suppress all opponents and dissent including that from long time fellow emigrés and allies. It is true that he did not make as liberal use of the death penalty as Stalin ultimately did, and that he would on occasion allow enemies to emigrate rather than imprison them, but it is also true that he reinstituted the secret police and camps for political prisoners. As Solzhenitsyn points out, it was Lenin who in his 1918 essay, "How to Organize the Competition," decreed that it was necessary to "purge the Russian land of all insects" by which he meant class enemies, malingerers and saboteurs. In some cases the "eliminate" meant arrest, imprisonment, forced labor, or when necessary, the firing squad.[14] Moreover, Lenin staffed many of the new camps with former inmates. And as so often happens when the ins become the outs, the new administrators ran the camp with a firmer hand than had their predecessors. Based on their personal experience, these new camp directors and guards knew what was wholly effective and what was not; the camps were no longer ordinary prisons administered by "dilettantes."[15]

Stalin took over from Lenin with hardly a moment's hesitation. By the time he was through, nearly thirty years later, the country had been traumatized. As Stalin intimated to Churchill, "millions of men and women [had been] blotted out or displaced forever" simply because they resisted the process of collectivization.[16]

Stalin was determined to industrialize the country without regard to sentimentality or cries of mercy. He out-bourgeoised the bourgeoisie. Stalin's industrialization drive was primitive accumulation with a vengeance. The main task was to produce and to build a solid capital industrial base. Agriculture and the peasantry were forced to finance the bulk of the accumulation needed for this industrialization. The prices paid to the peasants for their agricultural products were kept at below-cost levels. Accordingly, for decades afterwards, many peasants could not eke out enough from the collectivized sectors to sustain themselves. While keeping the procurement costs of agricultural products low, Stalin simultaneously imposed a heavy turnover tax on basic items such as bread, so that the retail store price turned out to be unusually high. Franklyn Holzman estimated that the turnover tax paid on ryebread amounted to approximately 86 per cent of the final retail price.[17] Such a tax was probably the most regressive any government could construct. Thus the peasants collected little, the consumers paid a lot, and the government kept the difference, which it used to finance its industrial buildup.

Not by bread alone did Stalin impose his accumulation. Investment for housing and other consumer goods was postponed in favor of investment for heavy industry. This in itself imposed an enormous burden on day-to-day life.[18] Stalin's refusal to allow adequate investment for the amenities of life was compounded by the fact that, throughout the period, there was an enormous migration of peasants to the city. Since investment in housing was generally not enough to sustain the existing population, the extra pressure put on the housing stock necessitated the subdividing of apartments into increasingly smaller units. This meant that several families would be gathered together and squeezed into what once had been an apartment for one family. Before long, the norm for the typical Soviet family was one family per room, with the toilets and kitchen shared in common. Whereas the amount of living space per person in urban areas was 5.7 square meters in 1926, it fell to 4.5 meters in 1940.[19] The norm had been set at 9 square meters per person, but there was no way this could be achieved when Stalin cut the investment allotted to housing.

The all-encompassing role of the state and the lack of flexibility of the Stalinist model was not an unmitigated disadvantage. For some purposes, the Stalinist model of economic development functions well, especially when there is little need for flexibility or adjustment. For example, the Stalinist system served effectively to build up a massive heavy industrial and military infrastructure. Since the Soviet system could forcibly extract the needed capital from the public, capital was accumulated at a rate that, at the time, was historically unique. Moreover, it did all this after a costly and destructive civil war. By the 1930's, the Soviet Union was achieving rates of industrial growth that surpassed those of many other countries at the time. According to official Soviet statistics, by 1937, Soviet national income had increased by 4.6 times over what it had been in 1913 and almost fourfold since the start of the five-year plan programs in 1928.[20] This continued into the 1950's. The national income, as defined by the Soviet Union, increased by 14 times from 1913 to 1953. In the early 1950's, that meant that the national income was growing at unprecedented rates of 10 to 12 per cent per year.[21] In terms of specific industries, steel production increased from 4.2 million tons in 1913 to 17.7 million tons in 1937 to 45.3 million tons in 1955.[22] Coal, electricity, and many other products increased at even faster rates.

Many of the more exaggerated claims were subsequently revised downward by some outside observers. Thus Abram Bergson calculates that the rate of growth of net national product, as defined by more widely accepted Western procedures, increased at an average rate of 4.8 per cent a year from 1928 to 1958, and by 6.8 per cent from 1950 to 1958.[23] But even at the more modest growth levels, the Soviet record was impressive, particularly given the fact that much of the rest of the world was then suffering from the Great Depression. While Western Europe and the United States were contending with levels of unemployment of 25 percent or more and negative economic growth, the Soviet Union found itself with GNP growth-rates of 4 to 5 per cent and rapidly disappearing unemployment. The Stalinist model was so impressive that Western economists unaware for the most part of what had influenced them, began to argue that noncommunist countries in the developing world should adopt a growth model that generally had more in common with the Stalinist model than any other noncommunist prototype. Unconcerned about the Freudian overtones, economists like Paul N. Rosenstein-Rodan and Walter Rostow, with their "big pushes," "takeoffs," "thrusts," and "spurts," argued that the best way to industralize was to begin with a massive campaign of capital formation with priority assigned to the establishment of a heavy industrial base.[24] Although they were not seeking investment to GNP ratios as high as 30 per cent, their infatuation with the role of the state in capital formation is understandable. It seemed to promise substantial and rapid economic growth where nothing else did. At the time there were no other successful development models in the twentieth century to point to. The Japanese miracle had not yet been invented.

VI.

Granted that the Stalinist economic model has had some undisputed successes, it also has had its share of shortcomings that became increas-

ingly apparent in the later half of the twentieth century. Once the decision was made to grow at a very rapid rate while simultaneously reducing
the rewards allocated to the consumer, the leaders of the state were
forced of necessity to protect themselves by maintaining a very coercive
stance. If allowed to choose freely, the populace would probably not
have agreed to such an arrangement. Thus inevitably strong measures
were required to prevent protests and protestors. The absence of consumer sovereignty in an extreme situation like this dictates the denial of
voter sovereignty. The leaders arrogate to themselves the right to determine what is good for the masses. The "Uncle Joe knows best" spirit
bears a striking similarity to the attitude that "the Czar knows best."
In both cases the government must be repressive; accordingly only the
firmly committed can be entrusted with power. If anything, the situation
was worse under Stalin because he tried to do more in a shorter period
of time than the czars. Moreover, because Stalin's program was closely
tied to an ideology that threatened political and economic life in the
outside world, Stalin felt himself threatened by foreign intrigues and
possible attack much more than the czars did. Consequently, Stalin
always seemed to be distrustful of his associates no matter how loyal
they might appear to be. This made personnel selection a critical function. To reduce the likelihood of disloyalty, Stalin as well as subsequent
Soviet leaders have reserved for themselves the task of determining the
staffing of government and industrial posts beneath them, the so-called
"nomenklatura" or elite list. In turn, those in subordinate positions
exercise the same power over those beneath them. Thus power ema-
nates from the top down rather than from the bottom up. In a creative
use of language, this process is called Democratic Centralism and has
become a key feature of the Stalinist model.

Such careful screening by the party of these *nomenklatura* posts is
intended to insure party loyalty. It also filters the flow to the top so that,
as we saw, when Brezhnev died there were only two people under sixty-
four years of age on the Politburo. To the extent that younger leaders
may be better suited for ushering in innovation and change, the exclu-
sion of these people from leadership positions is likely to place an undue
emphasis on the status quo and make change more complicated.

Once the great surge of growth which took place in the Soviet Union
in the 1930's and the postwar reconstruction came to an end, there was
remarkably little room left for mobility. While he lived, Stalin induced
some artificial turnover by periodically purging his ranks—Brzezinski's

concept of the "permanent purge." His successors adopted a more humane policy of fewer purges which has meant fewer changes in personnel. For example, only six members of the Politburo were removed over a ten-year period. But by not allowing room for upward movement, the state increases the risk that someday a group may try to take matters into its own hands, particularly if the economy is not running too well or seems to be having more problems than usual. Under the circumstances, it is logical to assume that there are at least some in the Soviet Union who have been chafing for the opportunity to exercise power. Potentially this could be a destabilizing force that any new leadership will have to contend with.

Of course, there is also the even greater danger that someone down the line will rebel, not out of frustration at being unable to move up the ladder, but at all the deprivation and coercion he or she sees, and at the Stalinist economic model itself. To ward off such temptations, the Stalinist model protects party members, especially those entrusted with governing power, from the shortages which are a basic part of life for the average Russian worker. Party officials are provided access to special stores where otherwise unavailable goods are sold just to party officials. Ordinary workers are kept out. In a sense, these special stores are a bribe, like chauffered cars, special housing compounds, and special theater boxes. Access to these exclusive accommodations also serves to cut off communication with the average worker. As a result, it becomes a little easier to be convinced that conditions are not too severe, that workers are not too unhappy, and that the Stalinist model does not involve too much sacrifice. Of course, there are showcase sites—filled with model, happy, and atypical peasant workers, but such Potemkin or facadelike settings are meant more to impress outsiders than mislead insiders. For those who do realize the true state of life, the temptation to protest is generally tempered by the realization that muckraking may lead to the withdrawal of such privileges. The Stalinist political model yields to no one in using the most effective combination of the carrot and the stick.

VII.

It would be wrong however to blame all the problems of the Soviet economic and political models on Stalin. Reform has also been impeded by a sense of Russian cultural and historical isolation and a sense of inferiority. Caught between Asia and Europe, the Russians have developed not unnatural fears of both East and West. Whenever one group of Asians or Europeans seeks major territorial expansion, more likely than not that expansion sets off population and military movements that directly or indirectly spill over into Russia. Never mind that those both east and west of the Soviet Union had often felt themselves threatened by Russian expansion. As the Soviets see it, from the west have come the French, the Swedes, the Poles, the Teutonic knights, and the Nazis. From the east have come the Mongols and Tatars. According to the Russian historian Nesterov, from the thirteenth through the twentieth centuries the Russians have been subjugated to at least one destructive invasion per century—sometimes from several directions at once.[25]

Given what sometimes seems to be the almost continual stream of marauders passing through or threatening the country, the Russians have come to accept some extraordinary restraint on their individual lives, usually in the name of national defense. As explained by one Soviet historian, "In order to repulse the enemies that pressed it, the state that arose in the land had to demand from its people in an authoritative [authoritarian?] way as much wealth and labor, as many times as it was needed to assure victory. Because they wanted to defend their political independence, the people gave their all."[26] This willingness to surrender personal freedom, in the minds of some, is compounded by the infusion into Russian blood of what a few Russian intellectuals see as "the Mongols' acceptance of brutality," or "the Mongol inheritance."

While Soviet xenophobia is deeply rooted in an unfortunate past, it is further fueled by current Russian paranoia. The sense of encirclement is always present whether that encirclement is real or imagined, and whether the invasion is physical or ideological. To lessen the risk of subversion or defection, Russian leaders traditionally have tried to isolate the Russian people from contamination by foreigners. Centuries ago, foreign businessmen were restricted to special walled-in compounds in Russian cities. Remnants of these ghettos still exist today. For example, the wall just outside the Metropole Hotel in Moscow marks the boundary of one such historic area. Almost all foreigners, even those from communist states, such as Bulgaria, Afghanistan, or Cuba, or those whom the Soviets regard as special friends, such as the Palestine Liberation Organization, are collected into special housing and office compounds out-of-bounds to all Russians except those who have special authorization. With few exceptions, these foreign settlements are walled-in and guarded twenty-four hours a day. When asked, Soviet authorities explain that such precautions are necessary to protect their special guests. Undoubtedly this is true, but such protection also serves to make it all but impossible for Russians to visit foreigners without passing through a special guard and identifying themselves. With the completion of a new World Trade Center in Moscow, and its large complex of office and apartments, the Soviets expect to gather together foreigners from a variety of locations and thus maintain even tighter, although somewhat less conspicuous, control.

The suspicion of foreigners and the resistance to foreign ideas is a theme that runs throughout Russian history. In turn this is in part both an explanation and a consequence of the fact that the Russians never fully benefited from the enlightenment and the ameliorative affect of the Renaissance and the guild movement. It is also the reason why most of the first Russian railroads were built in a north-south direction. The Russians wanted to be able to move within their country but did not want to make access to their country too easy for foreigners and outside armies, especially from Europe. Moreover, when the east-west railroads were built, the Russians chose a larger gauge track than existed in Europe, again in order to make access more difficult.

This isolation has been the focus of a continuing debate since at least the nineteenth century. On one side, the Slavophiles have argued that Russia should look inward to the peasants and Orthodox Church for its guide—and away from the West. In contrast, the Westernizers in Russia argued then and argue today that Russia has for too long been isolated and insulated. They argue that the Soviet Union should look outward to the West for enlightenment, technology, humanism, and a democratic form of government. Only in this way will there be a relaxation of some of the more authoritarian, if not brutal, personal and political characteristics acquired during the Mongol conquest.

The Slavophiles may have been right. It may be that Russia, given its cultural, economic, and social isolation over all these years, is not well suited for the assimilation of foreign economic and political institutions and ideologies. Historically, they have not done well with what they have taken. Certainly their most ambitious Western import—the adaption of Marxism—has not been an unblemished success. Although Marx assumed that communism would not emerge in an industrially backward country, he did allow, toward the end of his life, that communism might come to Russia, but only because of the socialist nature of its rural communes, the *mir*. Because the rural communes already seemed to be operating along communist principles, Russia might be able to move directly into communism, if it were willing to forego industrialization. Marx, in any case, regarded Russia as better suited for agriculture than industry. The industrial products needed by the country would come from Western Europe, which would supposedly also go communist and thus supply Russia. This reasoning was not acceptable to the newly victorious Bolsheviks. More of them seemed to want industrialization without communism than communism without industrialization. In retrospect, it was inevitable that Marxism and Russia would be incompatible.

The unnatural fusing of a Marxist system onto an agrarian society which in turn made necessary the imposition of the Stalinist model of economic and political development has left deeply imbedded scars on the Soviet Union. In addition, the historic resistance to change makes it difficult to bring about reforms even when everyone agrees they are needed. In the chapters that follow, we shall examine how those scars and the reluctance to reform have affected the economy (Chapter Two), agriculture (Chapter Three), the social system (Chapter Four), Soviet international relations (Chapter Five), and Soviet relations with Eastern Europe (Chapter Six). In each instance we will examine not only the deformities and distortions that are a fetter on the type of development desired today, but also the obstacles that exist to any fundamental restructuring and reform.

For many Russians the combined effect of all these influences is very depressing. Their inability to implement gradual change, their xenophobia, their sense of encirclement, their inability to participate fully in the humanism and creativity of Western Europe, their toleration of authoritarian regimes and the country's resulting economic and social inadequacies have had a decided impact on how most Soviets regard themselves. At the same time they are proud of their very survival and that, under the circumstances, they have accomplished as much as they have. Thus it sometimes seems that members of the Soviet intelligensia have split personalities; they seem to have both inferiority and superiority complexes when it comes to dealing with the capitalist countries, especially the United States.

Against this background, what kind of change can we anticipate in the years ahead? Some observers both in and out of the Soviet Union pin their hopes on the younger generation. The hope is that the new generation will take a more relaxed view of the outside and inside of the Soviet Union. Anyone thirty-seven years of age or less will have had no memory of World War II and will not have lost a parent in it. Admittedly, no one can escape the constant drumbeat of how the Soviet Union suffered in World War II; the losses were enormous. But the Soviets tend to attribute all their current problems to the war, an event which occurred four decades ago. At the risk of being too callous, the outsider can be forgiven for suggesting that the regime has made World War II the opiate of the people. Since the war is to blame for almost everything, why should the current leaders be blamed for what is wrong now?

However, a larger and larger proportion of the Soviet population was born after the war had ended. According to a personal estimate by Murray Feshbach (formerly of the Bureau of the Census, U.S. Department of Commerce), as of January 1, 1981, over 60 per cent of the Soviet population was under forty years of age. Not only has this younger generation not known war, but they have experienced an era of detente. Presumably this younger generation should therefore be less consumed by the historic sense of encirclement and the resulting paranoia that is such a hallmark of the Russian leadership. In addition, many more of the younger generation have traveled and have come in contact with foreigners than their elders did at a comparable age. This exposure to the outside world should also lead to more rationalization and adaptation of Western methods. The prime example of what outside exposure might mean was Rem Victorovitch Khokhlov who was the rector or president of Moscow State University. One of the first Soviet graduate students to participate in the American-Soviet exchange back in the late 1950's, he rose rapidly upon his return to the Soviet Union through the scholarly and administrative ranks of the university until ultimately he was made rector. By common agreement, at least among intellectuals, he was one of the best rectors the university ever had. He liberalized university procedures that had not been changed for decades, and he improved the quality of schooling and the staff and opened the university to less parochial views in an unprecedented manner. Unfortunately, he met a premature death while mountain climbing but the hope is that new young leaders marked by a similar enlightenment will have a comparable impact on a growing number of Soviet institutions.

Young leaders with attitudes similar to those of Khokhlov may well work their way through the system in an increasing number of influential posts. However, it may be unrealistic to look for too much from the younger generation. To be a reactionary, one does not have to be over sixty-five. Extensive contact with Soviet bureaucracy quickly disabuses the visitor of any such notion. Hard as it is to believe, among many, including potential leaders from the younger generation, there is a frustration with the relatively lax ways of the present and a longing for the more regimented ways of the past. One illustration of this occurred while I was teaching at Moscow State University. To improve my Russian I went to a Russian language class two or three times a week. After class I would walk with one of my classmates, a Yugoslav lawyer, the few blocks from our class to the main corpus of the University. The main building is the hallmark of the university. It is a big Stalinist skyscraper dominating the city. I would go back to my room to prepare for my lectures while my Yugoslav friend would head off to the metro station in order to reach the old campus downtown across from the Kremlin which still housed the Law School. As efficient as the Moscow metro system was, this still involved an hour's trip in each direction, and what he regarded as a major waste of time. He would complain frequently to me about how much luckier I was that I could walk directly back to my rooms. Sooner or later, he said he too would be spared the trip. The university was constructing a new building between our language classroom and the main skyscraper, and this ordinary rectangular building which we could see under construction, would become the new site of the Law School, when completed. His exasperation, however, seemed to build each day, until near the end of his stay, he remarked that he had complained to one of his dormitory neighbors, a young Russian lawyer from the provinces. The Russian was also upset by the need for his own similar metro trip, particularly as he put it, ''because the new building has been under construction for so long.'' Addressing my Yugoslav companion, the Russian added, ''Do you know how long they have been working on this new law school? Eleven years!'' Then making a fist, the Russian asked again, ''Do you know how long it took Stalin to build the main and much more complicated and bigger corpus? Four years!'' The moral: we need to return to the good old days when work was work and leaders were leaders, and knew how to make people work. There are a surprisingly large number of young Russians who feel exactly the same way. Even though they probably don't remember much about Stalin, they want more discipline and control rather than less. There is no reason, then, to assume that the future automatically belongs to the liberals, or even to the centrists.

2. The Economy

Even though Stalin has been dead for over thirty years, his impact on the Soviet economy remains. While present Soviet planners devote much more attention to the consumer than they did under Stalin, the heritage of the Stalinist model pervades the economy. Although the Eleventh Five-Year Plan for the years 1981–85 stipulates that consumer-goods industries (Group B) are to grow by 26.2 per cent, or at a slightly faster rate than the 25.5 per cent growth of the producer industries (Group A), most likely this does not signal any major shift in priorities. First, the difference between the two percentages is not very large. Second, it should be remembered that relatively faster growth for the consumer-goods industry had also been promised for the Ninth Five-Year Plan, 1971–75. However, in the tradition of the past, the original Ninth Five-Year Plan was revised so that in fact Group A, producer goods, grew faster than consumer goods, despite the plan. Thus producer goods grew at an actual rate of 7.8 per cent, all but equal to the planned rate of 7.9 per cent. In contrast, Group B goods grew at only 6.5 per cent, far below the original target of a very impressive 8.3 per cent. Once addicted to the Stalinist model and heavy industry, it is hard to break away. The heavy industrial sector continues to lay claim to a disproportionate share of capital. It is unlikely that consumer-goods output will become mean-ingfully more significant until there has been a change in the capital allocation process. If and when that happens, however, it will probably lead, as we shall see, to a fundamental restructuring of the economy, which in turn would have major political consequences. The problem is that once a society decides to opt for central planning and a central plan, it almost always follows that there will be an overemphasis on heavy industry. This means that the decision to de-emphasize heavy industry of necessity is likely to result in the end of or the emasculation of central planning and the plan.

The Soviet Union was the first country in the world to adopt a central planning process. As part of that process, the Soviet planners automatically relegated to themselves the authority and responsibility for determining everything that was to happen in the economic system. This reflected the leaders' distrust of the market system. It was based on their conviction that growth would come faster and ultimately more equitably when economic affairs were handled centrally and in detail, compared to when they were left to industrial decision makers with only general guidance from the government. In the debate that preceded the decision to collectivize agriculture and adopt a five-year plan, some argued that more emphasis should be placed on growth from the bottom up.[1] In particular, Bukharin advocated that the peasantry should have more leeway to respond to market incentives. They in turn would then spend their money on consumer goods and agricultural equipment, which in turn would stimulate light industry. This meant, of course, that the peasant would end up with a higher share of the national income than Stalin's model would have provided. To have followed such a course as proposed by Bukharin, however, would have involved placing an even heavier burden on the proletariat. As it was, the proletariat was getting little enough, and any increase in the peasants' share would have to come in part from the allocation intended for the proletariat. Favoring the peasantry over the proletariat would have been ideologically embarrassing. In the end, Stalin chose collectization and strict control by the center over the economy.

I.

Most Westerners find it hard to appreciate just what it means to rely so heavily on the plan rather than the market. In a plan-system, very little happens without someone, somewhere in the bureaucracy, taking steps to order it. This means there will be no laundromat, no machine to make the washing machine, no railroad to carry the metal to make the machines, and no miners or drills to dig the metal, unless someone orders that each of these steps be taken. In the West, we seldom appreciate how many decisions are taken spontaneously and automatically by the market for us, until there is a malfunction in one step of the whole process.

The agency designated to plan all those details in the U.S.S.R. and to compensate for the absence of a market is called Gosplan, the state planning organization. To aid it in its work, Gosplan, has traditionally used a technique it calls "material balances." This involves drawing up a balance sheet for a large number of key commodities. The potential sources of supply, including importation and withdrawal from inventory, are then set against proposed demands. If the two sides balance—simple; if the demand exceeds the supply—shortages. In the latter case, new sources of supply must be found or, more typically, potential users with a lower priority are simply deprived of the goods they want. Satisfying consumer needs is deemed to have a low priority. Thus consumer-goods targets are often reduced.

Physically, it has proven impossible to draw up material balances for every item produced in the Soviet Union. The number actually subject to such manipulation by Gosplan varies depending on whether the country is in its centralizing or decentralizing phase. That does not mean the other goods escape regulation. On the contrary, the production and distribution of almost everything else is regulated by bureaucrats further down the line, such as Gossnab, the supply ministry, or individual production ministries. Inevitably the result is a massive amount of paperwork and, excuse the expression, "red-tape."

As awe-inspiring as they may be, the orders issued by Gosplan or the Council of Ministers or, for that matter, even Stalin, do not automatically mean that performance is assured. When drawing up the plan, Gosplan normally endeavors to see that there is at least the technical potential for fulfillment. That means there should potentially be enough iron ore, limestone, and coal in the Soviet Union to produce the steel in the plan and that there should be enough electrical generating capacity to generate the electricity called for.

Theoretically, such a calculation can be derived for any number of goods that the planner may want to include. Instead of using the rather complicated and trial-and-error material-balance system, which necessitates thousands of manual adjustments, the whole operation could be put into an input-output matrix and all the interrelationships between the goods calculated by use of a high-power computer. However, the number of steps required to make such a calculation is so large that the planners have never agreed to put the whole plan on a computer, nor have they found a computer large enough to process so much data. There is also the suspicion that the planners fear that the use of a computer would in effect transfer their power to decide what should be produced, and how, to the programmers, who could in fact adjust the program as they see fit. Consequently the dream of a systematic plan for an economic allocation of goods that would solve all planning and supply problems is still only a dream.

However, even if there were assurances that an adequate plan could be designed by the planners and a computer, there is no guarantee that Soviet workers and managers would respond positively and adhere to the plan's guidelines. Managers and workers in turn have to be motivated. There was a period early in Soviet life when it was argued that the Soviet worker and manager would work because of their enthusiasm for the revolution and their ideological fervor. That phase passed rather quickly. Out of necessity it was decided, therefore, to base rewards on how much the workers and managers produced. The more produced, the higher the pay and premiums. This fit in nicely with the planning procedure since Gosplan, when drawing up its material balances, worked conceptually in terms of so many tons of this and so many meters of that, which were to be produced and supplied. In the same way targets for both state and work incentives were also spelled out in the same type of physical targets. A good worker and manager was one who produced more tons and meters the current year compared to the year before. The larger the percentage-increase in production, the higher the wage bonus would be.

In contrast, then, to the manager in a capitalist economy, quantities, rather than profits and return on investment, have been the major considerations to a manager in the U.S.S.R. As a consequence, there has been little concern in the Soviet economy about selling what was produced, and very little regard for quality and product variety. The workers' and managers' salaries generally have not been affected by such considerations. The system stressed production for production's sake. Whether the goods were used by a purchaser was immaterial. Presumably someone would find a use for them sooner or later. Since everything always seemed to be in short supply, it was usually sooner. Therefore, the system put a premium on good production engineers who knew how to prevent production breakdowns, insure a steady flow of supplies, and maximize the production process. Those who excelled at quality control or sales served no purpose and thus, more often than not, were flushed out of the system. Inevitably, economic growth became the chief gospel of the Soviet Union, and Gosplan became its chief prophet.

The Stalinist production system did have certain strengths. It served to bring about the industrialization of the Soviet Union. Prior to the revolution, despite some promising beginnings at industrial production, Russia was among the most industrially backward nations of Europe; now it is among the strongest industrially. We shall explain later why we purposely use the word "strongest" rather than "most advanced." By its terms, it is not only the strongest in Europe, but may be the strongest in the world. If one accepts the Soviet emphasis on physical output in individual industries, rather than on profit or gross national product, the Soviet Union may have won the race set by Khrushchev between the United States and the Soviet Union. In the late 1950's during one of his visits to the United States, he boasted that the Soviet Union would overtake and surpass the United States by 1970, and at the latest, by 1980. However, the Soviet GNP in 1979 was about $1.4 trillion, or only about 60 percent of the $2.4 trillion that the United States produced.[2] But Khrushchev never referred to the GNP. Soviet leaders rarely use the concept. Instead, he had in mind surpassing the United States in the production of such special items as steel, oil, coal, cement, lead, nickel, tractors, metal-cutting and metal-forming machine tools, and wheat.[3] It turns out that in 1980, the Soviet Union produced more of each of these items than did the United States, and so in a strict sense, Khrushchev won his race. (See Table II-1.) Of course, the United States still outranks the Soviet Union in the production of many items, such as natural gas, electricity, and automobiles. But the Soviet Union has done suprisingly well.

However, Khrushchev won the wrong race. The rest of the world went off in a different direction, emphasizing finished products and the standard of living, not individual industrial commodities. But as it has evolved, it is hard for the Stalinist economic model to do anything else but concentrate on individual industrial commodities. The production of individual commodities that the planners and the plan stress, and for which the enterprise managers win their premiums, does not necessarily benefit the consumer. What good does it do a strong industrial society today to have an increase of 10 per cent in the production of steel, if the process all but comes to an end there? At any early stage of development, the rapid growth of the steel industry is important because it makes possible the growth of other industries. But after a time, the emphasis must shift from producing steel for its own sake to producing it for use in the manufacture of consumer goods for the ultimate enjoyment of the population.

Table II-1

PRODUCTION OF MAJOR PRODUCTS

	1970	1975	1979	1980 (Actual)	1980 (Plan as of 1976)	1985 Plan	1979 U.S. Prods.
Electricity (bil. KWH)	740.9	1038.6	1239	1295	1380	1550–1600	2432
Oil (mil. tons)	353.0	490.8	586	603	640	620–640	420
Gas (bil. m³)	197.9	289.3	407	435	435	600–64	570
Coal (mil. tons)	624.1	701.3	719	716	805	770–800	704
Steel (mil. tons)	85.9	103.0	149	148	168.5	n.a.	123
Automotive Vehicles (1000's)	916.0	1964.0	2173	2199	2297	n.a.	n.a.
Automobiles (1000's)	344.2	1201.0	1314	1327	n.a.	n.a.	8419
Trucks (1000's)	524.5	696.0	780	787	n.a.	n.a.	3037
Metal-Cutting Machine Tools (1000's)	202.2	231.4	229.5	216			65.2
Metal-Forming Machine Tools (1000's)	41.3	50.5	56.5	57.1	215–220	283–243	30.5
Grain (mil. tons)	168.8	140.1	179	189			294

AVERAGE ANNUAL PERCENTAGE INCREASE FOR PRECEDING FIVE-YEAR PERIOD

Electricity	7.0	4.5	5.9	3.7–4.3
Oil	6.8	4.2	5.5	.6–1.4
Gas	7.9	8.5	8.5	6.6–8.0
Coal	2.4	.4	2.8	1.5–2.2
Steel	3.7	7.5	10.3	
Automotive Vehicles	16.4	2.3	3.2	
Automobiles	28.4	2.0		
Trucks	5.8	2.4		
Metal-Cutting Machine Tools	2.7	−1.4		
Metal-Forming Machine Tools	4.1	2.5		
Grain	5.8	6.2	8.9–9.5	4.7–5.2

Concentrating too much on consumer goods, however, might result in very low capital formation and no investment. For a time, there was considerable worry that we in the United States had gone too far to the other extreme and were focusing only on today, with no regard for tomorrow. That would be just as ill-advised as the steel, heavy industrial, and investment obsession that besets nations addicted to the Stalinist model.

Subsequent Soviet leaders have since acknowledged the harmful consequences of Stalin's continual emphasis on increasing production of basic industrial commodities. Khrushchev, for example, tried to steer his country in another direction in the early 1960's. The fact that he personally had to issue decrees about the need to decentralize, of course, only highlights how the center dominates everything, even the effort to decentralize. But in Khrushchev's colorful idiom, the planners were in a rut. Moreover, it was a rut they had come to love and cherish. In fact, they flourished in it—so why should they trouble themselves to risk anything new? More than anything else, they knew how to produce steel, so naturally enough, they enjoyed producing it. To paraphrase one of our former vice presidents, once they knew how to build one steel mill, they knew how to build them all. Why, therefore, should the planners risk plan underfulfillment for something as exotic and unpredictable as electronics, computers, or sophisticated chemicals? It was much easier and safer to stick with steel. In the words of Khrushchev, "The production of steel is like a well-traveled road with deep ruts; here even blind horses will not turn off because the wheels will break. Similarly, some officials have put on steel blinkers; they do everything as they were taught in their day. A material appears which is superior to steel and is cheaper, but they keep on shouting, 'steel, steel.' "[4] As one communist economist put it, "I never again want to hear how many tons of steel we produced last year."

The concentration on steel was symptomatic of the types of distortions in the Soviet economic system that have risen in response to the stress on plan fulfillment. For example, Soviet factories tend to be very large and self-contained. A Soviet factory manager tries to produce as much as possible of his output within the confines of his own factory. In this way, he hopes to reduce the number of delivery delays of components from suppliers. With fewer delivery delays, there should be fewer instances of plan underfulfillment. The East European economies have the same proclivity for large-scale self-sufficient operations. The share of total industrial employment in Eastern Europe which originates in factories of a thousand or more employees is more than double that of Western Europe.[5]

Large size is not the only economic distortion resulting from the preoccupation with plan-fulfillment. All too often the means—that is, plan-fulfillment spelled out in some physical unit of production which is needed to build the country's overall economic capabilities—becomes an end in itself. What is lost sight of in this process is the final product and the final consumer.

Some of that final product, of course, should go for investment and some for military purposes, but because the planners are forced to focus so intensely on steel, investment, and armaments, it is likely that the consumer side will be neglected. Then, as Igor Birman has put it, "The Soviet economy" will produce "mainly for itself."[6] As a result, a disproportionate share of production never sees its way to the ultimate consumer but is diverted, instead, to a needless increase in the capital intensity of industry, or just waste. Since the payoff in the Soviet Union for the manager comes from the sole act of producing, he does not have to worry about competing for sales or high-profit earnings. Therefore, as long as the product is produced, the planners are happy. There is no distress if the commodity is then just stored and forgotten, or reshaped in such a way that no one can use it. That is why the communist economist is so upset with the emphasis on steel production.

Such a system leads to enormous waste and distortion. The classic example is the nail producer whose target is spelled out in terms of tons of production per month. He concludes he can most easily fulfill his production target by producing one large nail. When the planners try to correct for this by specifying the target in numbers of nails produced rather than tons, the nail manufacturer simply switches his production to producing numerous tiny nails. Similarly, paper manufacturers have been caught up in the same weight-unit cycle as they switch between thick and thin paper.[7]

There is the same type of distortion when an enterprise produces a variety of heterogeneous goods. The typical physical-output standard cannot be used to measure enterprise performance because it is impossible to determine how to balance off the fact that an enterprise produces ten pounds more copper but twenty meters less wire. This makes it necessary, therefore, to devise a measure which will allow the planner to compare the production of different products and different units. Soviet planners came up with what they called *valovaia produktsia*, or "*val*" for short, which is a measure of the gross ruble-output. The manager of a factory producing a batch of heterogeneous goods is judged according to how much the gross ruble-value of his output has increased in the current year as compared to last year. Soviet managers quickly discovered, however, that there were two ways they could fulfill such a target: a) produce more units at the same price as last year, or b) utilize more expensive inputs per unit, so that after the fixed markup had been added to production costs, the gross ruble-value of items produced would total more, even though fewer units might actually have been produced. The fact that wholesale prices of raw materials were held constant for fifteen years from 1967 to 1982 did nothing to discourage the use of large quantities of raw materials; in fact, it did just the opposite.

This stress on wasting inputs has led Soviet manufacturers to favor the production of goods that are big and wasteful of resources. Moreover, unit-pricing for Soviet products is spelled out in tons or kilograms.[8] Thus the heavier the product, the more gross ruble-value the enterprise will be able to claim, and the quicker the firm will be able to fulfill its plan and collect a bonus. No wonder the Soviet Union has trouble with miniaturization. Furthermore, expenditure of fuel per-unit of electrical power produced, fuel per-ton of open-hearth steel consumed, and metal per-unit of engine power and of cargo capacity of railroad cars is higher in the Soviet Union than it is in most other industrialized countries.[9] (Does this also explain why the Soviet Union builds bigger missiles than we do?)

The Soviet planning system stresses not only intermediate production targets, but also intermediate performance and service. These are measured against some quantitative target, and as might be expected, this also causes distortion and often downright waste. Thus geologists who are assigned to drill for oil are rewarded with premiums if they manage to drill a specified number of meters each month. The drillers quickly concluded that they should drill only shallow holes. The deeper they go, the slower the drilling process becomes. It takes more time to put in a drilling pipe at deeper depths, compared to putting it in at shallower depths; also there are more pipe-cracks at deeper depths when the tension is greater. As explained by *Pravda,* "deeper drilling means reducing the speed of the worker and reducing the group's bonuses."[10] Accordingly, Soviet drillers soon came to regard the drilling for petroleum as being incidental to the drilling for meters. As a result, "there are geological expeditions in the Republic of Kazhakstan that have not discovered a valuable deposit for many years but are counted among the successful expeditions because they have fulfilled their assignment in terms of meters. The groups which conscientiously turn up deposits are often financial losers.''[11]

If such experiments were possible, it would be interesting to see whether Soviet planners would have adopted such a wasteful planning system were the country smaller and more poorly endowed. The fact that the Soviet Union is so large and so rich with raw materials has meant that the planners, until recently at least, have had no need to worry about exhausting their resources. Whenever the resources of one deposit appeared to be running out, the Soviet geologists have almost always managed to find new deposits somewhere else. Thus when the petroleum deposits at Baku became depleted, Soviet geologists found a new and larger field in the Ural-Volga region. When fears about the depletion of the Ural-Volga field began to increase, Soviet petroleum experts found the West Siberian fields. Under the circumstances, there was never much concern about conserving raw materials. What would have happened, however, if the communists had come to power in a resource-scarce country such as Japan or Switzerland? Would the Japanese or Swiss communists have adopted "*val*" and the quantity-type of success-indicators? There is nothing particularly sacred about such techniques in Marxist ideology. Yet once adopted, *val* and quantity indicators become hard to alter. They take on the aura of orthodoxy. But given the insistence on spelling out such tasks in quantitative terms, distortions seem to be all but inevitable. Because his bonus depends on the fulfillment of such quantitative targets, the factory manager comes to care only about fulfilling his specific target. But it is difficult to find specific micro-targets that over time always coincide with an improvement in the macro-economy. As a result, the fulfillment of micro-management targets seldom leads to comparable improvement in the country's economic well-being. In the process not only raw materials, but also human labor, is wasted. Thus in an effort to speed up the flow of railroad traffic, stationmasters in the Soviet Union were told that they would be rewarded with increased bonuses if they managed to reduce the number of train delays at their stations. Soviet planners were concerned that trains were being forced to wait idly in station yards while other trains ahead of them were being unloaded. The stationmasters responded quickly. Rather than seek to speed up the unloading of the trains, they simply ordered that incoming trains stop outside their station yards until the trains in the yards had completed their unloading process. This immediately reduced the number of trains standing by idly in the station yards, but it increased enormously the number of trains standing idly by outside the station yards.[12]

II.

Quantitative success-indicators generate similar distortions in the construction industry. The emphasis in construction is on work performed, not buildings completed. In addition, interest charges on the use of capital are applied imperfectly. Access to capital is dependent more on the decisions of planners than on financial considerations. Thus, once allocated, there is no urgent need to complete construction. It is not unusual, therefore, as in the case of the Law School at Moscow State University, to find buildings that have been under construction for a decade or more.[13] In fact in 1980, 87 per cent of the capital investment undertaken in the course of 1980 was unfinished by the end of the year.[14] That represents a sharp increase from 1970 when the figure was 73 per cent.[15] Even then it was considered to be too high. No wonder visitors to the Soviet Union are always impressed by the amount of building activity that is taking place. But it goes on and on, so that the construction industry is stretched too thinly. Soviet economists have concluded that probably more would be accomplished if construction officials restricted themselves to fewer projects and concentrated on finishing up those projects.[16] As a consequence, Soviet leaders periodically call for a moratorium on new construction in order to finish up the old construction.[17] But the frequency of such calls suggests how unsuccessful such efforts have been.

Of all the Stalinist model's shortcomings, the one that probably most hinders Soviet economic development is its inability to do away with the old and obsolete and foster innovation and technological change. The Stalinist model works best when it increases the production of the existing basket of goods. Any change, whether it involves shutting down the production of old goods or introducing new goods, is threatening.

Managers are unlikely to be concerned about obsolescence or innovation as long as their premiums are primarily dependent on increasing production. Since factory managers do not have to concern themselves with sales or market trends, they are under no pressure to do away with the obsolete. They have no need to respond to the normal signals and pressures which face managers in other economies. The system lacks an automatic mechanism for rewarding smart decisions and punishing dumb ones, at least as measured by what is good for the economy as a whole. On the contrary, as long as Gosplan continues to include a particular item in its plan, the manager will continue to produce it. Therefore, Gosplan somehow has to be notified that an item is no longer in demand. In order to know that, someone has to monitor inventory accumulation. However, due to poor communication and, more important, because increased production, not decreased inventory, has been Gosplan's main concern, Gosplan has generally been insensitive to the problem of the accumulation of either specific items in specific locations or total inventory. One indication of the problem is the growth of very large inventories.[18] On occasion factories have continued to produce obsolete models for ten years or more.[19]

Ironically, Marx implied that a capitalist society would be more likely to hold on to obsolete products than a socialist state because a capitalist will insist on straining the last productive ounce out of his capital, and thus produce as long as the machinery holds out. However, much as a capitalist would like to act as Marx suggests, in fact as well as in theory, the capitalist more often than not has found that holding on to the same products for too long a period of time is a sure way to bankruptcy. Instead, particularly if the market is a dynamic one, the capitalist's competitor is likely to come up with a more suitable product which will drive the old one out of the market, whether the capitalist's machinery has been fully depreciated or not. Thus the capitalist must be responsive and innovative and move to new products to stay in business. Bankruptcy is the final solution for obsolescence.

Ministry and Gosplan officials would just as soon not deal with bankruptcy. It is much easier to authorize a subsidy and thus avoid a shutdown of facilities.[20] Bankruptcy is not only messy from a bureaucratic point of view, but it also involves unemployment. Since the Soviet Union has overemployment, not unemployment, it normally would not be difficult to absorb any unemployed workers. Thus the reluctance to encourage the firing of workers is not due to a fear that they will be unable to find alternative work somewhere in the country, but because of the political implications of the act. Unemployment is something that is only supposed to happen in a capitalist society. Indeed, the guarantee of full employment is included as a part of the Soviet Constitution, and the Soviet leadership counts this as a human right generally not guaranteed in other countries. Such a guarantee, they imply, helps to balance off other shortcomings that might exist in the Soviet Union. However, this political concern reduces the country's economic flexibility and makes it difficult to cope with obsolescence. Guaranteed full employment may be a more humane policy, but unless administered with greater adroitness than the Soviets have so far demonstrated, it is also economically stultifying. As we in the United States have discovered because of similar political concerns, bankruptcy is not always inevitable here either. Where a corporation has political or military importance (Lockheed) or there is the prospect of massive unemployment (Chrysler), the government has so far found it expedient to step in with financial support. The government finds it expedient, therefore, to cushion the callousness of the market. In the Soviet Union, where the government owns and therefore is responsible for all industry, it is therefore almost always compelled to step in.

The reluctance to fire workers encourages the unproductive utilization of the labor force and the illusion that there are more jobs than employees. If managers are forced to use their work force efficiently, there would probably be a surplus of workers even in the next decade. But failure to utilize workers more efficiently will have serious consequences for future economic growth. Soviet planners rely heavily on increases in the labor force to provide the input necessary to increase industrial production. But because of a fall in the birth rate, there is due to be a serious drop in the next decade in the number of new employees who will be available to enter the work force.[21] Therefore, it is all the more important that Soviet managers be encouraged to fire nonproductive workers. The reluctance of a manager to winnow his work force reflects not only the political inappropriateness of such an act, but also the fact that the wage fund of the enterprise depends on the number of workers employed by the enterprise. Thus reducing the number of employees means that the overall wage-fund will be reduced as well, which in some cases also precludes the awarding of higher manager premiums.

The mirror image of product obsolescence is product innovation. Closing down factories might be a little easier to implement if new factories could be opened to absorb the released work force. Because of the retraining and retooling involved, that has been very difficult to do even in the most benevolent societies. Moreover, Soviet planners and managers seem, at least in the civilian sector, to have an almost phobic reaction to innovation.[22] The main reason is that the Soviet manager usually has little to gain and much to lose from innovation. In order to revamp his production line to make way for a new product, the manager usually has to halt production. This means he would be unable to fulfill his present production targets, and thus he will not qualify for his bonus. At the same time, the Soviet incentive system does not provide for any substantial increase in bonuses for the production of new goods. Thus there is little in the way of extra inducement for innovation, but considerable disincentive. Not surprisingly, the Soviets have found it virtually impossible to produce certain advanced and even not-so-advanced products long after they have become obsolete in the West. Their ineptitude with computers and computer software is particularly striking.[23] After all, not only are computers important for the economy, but they are critical for military purposes as well. The Soviet failure to master computer production is not due to a lack of effort. Indeed, the Soviets have produced a few prototypes of advanced computers but so far have been unable to produce them with the capabilities and in the quantities needed. In retrospect, this should have been anticipated. One of the major explanations for the success of American companies like IBM in the manufacture of computers is that the American companies, in order to survive, maintain a policy of catering to their customer's needs. This comes not only from frequent calls by computer salesmen, but from repairmen as well. Thus there has always been a good flow of feedback from the user to the manufacturer, and consequently, the manufacturer usually has a good idea of the improvements he should make in his products. There is almost no comparable feedback in the Soviet system. For that matter, when American manufacturers sell their products to Soviet buyers and offer to provide followup service in the same way they would do at home, the Soviets almost always refuse the offer. Sometimes this is done for reasons of national security, but more often than not, such offers are refused simply because that is not the Soviet way. The Soviet manufacturer engages in no such practices and has no such worries or expenses. All he has to do is produce, not sell; nor does he have to worry about repeat sales. Until a remedy can be found to mitigate the lack of concern for consumer needs, the Soviets will find it hard to catch up. In one instance, because they realized they were so far behind, the Russians found it necessary to pirate a complete set of six-hundred volumes of an IBM software manual, and translate those manuals into Russian, keeping the English names and terminology regardless of how inappropriate such names and terminology might have sounded when transliterated into Russian.[24]

Undoubtedly, the Soviets are not the first to pirate in such a blatant fashion, but what is striking about the Soviets is that they do not seem to be able to take the technology they copy, buy, or borrow and improve on it. Unlike the Japanese who flourish on upgrading foreign technology or improvement engineering, the Soviets seem as unable to improve on foreign technology as they are to invent their own technology. Taking an extreme point of view, Anthony C. Sutton, goes so far as to assert that the Soviet Union has had to buy, borrow, or steal all the technology developed in the country since World War I.[25]

While acknowledging Soviet problems, there are good reasons to dispute Sutton's contention. After all, the Soviets have led the world in putting a man in space and developing other technologies, particularly in the field of welding. However, whether the Soviets have borrowed as much or less than Sutton claims, the fact is that they must borrow more than might be expected. After all, they do not suffer from a lack of well-trained scientists and engineers, nor from a lack of impressive laboratory research. In addition, the Soviets are able to innovate when it comes to producing military hardware. They run the military sector, however, in a more flexible and imaginative way. The managers in weapon factories are not as dependent on plan-fulfillment for their premiums. Furthermore, they are given more flexibility to experiment and more capital to use in a more decentralized fashion. It also helps that production in such factories is considered to be a priority matter. However, there can only be so many priorities. Generally production of the nonmilitary items is not regarded as a priority, even when the same factory produces both military and consumer goods. Most important is the fact that when a factory manager in a civilian sector is shown a laboratory prototype with enormous potential, he is reluctant to introduce it on the factory floor. As with so much else in the Soviet economic system, the reason is that such experimentation might jeopardize his schedule for fulfillment of the plan and thus jeopardize his own bonus.

Another factor which hampers innovation is that capital financing is tightly centralized. This makes it very difficult to nourish any innovation outside the laboratory or at an unofficially authorized shop. This frustrates on-the-job or backyard inventions, an important source of innovation in the West, particularly in the United States. Soviet planners are almost always reluctant to allocate money to such groups because the utilization of capital is then harder to police, and as a result, there is a greater likelihood that the money will be diverted for unauthorized and conceivably even seditious use. Investment of this sort scattered in a buckshot way is much harder to control than when dispersed to a few firms, even if it is given in large amounts. Moreover, the cost of processing such a loan is almost always the same whether money is set aside for a large grant or a small one. Thus the tendency is to make large grants to large laboratories and factory units. Consequently the Soviets tend to deprive themselves of the growth that springs from small-industry creativity.

Some Soviet analysts have concluded that the Soviet Union may actually be better off if it takes promising laboratory results to Western companies and licenses those companies to produce the Soviet-invented products. This way, at least the Soviet Union can earn something from the sale of the license. Indeed, the Soviets have managed to license some important technology, such as diffusion-welding in a vacuum and the polymerization of ethylene, to Western companies before either process was used by industry in the U.S.S.R. itself.[26]

Such economic distortions and lack of innovation reflect how, in the Soviet Union, the true ends in the Soviet Union, have so often been lost sight of. This is an inevitable result when the incentive system no longer serves to stimulate the manager toward the proper ends. This is not unique to the Soviet Union. Some U.S. analysts fear that the same type of distortion has been occurring in the United States. Some critics warn that American managers have become mesmerized with the need to maximize short-run earnings.[27] This is because corporate stockholders have increased their insistence on higher short-run return on investment. Therefore, the manager's performance is judged from quarter to quarter, and inevitably, he tends to downgrade the importance of his long-run efforts. In some instances, that poses no problem. However, in most cases the maximization of short-run returns comes at the expense of the maximization of long-run results. Capital investment and long-run development projects, which might increase earnings in the long run, are scrapped because they increase expense and thus reduce earnings in the short run. The point is that the distortions so endemic to the Soviet Union are not necessarily a sign of the moral depravity of the Communist system. They exist whenever the incentive system becomes outmoded.

III.

The fact that such difficulties are not unique to the U.S.S.R. is not likely to be all that comforting. It is bad enough that the Soviet Union finds innovation so difficult to master and that the rest of the world has mastered new industrial techniques which leave the Soviet Union further and further behind. There is now even reason to worry whether the Soviet Union can continue to compete effectively on its own terms—that is, with heavy industry. By its own standards, the rate of growth seems to be falling, and indeed, in some cases has become negative. While Table II-1 shows that the Soviet Union may have outproduced the United States in several important areas, it nonetheless produced less coal and less steel than it had the year before. Similarly, in 1979, the Soviet Union also produced less coal and steel than it had in 1978, but in addition, it also produced less grain, fertilizer, paper, cement, vegetable oil, and fewer radios, metal-cutting machine-tools, and tractors. Such production declines clearly had the makings of a good-sized recession.

There are many possible explanations for this economic downturn. The bad weather hurt not only agriculture, but industry. In late 1978 and early 1979, it was simply too cold to work effectively. There were also floods in April and May, 1979. It is also true that some of the most conveniently located mineral and raw-material deposits have been depleted and thus it became more difficult and costly to produce such materials than it was a decade ago.[28] There is no doubt that the fall in the number of workers entering the labor force and the drop in the investment rate also began to have an impact.[29] Finally, for reasons we shall explain in the chapters ahead, worker morale became even more of a problem than before.

The important question facing Soviet leaders is whether or not anything can be done to reverse this falling rate of growth and drop in production. As indicated in Table II-2, there has been a fairly steady fall in the growth of factor inputs over the years, as well as combined factor productivity, particularly since the early 1960's. Nor is there much to indicate that this deterioration will be arrested.[30] But even if the Soviet Union somehow discovers how to revitalize its traditional industries, that would still not be enough. The most important challenge remains the revamping of the Soviet economic structure in order to bring it up to date with the world's new industrial techniques, but that will likely require radical surgery. Even then, there is no guarantee that such surgery will be successful. The ability to make midcourse corrections within the framework of an existing economic model is difficult to implement under the best of circumstances.

The economist Egon Neuburger has suggested that an economic model should be judged not only as to how well it meets the tests set for it within an existing framework, but as to how well it is able to adjust to

Table II-2

AVERAGE ANNUAL RATES OF GROWTH FOR SOVIET GNP FACTOR INPUTS,
FACTOR PRODUCTIVITY, AND CONSUMPTION PER CAPITA

	1951–55	1956–60	1961–65	1966–70	1971–75	1976–80
GNP	6.0%	5.8%	5.0%	5.5%	3.8%	2.8%
Labor[1]	1.9	0.6	1.6	2.0	1.7	1.2
Capital	9.0	9.8	8.7	7.5	7.9	6.8
Land	4.0	1.3	0.6	−0.3	0.8	—[3]
Combined factor productivity	1.4	1.8	0.9	1.5	−0.4	−0.7
Per Capita Consumption[2]	5.3	4.2	2.5	4.7	3.2	1.6[3]

[1] Man-hours.
[2] Total consumption.
[3] Refers only to 1976–79.
SOURCES: Office of Technology Assessment, *Technology and Soviet Energy Availability,*
Washington Office of Technology Assessment, 1981, p. 250.

an entirely new set of tests and needs.[31] Since the Stalinist model no
longer seems to be meeting its original performance tests, does it do
any better meeting Neuburger's second set of criteria; that is, does it
allow for flexibility and a relatively easy transformation into some new
kind of model? Or are the legacies of the past so fundamental that any
major adjustment will set off enormous economic disruptions?

Based on the evidence that is available so far, there is good reason to
believe that while the Stalinist model is well-suited for one type of effort,
it does not lend itself to switching to a new set of priorities, or to a
different mix of goods.[32] In fact, of all the world's economic systems,
the Stalinist model is probably the one that is the most difficult to re-
structure. It lacks an ability to adapt. Once in place, the Stalinist model
builds up strong vested interests. Not only economic surgery, but even
economic tinkering sets off disruption and distrust among all levels of
Soviet society. Soviet leaders fear change because in the past these
changes have had a tendency to escalate out of control. Managers fear
change because it may become harder for them to earn the premiums
they have been accustomed to earning. While the workers are probably
more open to change than either the leaders or managers, they favor
change only if it is clear that their jobs will not be affected.

Reforms have been attempted in the past, but at least since World War II, most officially proposed Soviet reforms have not sought to break too far away from the Stalinist model. For example, no reform has seriously proposed doing away with Gosplan, planning, plan-fulfillment, or the large investment-to-GNP ratio, or the continued emphasis on heavy industry. One of the most far-reaching proposals came from economist Evsei Liberman, who, along with several other economists, provoked a nationwide debate in the mid-1960's when he suggested that instead of plan-fulfillment, specified in some physical quantity, it might make more sense to switch to a plan measured in sales and profits.[33] He also advocated the elimination of several other targets such as labor productivity, number of workers, wages, and capital investment, which he said often caused the manager to divert his resources to nonproductive activities. The effect of these so-called "Liberman proposals" would have allowed prices to fluctuate some-what more freely and enterprises to operate with somewhat less inter-ference from the center. Admittedly, these reforms had the potential for setting off some far-reaching changes. Yet even Liberman did not chal-lenge the basic nature of the Stalinist model. While many foreigners saw his proposal to upgrade the role of profits as a sign that Liberman and the Soviet Union were moving towards a more market-oriented economy, Liberman himself denied this. He repudiated it not only for political reasons, but also because he did not really intend to do away with Gosplan, heavy industry, and heavy investment. His goal was sim-ply to make the existing process a more efficient one and improve the decision-making procedure.

In 1964, just before he was ousted from office, Khrushchev sought to implement some of the proposals put forth by Liberman and other economists. However, most of the reforms soon came to naught. They did not seem to bring about the hoped-for results. For the nation as a whole, the reported rate of economic growth began to decline. In all fairness, that was not just a reflection of the inappropriateness of the proposed reforms. Rather, the Soviet economy in the mid-1960's was racked by a series of disastrous harvests and other economic problems that would have caused serious growth retardation with or without such reforms. For example, the fact that some of the more conveniently located mineral deposits had begun to run out would have added extra costs to the economy, whether it were a Stalinist or even capitalist model.

But there were at least three more serious reasons for the failure of these reforms: one economic, one linked to domestic issues, and one involved with international political concerns. Economically, the reforms were doomed to fail because of the way they were introduced. A few factories at a time were singled out and told they could choose their own basic product mix, set their own prices, and measure their results in terms of profits rather than in terms of physical output produced. However, the enthusiasm for the experiment quickly waned so that as additional firms were converted to the new system, their authority to operate independently was cut back. As a result, there were never enough firms operating under the new guidelines (there was no critical mass) and those firms in the experiment never had the power they needed to act decisively. That turned out to be a crucial matter. Presumably, if enough firms had been converted to the new reforms, quantity would have made a qualitative difference. As it was, the few enterprises selected for the experiment kept running up against the inflexibility of the Stalinist model. What good did it do to allow the Bolshevik Mens Clothing Factory to choose its own product-mix when the plant's director quickly found that the new synthetic fabric he wanted to utilize in his clothing was either not being produced in the Soviet Union or had already been consigned by the plant to some other manufacturer. Even if the cloth had been found, the Bolshevik manager would have discovered that he could do nothing with it because he would have needed a more modern set of cutting and sewing equipment especially designed to handle synthetics. However, this machinery was unavailable in the Soviet Union because the textile machine manufacturers' targets were specified only as to the number of machines produced. Accordingly, the machine manufacturer had absolutely no interest or incentive in risking ongoing production in order to master these new and more complicated machines.

The second cause for the failure of the reforms stems from the tension that arises out of domestic political relationships. If the experimental firms were to be as flexible and responsive as planned, they would have to be freed from the "petty tutelage" or strict controls normally applied by the ministries which supervise their subordinate enterprises. Under the new system, the enterprises were to be guided by the market and its signals rather than the ministries and their orders. However, this assumed that the market would function properly and that the prices that were posted were meaningful ones that reflected demand and supply pressures. Only in this way would the manager be guided properly. Collectively, each manager's actions would in turn be digested by the market and to the extent these managers increased or decreased their demand for various inputs, these decisions would be transmitted through the pricing system. In effect, prices as they evolved within the market system would serve as a self-regulating feedback mechanism. But if prices were to perform such a function, that implies that there had to be enough firms, enough competition, enough flexibility in the market and enough give-and-take so that market forces could be reflected properly. Given the fact that initially only a few firms were selected for the experiment and that the Soviet Union had heretofore maintained strict control over prices (seldom changing wholesale prices more than once a decade) there seemed to be little chance that the prices and, thus, the market would function properly.

The best analogy is the way the Council of Mutual Economic Assistance (CMEA) countries decide how to price the goods they sell to one another. Because their currencies are not convertible, and because their internal pricing systems are so irrational and arbitrary, they find it simpler just to use analogous foreign-trade prices charged for similar goods by private corporations to each other in the capitalist markets. When a Soviet planner was asked how CMEA would decide prices when, as promised, the whole world became communist, he answered with a knowing wink, "We will keep one country capitalist just for this purpose." Whether he realized that world market-prices could only be meaningful when there are numerous parties involved was unclear.

Some have argued the contrary, insisting that state-owned firms can operate efficiently with meaningful prices. They point to the success of such nationalized corporations as Renault and Volkswagen, which even though they are basically state-owned, seem to function very well. However, what those making such contentions ignore is that these state-owned firms operate within the overall context of a capitalist market with countless other buyers, suppliers, and competitors who for the most part are reacting to market signals and therefore make the market function relatively efficiently.

Yet even if there were a critical mass of Soviet enterprises interlinked to a market system, that alone would still not guarantee that the prices would function effectively. In order for prices to function effectively, ministry and planning officials must refrain from interfering with local enterprise decisions. Yet despite instructions to refrain from interfering with the firms involved in the Liberman Reforms, the ministries intervened. They did this partially because they felt the market was giving off faulty signals, and partially because they always seemed to insist that the enterprise produce something that the enterprise did not wish to produce because the market dictated otherwise. Such interference, especially when a senior official would order that a firm *not* cease the production of a certain item, had the effect of emasculating efforts at creating fiscal discipline.[34]

It was impossible to head in two directions at once. The frustration the reformers felt was reflected in a widely circulated joke Soviet reformers used to tell at the time. It seems, the joke went, that the Moscow traffic authorities noticed a very sharp increase in traffic accidents. After various unsuccessful attempts to bring the accident-rate down, the chief of the traffic bureau had an inspiration. Someone told him that London's traffic accident rate was one of the lowest in the world. "Let us send someone to see how the British do it," he said. After a short visit, his deputy returned with the solution. The main difference between the way traffic operated in Moscow and London was that, unlike Moscow, London traffic moved on the left side of the street. The solution for Moscow was obvious; as of July 1, the traffic should be switched from one side to the other. However, an older specialist argued that this might be too much of a change to make at once, especially for those who did not drive for a living and therefore had less driving experience. Consequently, it was agreed to introduce the switchover in stages; on July 1st all trucks and taxis would be shifted to the left side of the road, while all private passengers cars would stick to the right side of the road until December 1st, by which date they too would make the switch!

International events were the third reason for the failure of the Liberman Reforms. It was something that the reformers had no way of anticipating. At about the same time that the Liberman Reforms were being discussed and implemented in the Soviet Union, the Czechs began an experiment of their own. Initially there was some similarity between the two reforms, at least in terms of the increase in authority that was to be turned over to the enterprise manager. However, as it evolved, it became clear that the Czech reform had become much more far-reaching. Not only had the Czechs radically decreased the emphasis on heavy industry, planning, and centralized control, but they began to change the political structure. The Soviet leaders interpreted these events as a threat to the role of the Communist Party inside Czechoslovakia, and to the Czech commitment to the Warsaw Pact and its close ties to the

Soviet Union. To express their disapproval, the Soviet leaders ordered an end to the Czech experiment, and on August 20, 1968, they sent Soviet troops into Czechoslovakia to insure that their orders were carried out. Having suppressed the Czech reforms, the Soviet leaders could hardly pursue their own reforms. Given the difficulties mentioned earlier, the Liberman experiment seemed to be going nowhere anyway. After the Czech invasion, for the most part it was quietly ignored and only a few inconsequential remnants remained.

The sad fate of the Liberman experiment did not mean the end of Soviet economic experimentation. Over the years the Soviets have proposed a variety of measures, but almost all were little more than superficial changes. In searching for some way to improve their economic efficiency, Soviet economists have frequently looked to the capitalist world for guidance. Undoubtedly Liberman took some of his inspiration from the West's private-enterprise sector, but so have some of the other reformers. Back in October, 1967, a planner near Tula suggested to the management of the local Shchekino Chemical Factory that instead of increasing the work force, the manager should shrink it and take half of the reduced payroll and divide it up among those who had not been fired. After two years' time, the labor force had been reduced by one thousand, while factory output increased by over 80 per cent, labor productivity doubled, and wages increased by 30 per cent.[35] Unfortunately, the plan seemed to have had a one-time-only impact. After the initial saving, there was considerably less that the management could do for an encore. And even though the planners had promised that the workers would continue to share the enlarged wage-fund, after a while the planners began to jack up the work norms and reduce the wage-fund. There was also a Catch-22 clause in the proposal. The incentive fund for the enterprise was set as a proportion of the total wage-fund. Obviously, reducing the work force had the net effect of reducing premiums even if a part of the reduced wages were distributed to the remaining work force. Therefore, the size of the bonus and overall take-home pay turned out to be much less than it initially appeared to the unsophisticated observer.[36] This experiment tended to generate distrust particularly among those workers who found themselves unemployed. They had come to believe the holy promises about the sanctity and constitutional guarantee of full employment. Like their counterparts in capitalist countries, those marked for dismissal began to protest, and morale, even among those who ultimately stayed, suffered.[37] Not surprisingly, the experiment was not widely adopted. Soviet experimentation has not been limited to shrinking the work force. An effort has also been made to rationalize the organizational structure of Soviet industry. Relying again on what they observed to be happening in the noncommunist world, Soviet administrators have sought to amalgamate related enterprises. The resulting "syndicates" or production associations resemble holding companies which combine enterprises producing related products that are at various stages of the production cycle. In addition to increasing the economies of scale, the Soviets hope these production associations will make it possible to short-circuit some paper work. The expectation is that the director of the production association will be able to make decisions within the production association that previously had to be referred all the way up to the respective ministries or Gossnab or Gosplan level. Thus, to a limited extent, the production association is given more of a say in the allocation of a restricted amount of investment funds. This is intended to increase flexibility and allow for a modest amount of innovation. Toward the same end, many production associations are designed to include a research laboratory within their jurisdiction. Since the production association is to operate on a profit-and-loss basis, in theory the production association will do all it can to insure that the inventions produced in the laboratory earn a pay-off. Therefore, the production associations should apply pressure on the managers of their subordinate producing enterprises to adopt some of these new inventions. Since they have investment funds to allocate, they should be able to finance and facilitate the effort. As of mid-1981, four thousand production and research enterprises had been combined into production associations.[38] Since the rate of industrial growth has continued to slow, the production associations obviously have not proven to be a cure-all. Nevertheless, the growth rate might have fallen more without them. It also might be too soon to see the effect.

Finally, the Soviets have also tried to improve the system of targets. The distortion created by the emphasis on physical production targets and on gross ruble-value of production (*val*) is not a secret shared by only a few Soviet economists but is widely acknowledged. As an alternative, Soviet authorities in July, 1979, announced a new system. Instead of targets spelled out in tons-produced, managers were to be judged by whether or not they had fulfilled their delivery contracts. Instead of increasing gross ruble-value of production, they were to fulfill net-normative output targets. Net normative output is a measure of value added. If effective, this would lead managers to cut back on their extravagant use of raw materials and focus instead on the efficient utilization of labor, capital, and managers. But like almost all the other reforms introduced by Brezhnev and his predecessors, most of these reforms have been ignored as much as they have been honored.[39] Consequently, the impact thus far seems to have been neutralized. In no case, however, were these reforms intended to do more than make cosmetic changes in the Stalinist model. Will Brezhnev's successors be able to make a more cosmic change, or will they also find themselves unable to break away from the model?

IV.

What is there about the Stalinist model that makes it so difficult to alter? First, there is the reluctance to tamper with the status quo. Soviet planners know what to expect from their model and they feel comfortable with it, particularly since those in control with their access to special consumer shops tend to be protected from some of the system's more serious shortcomings. Most Soviet planners are not all that convinced that the system has performed so badly.

Even those who feel a change is long overdue are hesitant about moving too fast. This in part explains why there is so much experimentation rather than an across-the-board adoption of a uniform change. There is a realization, even among those who are not satisfied with the existing situation, that significant changes have been delayed for so long that a change, when it does come, is likely to be convulsive. Thus it is not entirely irrational when some of the reformers try to implement their reforms on a piecemeal basis. Too much reform too fast is likely to be destabilizing, especially for the bureaucracy. Unfortnately, this reduces the likelihood of the reform's ultimate success. It also explains why our fabled traffic authorities suggested that only the more sophisticated drivers be moved to the left side at first, while keeping the less experienced to the right side. But this, too, is likely to be disastrous. Unfortunately, economic change has been delayed too long. The Soviet economic system would undoubtedly be in better condition today if it had undergone a series of evolutionary changes over the years. The pent-up distortions caused by the failure to make incremental economic changes are analogous to the pressures which have piled up on the political side. Once released, the dynamic of change may swee along everything with it.

Given the conservative, even paranoid, perspective of so many Soviet officials, that could be a frightening prospect. Even if a fundamental reform of the economy were gradual, it could unleash uncontrollable forces. The main problem is that the economy has made so little effort to serve consumer needs. This frustration, built up over sixty years, is reflected in the unprecedented hoard of disposable income accumulated by Soviet consumers. Thus for the period, 1975–79, the amount of increase in savings deposits in Soviet savings banks, the best measure we have of Soviet savings, increased faster than the increase in retail sales. (See Table II-3.) Only in 1980 did sales increase faster (17.1 billion rubles), than savings (10.3 billion rubles). However, even though the ruble increase in retail sales was larger than the ruble increase in savings, the relative savings increase of 7 per cent exceeded the relative retail sales increase of 6.6 per cent (sales increase over total savings). This continues to reflect the growing dissatisfaction with the type of goods being offered for sale and the increase in the enormous hoard of liquid funds which is waiting to set off in pursuit of more desirable goods, should they ever become available from either domestic or foreign suppliers. It also serves an enormous private black market, or second economy, that some estimate to amount to as much as 25 per cent of the GNP.[40] Goods sold in black market channels at both the manufacturing and consumer levels are often stolen or misappropriated from official state channels. Fortunately or unfortunately, as evidenced from the way the size of savings accounts continue to grow, the second economy is in no way large enough to satisfy the gaps between supply and demand.

Under such circumstances, a sudden decontrol where manufacturers

Table II-3
CHANGES IN SAVINGS BANK DEPOSITS AND RETAIL SALES
(billions of rubles)

Year	Total Savings	Increase	Retail Trade Volume	Increase
1975	91.0		215.6	
1976	103.0	12.0	225.9	10.3
1977	116.7	13.7	236.4	10.5
1978	131.1	14.4	247.8	11.4
1979	146.2	15.1	260.7	12.9
1980	156.6	10.3	277.8	17.1

could produce or import what they wanted to, and consumers could freely bid for what they wanted to, could easily set off a panic. The manufacturers would rapidly try to reorient their production focus. To do this they would have to search out new, more suitable supplies from other manufacturers, who like them, are trying to revamp their production facilities. The result would be an enormous bottleneck and a scramble for capital resources that could generate immense inflationary and import pressures. At the same time, unemployment will likely be created all over the country as outmoded plants are closed and as unproductive workers are fired.

Similarly, the Soviet Union will find itself, just as did Czechoslovakia, Yugoslavia, and Poland, with a considerable amount of wasted capital that has been expended in the past on ill-conceived projects in unsuitable places that were designed more to satisfy local political and outmoded economic cravings than basic economic needs.[41] At the same time, there is almost no likelihood that any sudden campaign for rationality will be able to satisfy the demands placed on it in a reasonable period of time. The distortions have grown too large and the backlog too great. Whichever generation of Soviet leaders sets off this explosion will then have to deal with a prolonged period of inflation, unemployment, and supply bottlenecks, and shortages of desirable capital, surpluses of outmoded capital, profiteering, and a severe balance of trade deficit as the demand for imports soars.

It is doubtful if the political fabric can withstand such an upheaval. The Soviet Union will find itself with all the evils previously associated with capitalism, which the Soviet Union had prided itself on being able to avoid. However, such a change, when it comes, will involve even more extreme enormities, because change has been held back so long. In a short period of time, there could be a counterreaction as those who feel repulsed by the excesses and those who find themselves displaced join together to restore what they view as order.

V.

The above scenario for chaos is more than just a fantasy of a bourgeois apologist. There are precedents in which other countries have tried to break away from the Stalinist model. Brezhnev's successors will not be reassured by what they find. Yugoslavia was the first country to try to break out of the Stalinist mode. Even though Yugoslavia only adhered to the Stalinist pattern for a few years, the Yugoslavs have never satis-factorily solved their inflation, their unemployment, their misallocation of capital, and their foreign-trade deficits. By comparison, however, the Yugoslav economy has performed far better than any other in Eastern Europe. But even in Yugoslavia, there are complaints about politically inspired and ill-conceived investments. The impact of the political and economic distortions built into the country's political structure has become even clearer after Tito's death, and these distortions will not be easily resolved.

Because they have waited so long, the economic reformers in China and Poland are having a much more difficult time in breaking the Sta-linist economic mold. The Chinese find themselves with serious unem-ployment, inflation, profiteering, corruption, unrealistic demands for capital, excess capacity, and in some sectors of the economy, an enor-mous balance of trade deficit. Complicating these problems is the fact that Chinese leaders cannot seem to agree on how far to go with their reforms. Ominous voices have been warning for some time that the reforms may have already gone too far, and that the system has ended up with what is most distasteful from both communism and capitalism. There are some who fear it is only a question of time before the pen-dulum swings back to a new set of leaders who will reimpose the Sta-linist model.

Attempt at reform from below by the workers in Poland is more dif-ficult to evaluate because so much of what has been proposed and implemented, while bold to begin with, was ultimately tempered by fear, not only of provoking the Stalinists within Poland, but of the Soviet Army as well. Amidst all the debate about how the union Solidarity had encroached on Communist Party prerogatives, many have lost sight of just how disrupted Polish economic life had become. At one point, con-sumer goods had all but disappeared from the stores, and factories could operate at no more than 75 per cent of their capacity because of their inability to obtain the necessary inputs and components they needed for production.

Given these various precedents, Andropov and his successors will probably be even less tempted to make the fundamental reforms they need. Indeed, because there is so much more to undo in the Soviet Union, the upheaval may be considerably greater than anything we have seen so far. At least the Yugoslavs, the Poles, and Chinese could call on some of their older countrymen for advice about how the economy ran when the plan and heavy industry were not so dominant or distorting. The Soviets do not have such an option. Because the planning system has been in place for over fifty years and the party has been in control for about sixty-five years, there is almost no one who has a familiarity with the market system before World War I, and thus no one who could guide the economy through the transition. The Politburo leaders may stay in power a long time, but even they do not seem to have lived that long.

Those who have known nothing else but the Stalinist model during their lives do seem to have more trouble adjusting to new economic measures than those who have lived at least a portion of their lives under another system. The Soviets themselves reflect this when they tell the story of the woman who urges her neighbor to run quickly to GUM, the Red Square department store, in order to line up for a recently arrived shipment of shoes from Czechoslovakia. "Why all the excitement?" the neighbor responds coolly. "The Czechs' shoes are still communist-made shoes." "Yes," her friend concedes, "but Czechoslovakia has only been communist for thirty-five years, not sixty-five years." It is also reflected in the greater difficulty that recently arrived Russian emigrés have had in adjusting to the market economy in countries like the United States and Israel. When they arrive in the West, an astonishing number of them are disoriented, and unlike their counterparts who arrive from Hungary, Czechoslovakia, Poland, Rumania, and even China, most Soviet emigrés are unable to comprehend how the system operates. They assume the state will take responsibility for finding them jobs. When somehow they manage to find themselves with a business, they assume the state will send them customers. This attitude is less evident in the East European emigré community.

The lack of experience with less centrally dominated economies also makes it unlikely that the Soviets would have been any more successful if they had tried to emulate the rather more sophisticated Hungarian economic reforms. Cognizant of all the pitfalls, the Hungarians have been trying to maneuver their way through the overdominance of the Stalinist model and the spontaneity of the market system. Better than other communist nations so far, including Yugoslavia, the Hungarians seem to have learned how to drive simultaneously in opposite directions on one lane of the highway. They have increased the role of the market; they have relaxed price controls; they have removed the ban on small private businesses, which has helped improve the quality of service;

they have increased productivity and the quality of their goods; they have managed to hold down the size of their foreign-trade deficit; they have almost brought their currency up to world standards so that it is almost convertible; and they have improved their innovative capabilities, although they still lag seriously behind most Western countries on most of these matters. At the same time, they have not abandoned the plan, the predominance of the Communist Party, nor their adherence to Soviet foreign policies.

Cynics insist that only a Hungarian can understand how two such contradictory policies can be carried out simultaneously. Be that as it may, there is no doubt that the Hungarians have had to muster enormous self-discipline. Unlike the Poles, the Hungarians have endured price increases, a curb on the importation of foreign goods, and some economic disruption with virtually no protest. In part, the way was prepared with very careful warnings about what was to come and for what purpose. The Hungarians were told that there would have to be some belt-tightening and a lowering of aspirations. Otherwise, they might never free themselves from the addiction to the Stalinist model. A policy of this sort entails enormous risks and does not necessarily ensure success. For example, in Poland similar price hikes and belt-tightening sparked strikes and the formation of an independent union. In addition, the Hungarian effort undoubtedly required a clearly perceived political consensus that such a program would be best for the whole country and, of course, that required a basic minimal trust in the Hungarian leadership's ability to navigate through such hazardous waters. Doubtlessly the Hungarians have also concluded that after their misadventure in 1956, they could probably accomplish more through gradual, than through extreme change.

The likelihood that the Soviet government can develop the consensus that exists between the Hungarian government and its people is rather slim. As some Soviet officials have put it, Hungary is not a useful model for the U.S.S.R. because it is so much smaller than the Soviet Union. Its population is only about 10 million compared to about 266 million in the Soviet Union. Such arguments also reflect the fact that there is too much resentment in the U.S.S.R. between the powerful and the powerless, the Russians and the non-Russians. Short of an invasion by the United States and China, the Soviet people are unlikely to rally together to form the consensus they will need. Moreover, if there should be such an invasion, that would hardly be the occasion for an economic reform designed to bring about a decrease in the government's role. Because they recognize how difficult it would be for them to attempt such reforms, Brezhnev's successors are unlikely to try anything so venturesome, no matter how serious their economic need. It may be that one day the Soviet people will ultimately take matters into their own hands when they find that they can no longer tolerate the way in which the economy fails to serve them. This is what almost happened in Poland. As the czars discovered, if pushed too far, the patience of even the Russian people has its limits. But that day of protest always appears too far off and unreal. In contrast, the avalanche that could be set off by a series of small changes tends to seem much more immediate and threatening. Thus the chance for such a major change is unlikely to be consciously or dispassionately introduced in the Soviet Union, at least as long as Soviet leaders continue to fit Brezhnev's mold.

Brezhnev's successors will therefore probably try to do all they can to maintain the status quo. What are the prospects that they will succeed? Fortunately for the Soviet Union, they have enormous territory at their disposal. While such a land mass generates serious communication problems, it also generates an abundant supply of raw materials. As we shall see, the country is too far north to put all that land to good agricultural use, but there is no doubt that the raw materials are there. Yet as we noted earlier, all that land can also cause other problems. The abundance of Soviet raw material deposits has contributed to the wasteful way in which the Soviet Union has used those deposits. Given its relative resource endowment, however, the Soviets may not have been all that irrational to squander their abundant raw materials and instead seek to conserve other, more limited factors of production, such as labor or even capital.

Assuming the Soviets do take steps to rationalize their use of raw materials, will they have enough to continue producing more or less of the same product mix in the same way that they have been doing for so many decades? If they can, life will be easier for Andropov and his aides. If there is any country in the world where raw materials and basic heavy industry can serve as the main focus of production, it is probably the Soviet Union. After all, not every country can or need specialize in high technology. If the Soviets can import Western technology which will help them mine their resources more effectively, and if they can design an incentive system which will stimulate them to search out and explore their mineral fields more effectively than they have been able to do so far, then it may be that the Soviet Union will find a niche for itself as the world's raw material base. In this way, the Soviet Union may also gain the wherewithal to finance the purchase of consumer goods for its citizens.

If the world's supply of raw materials should continue to tighten, relative to the world's demand, as it well may, the Soviets could find themselves in a strong financial position if they concentrate on developing their raw materials. With time, of course, some of their raw material stocks will be depleted; some have already been exhausted. But as more and more of the industrialized countries switch to the production of services and high-technology products, and away from their traditional industrial activities, there will be a greater need for the basic products of Soviet heavy industry. This may put the Soviet Union in increasing competition with the developing countries. In effect, the Soviets could become a raw-material-producing colony for Japan, Germany, and even the United States. This would hardly be a satisfying solution, politically or psychologically, and maybe even economically, especially for a country like the Soviet Union, with such an unrequited sense of inferiority, but it would avoid, or at least postpone, the need for a more thorough shakeup of the economy.

VI.

The choices facing Soviet leaders in the next decades are not very pleasant ones. A pessimist looking at the economy might conclude that the whole economic system is on the verge of collapse. To the optimist, the Soviets may, at best, be able to go about their business as usual and probably survive. In neither case, however, does there seem to be much hope of a major breakthrough or improvement—indeed, all of this merely postpones the ultimate day of reckoning. Nor is there any guarantee that if, despite everything, the Soviets should do well economically, they will be able to channel their gains so that they can be enjoyed by the people. As long as the Stalinist model remains intact, there is little likelihood that the planners will ever do much to increase consumer welfare.

In all likelihood, the Soviet planners will sustain their decades-long habit of pumping funds into heavy industry in a misguided effort to reduce the gap between the Soviet Union and the rest of the industrialized world. The realization that the Soviet model is not well-suited for this kind of effort has apparently not yet completely penetrated the existing leadership, and when it does, there remains the question of whether they will still hesitate to act for fear that they will set in motion a breakdown of the whole system.

Given their choices, there is good reason for Soviet leaders to postpone a reform of their economy for as long as they can. It probably is the safest course of action to follow, at least in the short run, but it does nothing to solve the Soviet Union's long-run needs. However, a systematic effort to resolve those long-run needs is likely to set off a chain effect that could be explosive. In addition, the Soviets, unlike the Hungarians, have done little to inspire their people with the need for belt-tightening. Even though the Soviet Eleventh Five-Year Plan is much more modest in scope than previous plans, the rhetoric that surrounds this plan continues to promise more in an unrestrained fashion. Understandably, such a belt-tightening campaign would not be warmly received in the Soviet Union where many of the workers feel they have been wearing tightened belts since the revolution. Therefore, why risk drawing needless attention to the problem, particularly when the patience of the average Russian is so great? They have the capability to endure enormous suffering, as most of the last sixty-five years have shown. As long as the quality of life shows slight improvement or no serious deterioration, there should be no trouble. The ever-growing disparity between the Soviet standard of living and the rest of the world may increase discontent, but it is unlikely to be so great as to provoke revolt, at least as long as the food supply is adequate and the production of nonfood consumer goods improves, even if marginally. But that assumes that things go well, not badly. In the meantime no one is doing anything to address the long-run problem.

Those who would tackle the long-run structural changes in the economy may have the best interests of the Soviet Union at heart, but they run the risk that the process of change will set off a dynamic of its own that will be impossible to contain. Yielding a little is likely to excite popular expectations which might be better kept bottled up. Yet failure to face the long-run needs of the economy may test Soviet patience beyond the point to which the Soviet population is willing to go. As the pre-Revolutionary czars can attest, great as the patience of the Russian citizen is, it is not infinite.

3. Soviet Agriculture

From what we have seen so far, political unrest in Russia has frequently been sparked by a marked drop in the peoples' standard of living. Insuring that this does not happen again must be a top priority for the Soviet leaders. As long as conditions improve each year, even marginally, there is less likely to be uncontainable pressure for radical reform of either the political or economic structure. Of course, the more such reforms are delayed, the more unpredictable and more far-reaching an upheaval it will be when it comes. However, Soviet leaders will probably try to hold the lid on as long as they can. It is always easier to tend to a country's short-run rather than to its long-run needs. Therefore, Soviet leaders must by all means insure an adequate supply of food.

For that reason, agriculture must be a priority area of concern for Brezhnev's successors. Despite the fact that in times past Russia served as the breadbasket of Europe, the Soviet Union in recent years not only has been unable to maintain its net exports of grain, but also has been unable to satisfy the basic food needs of its own population. Increasingly it has had to turn to exports. From 1909 to 1913, before the revolution, Russian grain exports averaged 11 million metric tons a year. This amounted to 30 per cent of world grain exports and made Russia the world's largest grain exporter.[1] Yet despite a vastly increased stock of machinery and the eventual introduction of pesticides and fertilizers, Soviet grain exports since the revolution have never exceeded 7.8 million tons.[2] That postrevolutionary peak was reached in 1962, but by the 1970's, net grain exports had become a rarity. In fact, in bad harvest years the Soviet Union has had to turn to foreign suppliers for as much as 35 to 45 million tons of grain a year. Prior to the Afghanistan embargo on grain exports by the United States, they had arranged to purchase almost 25 million tons of grain in 1980 from the United States alone.[3] What is there about Soviet communism that turns the world's largest exporter of grain into its largest importer?

I.

Most specialists both in- and outside the Soviet Union agree that grain is one of the laggard areas of the Soviet economy. It is often called the "Achilles heel" of the Soviet Union. True, in the 1970's when there were a few isolated good crop years, the harvest and crop-yield figures rose significantly over the earlier decades. But in recent years the harvest and yield never have risen enough to satisfy all Soviet grain needs. (See Table III-1.) Nor have they been able to do much about inefficiency.

Over 20 per cent of the Soviet labor force still works in agriculture. That is a major improvement from the years after the revolution when the comparable figure was 75 per cent. Nonetheless, by comparison, agriculture requires less than 3 per cent of the American work force.[4] Moreover, those American farmers usually have to be told to cut back production. By contrast, despite the large number of people still employed in Soviet agriculture, the Soviets have occasionally found it necessary to import as much as 25 per cent of their grain.

The fact that one Russian peasant can barely feed himself and four others, while an American farmer can feed himself and forty-nine others is due to more than the superior efficiency of the American work force. As we shall see, geography and nature also have something to do with this difference. However, even if allowance is made for the argument that prerevolutionary exports were only as high as they were because czarist officials chose to export rather than feed their own starving people, there is still something more involved. For that matter, the Soviets under Stalin also exported grain, despite the fact that the peasants were starving in the fields.[5] It may be that the Soviets will simply decide to throw up their hands and abandon their attempts to be self-sufficient or net producers. But as they discovered after the American grain embargo in 1975 and again in 1980, relying on others for food supplies leaves them vulnerable. Moreover, their vulnerability is not only political, it is also economic. On occasion they have had to spend as much as $5 to $6 billion a year in hard currency for their grain imports. Nor is grain the only food the Soviets have imported. As part of their effort to broaden

Table III-1
SOVIET GRAIN HARVEST, EXPORTS & IMPORTS
(million metric tons)

	Harvest	Export	Import
1950	81	2.9	.2
1955	104	3.7	.3
1956	125	3.2	.5
1957	103	7.4	.2
1958	135	5.1	.8
1959	120	7.0	.3
1960	126	6.8	.2
1961	131	7.5	.7
1962	140	7.8	—
1963	108	6.3	3.1
1964	152	3.5	7.3
1965	121	4.3	6.4
1966	171	3.6	7.7
1967	148	6.2	2.2
1968	170	5.4	1.6
1969	162	7.2	.6
1970	187	5.7	2.2
1971	181	8.6	3.5
1972	168	4.6	15.5
1973	223	4.9	23.9
1974	196	7.0	7.1
1975	140	3.6	15.9
1976	224	1.5	20.6
1977	196	3.0[2]	10.5[1]
1978	237	1.5[2]	23.0[1]
1979	179	3.0[2]	25.5[1]
1980	189	2.0[2]	30–35[1]
1981	160[2]	3.0[2]	43.0[1]
1982	170[2]	2.0[2]	35.0[2]

[1] U.S. Department of Agriculture estimates
[2] Author's estimates
SOURCE: VT SSSR

the population's diet, Soviet leaders have sought to increase meat consumption. Thus throughout the 1970's, the Soviets imported an average of almost 300 million tons of meat a year. Of course to the extent that there was a bad grain harvest, that meant that there would be less grain for fodder. Presumably that should have resulted in higher meat imports. It did at least in 1975, 1979, 1980, and 1981. In fact in 1981 (as indicated in Table III-2), the Soviets imported almost one million tons of meat. Incredibly that amounts to about ten pounds of meat for each Soviet citizen. The cost of such imports totaled about $2.5 billion, of which about $1.5 to $2 billion was in hard currency. Consequently, the cost of combined grain and meat imports in 1981 amounted to at least $6.5 billion and maybe as much as $8 billion, or almost one-quarter of the Soviet Union's hard-currency imports. The need to import so much food is perhaps the clearest measure there is of the extent of the failure of Soviet agriculture, and illustrates the burden that Soviet agriculture now places on the Soviet economy. Though agriculture used to be the strongest sector prior to the revolution, it now has become one of the economy's greatest weaknesses. As we shall see, the need to import this much food has forced the Soviets to divert some of their hard currency from more productive industrial imports. Alternatively, they could have reduced their exports. Normally the Soviets only export to earn the hard currency they need to pay for their imports. Since petroleum accounts for over 50 per cent of their hard-currency exports, this means that if

Table III-2
SOVIET MEAT & MEAT PRODUCT IMPORTS
(thousand metric tons)

Year	Imports
1971	225
1972	134
1973	129
1974	515
1975	515
1976	361
1977	617
1978	183
1979	386
1980	576
1981	980

SOURCE: *Vneshniaia torgovlia SSSR v 1971–78 Ekonomicheskaia gazeta,* April 1, 1982, #14, p. 21.

they could have produced enough of their own grain and meat, they would have been able to keep more of their own petroleum at home. After all, the Soviet Union is not like Japan which has comparatively very little land available for agricultural purposes. Under the circumstances, it is very embarrassing for a great power to admit that it is unable to utilize its vast agricultural resources efficiently. Consequently, the next few generations of Soviet leaders will have no choice but to seek some fundamental solutions to their agricultural problems.

II.

It is not as if agriculture in the Soviet Union has been ignored. Ironically that may be its problem. In many ways, Soviet peasants probably would have been much better off if they had been left alone to go their own way. After all, the debates which began in the 1920's over the extent of the guidelines to be imposed on the peasants were not new. Levin in Tolstoy's novel, *Anna Karenina,* worried whether the peasants or Levin really knew best. Levin questions whether he should take a more active hand and introduce more sophisticated agricultural techniques. In response to an argument he had with one of his acquaintances who took a dim view of the capability of the Russian peasant, Levin thought, ''I ought to have said: You say that our farming industry is a failure because the peasant hates every kind of improvement and that improvements must be introduced by force; but if farming did not pay at all without these improvements, you would be right. But it does pay, and it pays only where the laborer is working in conformance with his habits . . . your and our common dissatisfaction with farming shows that it is we and not the laborers who are at fault. We have for a long time been trying to run the industry in our own way—in the European way—without bothering about the nature of the labor force at our disposal. Let us try looking upon labor not as an abstract labor force, but as the *Russian peasant* with his instincts, and let us organize our farming industry accordingly.''[6] Change a few words here and there and the argument would be as appropriate today as it was a century ago.

The obsession with agriculture is only natural considering Russia's past and the immensity of its land mass. Moreover, since over 80 per cent of the population was living in the rural areas at the time of the revolution and as much as 50 per cent of it was living there as recently as 1961, most Russians are not too many generations removed from the soil.[7] Yet even if Soviet peasants should suddenly become the most motivated agricultural workers in the world, and if Soviet agriculture should suddenly become a model of efficient organization, the Soviet Union would probably still have periodic production problems, as we shall see, and might still find it necessary to import over ten million tons of grain a year. However, given the way the present farming systems has evolved, neither the peasants' motivation nor organizational efficiency is likely to change markedly in the next decade. Thus Soviet agriculture will probably be the cause of even more soul-searching in the years ahead.

More than anything else, Soviet agricultural officials have to contend with the fact that the Soviet Union is located too far north and too far east. This gives it a northern continental climate. What this means is that despite the thousands of square miles of land that are available, only a relatively small fraction of the country has a long-enough growing season and enough moisture at the right time of year. Thus, although the Soviet Union has some of the richest soil in the world, most of this black-earth region is in the Ukraine, which is located on approximately the same latitude as southern Canada. There is nothing wrong with Canada, and indeed it is a major wheat-exporter, but Canada has a smaller population to feed and therefore more surplus for export. Also, Canada's weather tends to be subject to fewer extremes. In contrast, the best agricultural regions of the Soviet Union seem to be affected by drought about once every five years. From 1979 to 1982, there was a period of four consecutive years of inadequate moisture, extreme heat or cold, and as a result poor crops. Moreover, impressive as Canada's agricultural production is, the Canadians grow relatively little corn even in good crop years. To be successful, corn requires the warmer weather of the more southern states of Iowa and Illinois. Except for some farming areas in the Kuban and Caucasus, the U.S.S.R. does not have much suitable land south of Odessa. Consequently, it is extremely unlikely that the Soviet Union will ever produce more corn. Thus as long as the Soviets try to increase the meat supply available to their population, they will have to import corn, livestock, or meat.

Because of the extremes in climate, the most suitable agricultural land in the Soviet Union is restricted to what approximates a crudely drawn triangle with the narrowest side of the triangle stretching north and south through the Ukraine and with the other two legs of the triangle extending into Siberia. The continental nature of the climate produces very extreme weather conditions, especially in the winter. Indeed, some analysts have argued that a good portion of the Soviet Union is really not meant to sustain year-round human life, let alone agricultural life.[8] In their minds the harshness of life has also forced inhabitants of the region into a closer dependence on one another. In contrast to the pattern of farming life in the United States, where American farmers live in separate homes surrounded by their land and where their nearest neighbor may be a mile or several miles down the road, the homes of Russian peasants' both before *and after the revolution,* have been clustered together in villages with their land surrounding the whole village. It was simply too dangerous to live alone, exposed to the elements, when the cold was so extreme. However, whether clustered into villages or not, it may be that it is unrealistic in terms of its geography to expect Soviet agriculture ever to produce at levels comparable to other more southerly located lands.

Whatever the natural shortcomings of Soviet agriculture, the political reality is that the agricultural sector has always been expected to provide an important, if not the key, underpinning for the total economy. Even before the revolution, most leaders believed that Russian agriculture would have to serve as the instrument for building up the country's industry. This in part explains why some peasants may have starved despite record grain-exports prior to the revolution. In the vocabulary of the Soviets after the revolution, agriculture was considered to be the source of primitive capital accumulation. Almost no Soviet leader disputed how important agriculture was to be as a source of funds for the rest of the economy. But from the beginning, there have been serious disagreements about how this might be best accomplished. One thing is certain: in the process of reaching for a solution, the peasants have been treated badly. In turn, agriculture has become one of, if not the weakest, link in the Soviet economy.

That Soviet agriculture would prove to be such a weak link was all but preordained once Lenin decided to bring his Marxist revolution to an industrially backward country like Russia. As we saw earlier, Marx did not design his revolution for a country without industry and a proletariat. Lenin quickly discovered why. As he sketched out the strategy for his proletarian revolution, Lenin realized that since the proletarian class constituted considerably less than 15 per cent of the Russian working force, it was by itself simply too small a fraction of the population to bring about a revolution. Consequently, Lenin had to seek out additional support. The most likely ally was the peasantry that made up about 80 per cent of the population. As a result, Lenin lost little time in trying to attract large numbers of peasants to his cause and away from other revolutionary groups such as the Social Revolutionary Party. His effort to build a coalition was clearly reflected in his revolutionary slogan, "Peace, Bread, and Land." Peace was for everyone, bread was for the proletariat, and land was for the peasantry. The latter was a promise to carry the emancipation of the serfs and the Stolypin reforms begun in 1906 to their final conclusion. This time not just the strong and able peasants, as Stolypin and the czars had envisaged, but all the peasants would be given land.

Lenin made his revolution and the peasants quickly demanded their share of the bargain. Indeed, many urban dwellers who had only recently left the countryside returned to it in order to claim their stake. The number of peasant households rose from 21 million in 1916 to 25 million after the revolution.[9] For an unusually large number of peasants, this was the ultimate realization of a centuries-old dream.

However, conditions in the countryside were harsh, particularly during the initial stages of the civil war after the revolution. There was fighting and a breakdown of the country's infrastructure. Agricultural supplies were frequently confiscated in order to provide food for the cities. Ultimately, the sailors based on the Kronstadt Island naval base rebelled at the way the peasants were being treated. Since these sailors had played a key role in the revolution itself, this was a severe setback to Lenin who immediately decided to pursue a more relaxed and less Draconic policy. He ordered an end to the confiscation of supplies from the peasants. Instead, in 1921, each peasant was assigned a quota, and anything he produced above that quota he could keep. Thus began the New Economic Policy, or NEP. With this, conditions for the peasants improved markedly.

To Stalin, however, Lenin's agricultural policies had their drawbacks. As a temporary program, they served to bring an end to the previous chaos, but Stalin wanted more than that. He continued to insist that agriculture would have to serve as a source of capital accumulation for industry. Nikolai Bukharin, one of the early Bolsheviks and one of the party's leading theoreticians, thought the existing agricultural system set up by Lenin was well suited for that.[10] To be most effective, the process of transferring resources from agriculture to industry should be a gradual one. As Bukharin saw it, the peasants, after both the Stolypin reforms and the New Economic Policy, had demonstrated an ability to work hard and build up a marketable surplus. In both cases, the peasants were unleashed from the controls of the state and the village, allowed to produce for themselves, and permitted to keep the bulk of their earnings. If properly encouraged, Bukharin expected the peasant would continue to produce a large food surplus. This surplus would be used to feed the expanding urban proletariat and would also be channeled into the export market to earn money for the purchase of the machinery needed to modernize Soviet industry. At the same time, peasants would spend the income they earned on machinery and consumer goods. These sales would also stimulate the growth of domestic agricultural machinery and consumer goods industries, and the workers in these industries would then, in turn, spend the money on food. Thus there would be a ready-made market for both agriculture and industrial products. This would contribute to a self-sustaining growth from the bottom up. Thirty to forty years later the Japanese–Korean–Taiwanese economic model would come to bear a very strong resemblance to Bukharin's model.

The strategy did not ultimately appeal to Stalin. After some Machiavellian maneuvering, Stalin came down on what had been Leon Trotsky's side of the argument. It would be unseemly for the peasant to share so handsomely in what after all was still supposed to be a revolution for the proletariat. Moreover, Stalin like most Marxists was distrustful of the peasantry. They were too petty-bourgeois in their mentality: they were always accumulating, always hoarding. Yet in one sense, Stalin agreed with Bukharin. The peasant would work hard and seek to build up his production. However, in Stalin's mind, this would not help the state. On the contrary, the peasant would demand exorbitant prices from the state for his goods—and hoard, not spend, the proceeds. This would make it very difficult to divert much in the way of agricultural surplus to the state and it would be unlikely to do much in bringing about the rapid expansion of industry, even if that industry could serve the peasants.

Even if industrialization were to take place as Bukharin had predicted, it would still not have satisfied Stalin. He wanted greater certainty and much quicker action. He did not want to leave such matters to chance. The transfer of resources from agriculture to industry would be much more effective, Stalin reasoned, if the peasants were simply told to produce an assigned quota and turn it over to the state at a low price. In this way, the state would not have to worry about whether the peasant was happy or not with the terms set up in the market place. Moreover, there would be no uncertainty as to the share that would be collected by the state. Whatever was needed would be taken and utilized for the new urban work force and for exports. Agricultural surpluses could be used in this way to build up heavy industry. There would thus be no need to waste time, energy, money, and resources on "frills" such as light industry and simple agricultural machinery. Whereas Bukharin's strategy was indirect, slow, and full of uncertainties, Stalin's approach was direct and quick.

To justify the Draconic measures he was about to take, Stalin attempted to show that, given a choice, the peasants would not market their surpluses. According to his statistics, the peasants were as he theorized, withholding a larger and larger share of their production from the market. This he insisted made it harder to extract the surplus needed for exports and support of the urban work force. Thus to insure there would be a continuing flow of marketable crops and to prevent the collapse of his industrial strategy, Stalin decided to collectivize Soviet agriculture and take the land away from the peasants.

Some, particularly the late Jerzy Karcz, have attempted to show that there was no such drop in production and that even the marketed surplus did not fall as sharply as Stalin said. Apparently Stalin doctored the figures to justify the subsequent collectivization.[11] Moreover, Holland Hunter argues that the production potential of Soviet agriculture was such that if the peasants had been left alone, production could have increased throughout the 1930's. Production in 1939, Hunter calculates, could have risen by as much as 30 million tons above the 72 million tons produced in 1929. In contrast, actual production in 1939 only rose to about 75 million tons, a difference of close to 26 million tons.[12]

To the peasants, it was largely immaterial whether Stalin's figures were dishonest or not. What was important was that Stalin ordered the collectivization of their land. For a very large number of peasants, the period after the revolution was the first time that anyone in their family had owned their own fields. Yet only a decade later, Stalin embarked on a bloody drive to take this same land away. They had been double-crossed. Individual fields were consolidated in the name of the state into large collective ventures with the understanding that the rewards would also be shared collectively. It was clear immediately, however, that once Stalin had taken out the state's share, there would be little left over for the peasants. In fact, many of the farms frequently ran at a loss, unable to put enough aside for next year's seed. True, the land had not been returned to the old landlords. But to most peasants, it made no difference; they were again working for a landlord, only this time it was the state. For most of the peasantry, the prerevolutionary arrangement was a preferable one.

The peasants may have been less resistant to collectivization if the land had never been turned over to them in the first place. They would never have known what they came to miss. To mangle a metaphor, it may have been better never to have owned at all than to have owned and lost. If the revolution had occurred in an industrialized state as Marx had predicted, instead of an agricultural one like Russia, there would have been no need to woo the peasantry, no need to evoke a sense of betrayal, and no need to put such pressure on agriculture in order to finance the accumulation needed for heavy industry. The decision to exploit the peasants was not cheap; it incurred long term costs. The consequences are still being felt.

The resistance of the peasants to collectivization has been well-documented. Stalin's remarks to Churchill hinted of the overall dimensions of the struggle. Soviet literature itself, including Sholokov's *Quiet Flows the Don*, graphically depicts not only the human suffering, but the slaughter of what was once their own livestock by the peasants. Large numbers of them decided to destroy their own property rather than turn it over to the collective farms. Thus the cattle herd which totalled 70.5 million head in 1928 before collectivization was cut to 38.4 million after collectivization.[13] The pig herd and the stock of horses were actually cut by more than half. From a high point of 26.2 million in 1928, the number of pigs was reduced to only 11.6 million in 1932. The horse population fell from 34.6 million in 1929 to 15.7 million in 1934. The stock of sheep and goats was reduced to a third of what it had been.[14]

Despite the enormous losses, neither Stalin nor his successors have ever done much to mollify the peasants. After a time, Soviet authorities even dropped the pretense that agriculture was being run on a collective basis by and for the peasants. More and more collective farms were converted into state farms where the peasants were more or less treated as hired hands. For many that was actually a preferable arrangement, because that meant that a salary would be paid regularly for work when it was done. Previously most collective farmers had to wait until the end of the crop year to be paid for the work they had performed earlier in the year.

But if the state did not back down, neither did the peasants. Again in a throwback to Tolstoy's *Anna Karenina,* the modern-day peasant has been known purposely to malinger and neglect the care of the farm's machinery and fertilizer.[15] Viacheslav Molotov, Stalin's chief deputy, complained, for example, that once a horse was taken away from a peasant by a collective farm, the peasant, angry because the horse was no longer his, made no effort to care for it.[16] Other peasants who, prior to collectivization regarded theft as a major crime, simply assumed that theft from the collective farm was a normal part of life.[17] Stalin's forceful methods alienated the peasants to such an extent that they became enemies rather than supporters of the state. One of my students at Moscow State University reported that when he and his classmates were sent to help bring in the harvest, initially they attacked their job with youthful enthusiasm. After a time, however, one peasant drew him aside and called him a strikebreaker. Similarly, when Hitler's troops invaded the Soviet Union, the peasants in many regions of the country initially met the invaders with bread and salt, the traditional sign of welcome. For a brief, unrealistic moment, the Germans were viewed by the peasants as liberators from the neo-serfdom of the communist collective farms.

The reaction by the peasants to collectivization and Stalin nearly proved to be the undoing of Stalin; it has haunted his successors and will continue to haunt Brezhnev's heirs. Indeed, until Soviet leaders find some way to remedy these injustices and win the support of the peasants, not only will agriculture continue to be a burden instead of a blessing, but the country's inability to realize its agriculture potential will serve as a drag on the whole economic process. Ironically, despite the fact that this agricultural mistake has become common knowledge, virtually all other communist governments which have come to power since then have made the same mistake, and consequently, have come to find themselves with the same agricultural headaches.

III.

However abused the peasants have been, the nonagricultural population in the Soviet Union has relatively little sympathy for their cause. For that matter, even though most urban residents are only recent arrivals from the countryside themselves, they show enormous disdain for their peasant cousins. The term *kolkhoznik* (collective farm worker) or *sovkhoznik* (state farm worker) connotes something backward and unmodern. The image is much more of someone barely literate in big black boots who, in attitude and productivity, more closely resembles the peasants of Russia in the nineteenth century, or of today's Mexican, Indian, or Egyptian peasants, than the farmers of the United States. In fact, the Soviets seldom if ever use the equivalent of the word "farmer" in the same sense that someone in the United States or Western Europe would. Soviet urban dwellers not only look down upon the peasantry and find them a cause of embarrassment, but they resent them because of what seems to be the high prices charged by the peasants for the goods in the collective farm markets.

Once Stalin had decided to exploit the peasants, the relationship between agriculture and industry became even more strained. The more the peasants held back, the more the planning authorities in Moscow increased their control of agriculture. This tended to make the peasants less cooperative and all the less willing to show initiative as the peasants must do to cope with the unanticipated changes in the weather. Not surprisingly, the agricultural potential of the country has not been fully utilized since collectivization.

It was not until Stalin's death that any substantive effort was made to improve the peasant's well-being. The procurement price for agricultural products was increased in 1953, 1956, and 1958 by Khrushchev, and the turnover tax burden (a sales tax that was imposed on both consumers and farmers) was reduced. Khrushchev also began a massive investment program intended to increase agricultural productivity and overall production.

Although Khrushchev's heart was in the right place, his strategy was not. He tried a little of everything in the hopes that something would work. He switched from one campaign to another. After each shift, the peasants were a little worse for the wear, the treasury a little emptier, and production in 1963 about where it had been in 1955. He put millions of acres of virgin lands under the plow so that the total acreage under cultivation increased by one-fifth. He embarked on a crash program to create a fertilizer productive capacity for the state. Finally he decided that he would take a page from American agriculture and switch a substantial portion of Soviet agricultural production from wheat to corn. As an example of how disruptive some of his orders were, by 1962 Khrushchev had increased the crop area devoted to corn to a peak of 37 million hectares from the 3.4 million hectares it had been in 1953. The peasants, even if they had been fully cooperative, were simply incapable of making such sudden changes in their farming practices.[18]

Not all of Khrushchev's efforts were in vain. Indeed, from 1956 to 1960, there was a significant increase in agricultural output and a decided improvement in peasant life on the farm. Agricultural output in 1956–60 rose 40 per cent over what it had been in 1951–55.[19] But Khrushchev's programs also created problems. The growth in agricultural output began to fall off sharply in 1959–63. Because of poor weather, inefficient organization and continuing peasant resistance, average output in 1963 was up only 3 per cent above 1958.[20] As the country's grain needs began to outrun its production, Khrushchev, in a momentous break with tradition, found it necessary to turn to Canada, Australia, and the United States for wheat imports. More than that, the sharp increase in prices paid the Soviet farmers made agriculture an increasingly more expensive operation to run. It was not that the average Soviet peasant had suddenly become rich—he was not. Although his income had risen sharply, doubling from 1956 to 1966 and doubling again by about 1979, his income in 1966 was still only 59 per cent of the country's monthly income; that is, it was only about half that earned by urbanites.[21] To make even this improvement, however, proved to be very costly. Agriculture turned from being a source of primitive accumulation to being an enormous absorber of investment. Whereas investment in agriculture used to amount to 13 per cent of total national investment before and after World War II, from 1956 to 1960 it averaged 17 per cent of the total.[22] Moreover, it became necessary to subsidize the whole operation. Heretofore, agriculture had subsidized the rest of the country.

Part of this increase in cost stemmed from the fact that Khrushchev tried to do too much at once and too little with any one project. He switched campaigns so fast that the peasants never had a chance to see any one project through to completion. Moreover, many of his programs were ill-conceived or "harebrained," as they were called when he was subsequently thrown out of office. When he decided that fertilizers were to be agriculture's salvation, everyone had to become a specialist in chemistry. Khruschchev even tried to change Lenin's slogan about electrification. As Khrushchev put it, "electrification plus chemicalization and the Soviets equaled communism." Similarly, when he discovered corn, Khrushchev insisted that peasants all over the country demonstrate similar enthusiasm. As a result, farmers in such unlikely places as Ukhta in northern Siberia were ordered to grow corn. But the growing season was of such short duration in such places that the corn barely made it to a height of one or two feet before it was killed by frost.

In an effort to reduce the burden on the overall economy of some of these programs, in 1962 the government under Khrushchev ordered an increase in retail prices on several food products. The result was a rash of riots and protests. Since then the Soviet government has sought at great cost to avoid increasing basic food prices at the retail level. Given the violence which has accompanied similar price increases in most of the rest of Eastern Europe, Soviet planners will not be eager to change their policy. This poses a dilemma for Soviet planners. While retail prices of most basic food products have been kept at a fixed level, over the years the cost of production has increased sharply. As a result, it has been necessary to increase the annual subsidy for Soviet agriculture. By 1980 it totaled approximately 35 billion rubles (about $50 billion) of which 23 billion rubles (about $35 billion) were spent on wheat and dairy products alone.[23] This has been the cause of all kinds of distortions. For instance, because the retail price of subsidized bread is so cheap, many peasants find it cheaper to buy and feed bread and potatoes to their livestock than the unprocessed grain. But the distortions do not end there. In the same way, and for the same reasons, the peasants find it profitable to buy meat when they can find it and feed it to the fur-bearing foxes they breed.[24] The retail price of meat is about half the wholesale procurement price paid to the peasants who produce it. Not surprisingly, such practices increase and distort the demand for both bread and meat. Unless Soviet planners someday decide to muster the courage to increase prices, it is likely that the subsidies and resulting distortions will continue to grow from year to year.

At the same time there has been no apparent cutback in agricultural investment. Under Brezhnev, the relative share of investment in agriculture relative to the total has actually grown to about 27 per cent.[25] This is a substantial increase even over the 17 per cent of total investment Khrushchev authorized, and it is more than double the relative share set aside by Stalin. It is also substantially above the share of investment in American agriculture, which totals only about 5 per cent of total gross investment.[26]

Given this amount of investment, supposedly there should someday be a payoff in the form of either a reduced cost of operation or higher production. It would be wrong to suggest that conditions have not improved. A careful analysis by Douglas B. Diamond and W. Lee Davis shows that output per hectare in the Soviet Union increased 75 per cent between the periods, 1950 to 1954 and 1973 to 1977, while output increased only 59 per cent over the same period in the United States.[27]

If the Soviet Union were to have a succession of five good weather years, conceivably much of this investment would begin to pay for itself with larger harvests and thus smaller grain imports. However, there is reason to question just how useful the Soviet investment program in agriculture has been. According to Diamond and Davis, while the growth of total productivity in Soviet agriculture rose at a reasonably rapid rate from 1951 to 1960, the pace fell off sharply from 1961 to 1970, and despite the fact that investments in agriculture rose rapidly, agricultural production in 1971 and 1977 barely increased.[28] In large part the disappointing increase in productivity reflects the bad weather that plagued the Soviet Union in 1972, 1975, 1979, 1980, 1981, and 1982. It also suggests just how low productivity was prior to 1954. In addition, it may be that Soviet investment policy in agriculture has not been particularly effective. After all, the size of Soviet investment in agriculture each year has been enormous. According to a CIA calculation, in 1977 the Soviets invested the equivalent of $78 billion in agriculture, compared to $11 billion in the U.S.[29] Given the large percentage of total investment that went into Soviet agriculture, that is not such a surprising figure. This large sum reflects not only the lower labor productivity of Soviet agriculture, but what appears to be the urgent effort by the Soviets to free themselves from costly agricultural imports.

Yet regardless of the massive sums involved, the Soviet investment program has been and continues to be ill-conceived. Seemingly, the Soviets are trying to compensate for the earlier years when agriculture was drained in favor of heavy industry. But investing more later is not enough to compensate for the inadequate investment of the earlier period. It is like starving a baby and then overfeeding him in adulthood in order to compensate for the initial neglect. The Soviets are not only spending the money too late, but unwisely. What they need is a very careful strategy and a very thoughtful set of targets. Instead, the Soviets appear to operate on the premise that regardless of where they put their funds, if they throw enough money at their agricultural problems, their difficulties will go away. This reaction may reflect their "quantity rather than quality" mentality.

Because the organizational structure of Soviet agriculture is so different from what it is in the United States, we should not expect to find precisely the same type of investment profile in both countries. Nonetheless, it does come as a surprise to find that the Soviet pattern is almost the exact opposite of what it is in the United States. Because of the system of private farming in the United States, the overwhelming share of agricultural investment is carried out by the farmers themselves. Since they are the ones who are doing the borrowing, it is only natural that they will seek to use their funds for the benefit of their own farms. The United States government also invests some of its funds in agriculture, and as might be expected, a good deal of its money goes for large scale general projects such as irrigation, just as in the U.S.S.R. In contrast, since almost all investment in Soviet agriculture comes from the government, we should expect that very little of it will be used to finance projects that will benefit the individual peasant. Not unexpectedly, the bulk of this investment is concentrated on large-scale macroprojects. First, it is easier to administer government money when a few major projects, rather than numerous minor projects, are involved. Second, when the investment decisions are made in Moscow or the other Soviet republic capitals, the interest of the local farm units do not weigh as heavily as do those of the government bureaucrats. Under no circumstances does the manager of the Soviet *kolkhoz* collective farm have as much influence on determining the pattern of investment as does the American farmer who uses his own money for his own benefit. In the Soviet system, except for relatively meager amounts, the *kolkhoz* or *sovkhoz* manager does not have "his own funds" to invest.

Given the vested interests involved, the investment profile in the United States and the Soviet Union is about what we would expect. Thus according to CIA estimates, approximately 75 per cent of the money invested in American agriculture is used for increasing the stock of machinery.[30] In the Soviet Union, the comparable figure is about 50 per cent. At the same time, about 40 per cent of Soviet agricultural investment goes for construction, compared to only about 25 per cent directed to construction in the United States. Thus a disproportionate share of Soviet investment goes to massively conceived projects, particularly irrigation and drainage. Since extreme weather changes, especially droughts, do account for major crop losses on a regular basis in he Soviet Union, such projects do make some sense. However, when it comes to water projects, the Soviets seem to go overboard. They seem almost to have a Freudian fixation with water. Nothing seems to satisfy them as much as building a dam or draining a swamp.

Unfortunately, these giant projects do not always bring about the hoped-for increase in productivity. Because existing land resources are handled so poorly, it is a challenge for the Soviet Union merely to keep the total amount of arable land from falling. For every acre of land added to agricultural use because of irrigation in Central Asia, an acre disappears, most often because of salination.[31] In many cases the same exchange results when new land is irrigated but equally valuable land is lost when comparable acreage is flooded to create a reservoir behind the irrigation dam. Because of overcropping and poor agricultural techniques, the Soviets have also been troubled by periodic dust storms. One economist writes that from 1960 to 1980, while the Soviet Union added 2 million hectares of land for use in agriculture, overall it lost 7.5 million hectares, including 1.6 million hectares that were being cultivated.[32]

Dust storms and erosion were also problems prior to the revolution. However, the magnitude of the current problem undoubtedly has grown as the central planners began to intervene more and more directly in day-to-day agricultural operations, and the peasants found themselves having to respond on call to outside orders rather than to their own sense of nature's needs.

Because of their passion for major construction efforts, Soviet planners tend to ignore more specific needs such as barns and auxiliary facilities on the farms. A visitor to a Soviet farm is struck by the absence of general barn-like shelters in comparison to what he would find on an American or European farm. Again this can be explained largely by the lack of the individual peasant's influence on the allocation of Soviet funds. Given their problems with weather, the lack of barns, silos, and grain elevators means a much greater exposure to the weather for farm equipment as well as for the grain once it is harvested.

The weather also affects Soviet agriculture more than it should because Soviet planners have devoted almost no attention to building a farm to market road network. For instance, more than one-fourth of the *kolkhoz* and *sovkhoz* farms in the Russian Republic have no roads connecting them with the outside world.[33] In addition, the overwhelming majority of Soviet farms have no hardened roads at their disposal to bring in supplies and to take out their harvest. All they have are dirt roads. In the United States, where government spending on agriculture is much more responsive to farmer pressure, a farm-to-market road program is a central component of the government's investment program. In contrast, reflecting its Stalinist orientation, the Soviet investment program is much more in line with the planner's interest. Moreover, since peasant incomes were low in the Soviet Union and there were, and are, few peasants who own their own automobiles or trucks, there appears to be less need for such a highway program. Whatever the explanation, the fact is that the vast majority of Soviet farms have no year-round road at their disposal, which means they are often isolated by mud much of the spring and late fall. Not only do private automobiles not move on these roads, but neither do the trucks of the collective farms. The need to free up the trucks in turn immobilizes more than one-half of the tractor fleet which traditionally is assigned to tow the farms' trucks.[34] Devoting money to roads, machinery, and barns, rather than construction projects would probably have provided a better payoff for Soviet agriculture.

Recently Soviet agricultural planners have come to recognize some of their mistakes, and have belatedly embarked on a massive program to erect storage facilities.[35] However, as might be expected, given planners' not the farmers' preferences, these facilities have tended to be large complexes concentrated in a few locations. This reflects the gigantomania which characterizes so much of Soviet construction. Everything must be the biggest, albeit not necessarily the most efficient. Unfortunately these large complexes have not been of much help. The problem is that in the absence of a good highway system, it is very difficult for many of the farmers to deliver their harvest to these remote storage facilities. As a consequence, there is good reason to believe that an unduly large portion of the harvested crop never works its way into the distribution system. It simply rots in the field or on the way to the grain elevator. Each year, for example, approximately 20 per cent of the grain, fruit, and vegetable harvest, and as much as 50 per cent of the potato crop perishes because of poor storage, transportation, and distribution.[36] This may also explain why it is that while the grain harvest has appeared to grow over the years (except of course when the weather is unusually bad), it is always hard to see much improvement in the quality or quantity of the domestically grown food available in Soviet shops. Grain in the Soviet field is a bit like steel in the Soviet steel mill, it is hard to see what happens to it after it is produced.

Because their problems have appeared to be so intractible, Soviet leaders have devoted enormous attention and as we have seen, enormous sums of money toward trying to solve their problems. Only recently have they even begun to appreciate how wrong their policies have been. In a remarkable speech to the Plenary Session of the Central Committee of the Soviet Communist Party in November, 1981, Brezhnev in effect admitted that the whole pattern of Soviet agricultural investment has been counterproductive. What were needed, he insisted, were not just large grain elevators, dairies, and storage facilities, but small storage facilities located closer to the sources of production, not at remote locations from the farms.[37] As he acknowledged, all too often, livestock, grain, and milk have had to be transported hundreds of miles over nonexistent hard-surface roads. He also demanded the construction of hard-surface roads. All of this was embodied in Brezhnev's May 1982 agricultural programs.

Brezhnev's overdue but perceptive analysis is to be applauded. The first challenge has been met. Soviet leaders at least have come to see that most of the billions of rubles that have gone into agricultural investment have been for naught. But now the challenge will be to induce the planners to change their investment strategy. This will be an upending of everything they have been doing all these years. In effect, this will mean a shift away from Stalinist priorities and planner's influences, a switch that will not be easy for Andropov to bring about in a short period of time.

IV.

The Stalinist legacy has affected not only the agricultural investment program, but the character of crop production as well. Planning seems to lend itself best to the production of crops such as grain, which can be grown in big fields, and planted and harvested by large-scale machinery. It is true that vegetables and fruits in the West are produced on farms that grow larger and larger each year. But as large as such undertakings in the West may be, central planners in most communist countries seem to find it easier to concentrate their efforts on grain crops. With the exception of Bulgaria, almost all communist countries seem to have great difficulty in mastering the cultivation of fruits and vegetables. It may be that because fruits and vegetables are more sensitive and delicate crops, they do not lend themselves to mass, centralized decision-making. If it suddenly turns cold, there is no time to wait for authorization from Moscow to turn on the smudge pots. They also need more hand and less machine care. Whatever the explanation, in those countries where agriculture is still centrally planned, production is restricted primarily to grain or more labor-intensive crops. As a result, a very small percentage of fruits and vegetables come from the state or collective sector. The bulk of these crops is produced on peasants' private plots. Moreover, the state and collective farms also account for a surprisingly small percentage of meat production.

That the small plots of land allowed most Soviet peasants are the source of so much fruit, vegetables, and meat, illustrates just how important these plots are. Even though private plots in the Soviet Union occupy only about 4 per cent of the country's arable land, they account for about 60 per cent of the Soviet Union's production of potatoes and honey, over 40 per cent of its fruits, berries and eggs, and about 30 per cent of its meat, milk, and vegetables. Douglas Diamond estimates that private plots produce 25 per cent of the Soviet Union's total crop output.[38] For the peasants themselves, their private plots play an even more important role supplying them with 72 per cent of their meat, 76 per cent of their milk, and about 100 per cent of their potatoes and eggs.[39] Such crops require more care and flexibility than those grown in the collective fields. Nonetheless, considering that the private plots of the *kolkhozniki* utilize such a small percentage of all the arable land available to the collective and state sectors, the inescapable fact is that compared to the productivity of the collective and state sectors, the output of the small plots is enormous.[40]

Undoubtedly, the extra care lavished on their small acreage is essential to the growth of the more sensitive agricultural products grown on the peasants' plots. But whatever the explanation, the indisputable evidence that the private plot yields are so much higher poses some delicate dilemmas for Brezhnev's successors. If they are interested in increasing production, it would certainly make sense for them to increase the scope and size of the private plots. It was exactly such reasoning which led Mao's successors to increase China's private plots to 15 per cent of the country's arable land.

The Politburo's attitude towards the private plots has so far moved in cycles. In times of trouble, such as World War II, and the bad harvests of 1979, 1980, 1981, and 1982, the government reluctantly finds it necessary to encourage private activity. This may be awkward ideologically, but necessary economically. In the past, the usual practice has been to authorize a slightly larger plot, permit an increase in the number of livestock an individual may legally own, and ease the procedure for buying supplies. During the bad harvests of 1979 to 1982 and the American grain embargo of 1980 to 1981, the Soviets offered some new concessions to the peasantry as well. These concessions were necessitated by the fact that, initially, there was an abnormally severe shortage of meat. Soviet planners decided that the speediest way to increase the production of meat stocks was to provide the peasants with more of a personal incentive. But it was feared that if peasants were allowed too large an increase in the number of livestock, there might be too much profit–making and too much weakening of the collective system. Consequently, a compromise was reached whereby collective farm livestock was "farmed out" to the individual peasants. Ownership remained with the farm, but the profits realized from the sale of the livestock were evenly split with the peasants. Since livestock raised by individual peasants ostensibly requires only one-third of the grain needed by the livestock fattened on the collective farms, the system seems to make good sense. Undoubtedly, the closer attention shown the private livestock does make a difference. But it turns out that the peasants steal much of their feed from the collective sector and never report it. The collective farms were also instructed to make it easier for the peasants to acquire the additional stocks of feed grains they would need for their larger herds. This policy switch also seems to explain why the livestock herds did not shrink as much as they had during the poor harvests of the past.

During this be-nice-to-peasant-plots phase, some specialists even suggested that a special effort be made to supply the peasants with specially designed machinery to increase productivity on these plots. Almost all Soviet agricultural machinery is designed for large scale operations.[41] Therefore, anything the individual peasants use on their own plots, more often than not, is homemade. Occasionally, equipment is stolen from the collective sector and cannibalized in order to "downsize" it to the more restrictive confines of the peasant plot. The fact that it has taken over fifty years for Soviet officials to begin talking about the need to provide machinery for the peasant plots probably indicates how serious the situation was in 1979, 1980, 1981, and 1982. But it also highlights how ambiguous the Soviet leaders are about the role of the private plot. Clearly, the use of private plots is an embarrassment, but it is also a last resort. It is the tragedy of Soviet agriculture that this tiny portion of Soviet agriculture, which generates such a large fraction of Soviet production, is regarded as an embarrassment and that private agricultural activity is deprived of the resources which might make it even more productive.

The vested interests of the agricultural bureaucracy usually resist any increase of production by the peasants on their private plots just because such efforts normally prove to be so successful. The peasants become so responsive that those in charge of administering the collective sector complain that, when the controls are relaxed on the private plots, it becomes even more difficult to get the peasants to meet their collective-sector targets. Not only does it become harder to get the peasants to put in their time on their collective chores, but diversion of feed and other supplies by the peasants from the collective sector to the private plot sometimes leads to a breakdown of the collective-sector operations. Especially upsetting is the sense that the peasants are enriching themselves at the expense of the urban proletariat. After a time there is usually a reaction and an ultimate cutback in the scope of the private plot activities.[42] Since the Soviet Union presently has been extending the scope of private plot operations, Brezhnev's successors may find themselves at the extreme end of the collective versus private-plot cycle. This will provide them with a unique and potentially far-reaching opportunity. Since a fall-off in the collective sector would be more than offset by a sharp increase in the private sector, why don't Soviet leaders simply decide to risk the decline in the productivity of the socialist sector? If they were to do this, there is every reason to expect that agriculture, which has always been regarded as the flat tire in the Soviet economy, could become the accelerator. Because private activity has been tolerated almost since the beginning of the collectivization effort, the decision to increase the scope of the private sector would not be such a radical step. It could be rationalized as an evolutionary step even though, admittedly, the consequences might be far-reaching. In contrast, any decision to allow private activity in other areas of the economy would constitute a heretical step. In a real sense, then, agriculture may be the one economic sector that can be reshaped so that it yields a higher output and becomes more sensitive to consumer wants.

That the road to improved production in Soviet agriculture may lie through the private plot constitutes yet another oddity. For years American observers have argued that the only way the Soviet Union could solve its agricultural problems would be if it switched to the American family-farm type of operation. Work on the farm, such critics argued, requires the enthusiasm and tolerance of long, unrewarding hours only an owner will endure. Hired hands simply will not put in the time and effort required. Yet American agriculture itself has been changing. Although the family continues to be the main farming unit, more and more families have been incorporating their farms and expanding, with as yet no evident decline of productivity. With expansion has come an increase in the use of hired hands. In other words, American farming is now more impersonal and yet still more productive than it used to be, and with more of the impersonal hired help and characteristics previously associated with industry and, inappropriately enough, the *kolkhoz* and *sovkhoz*.

V.

Whether Brezhnev's successors opt for more private or more collective farming, the decision will not be easy. It is true that in some limited areas there has been an increase in agricultural production and yields. But Soviet specialists recognize there is enormous waste in the way Soviet farms presently operate. Thus despite approximately $78 billion of investment in agriculture a year, plus about $50 billion for subsidies, the Soviet Union seems to be moving further and further away from being the exporter it once was. The Soviet Union still finds it necessary to spend as much as $8 billion in hard currency on grain and meat imports. While Soviet leaders would love to be able to resume grain exports, they undoubtedly would settle for simple self-sufficiency.

Unless there should be five years, or even better, a decade of optimal weather that would make it possible to increase output with the existing inefficient methods and motivations, Soviet leaders will have to face the fact that given all their historical and geographical handicaps, the existing *sovkhoz* and *kolkhoz* system simply does not serve the needs of the Soviet people. For that matter, even if the Soviets do manage to increase grain production to much higher levels, this may still not solve their problems. The demand for grain products is fairly income-inelastic. Published Soviet studies show that as per capital incomes increase, consumption of such basic staples as grain and potatoes barely increases and, in many instances, actually drops.[43] Of course, such fundamental needs must be provided for, but if Soviet consumers are to be truly satisfied, they will also have to be supplied with more nutritious and frivolous products, such as fruits and vegetables. These items have a much higher income-elasticity, so that as income rises, the demand for such products will increase even faster. Since there has been such a dearth of these products in the past, and because as we saw when we looked at the buildup in savings-bank deposits, there is such pent-up liquid demand, it will take many years and enormous effort before the distribution system will be able to satisfy these demands.

If all the Soviet leaders wanted was an increase in agricultural productivity, the simple solution would be to increase the role of the private sector. But here, just as with so much else, an easing of restrictions on decentralized or private farming might start an unraveling process which would not be limited to the agricultural sector. Moreover, there is a specter behind any such move which haunts Soviet agriculture in particular, and that is the ghost of Bukharin. It may be that the only way Soviet peasants will enrich the lives of the Soviet proletariat is if the Soviet leadership decides first to enrich the lives of the peasants. But that is playing with class animosities and may be a politically impossible step to take.

Brezhnev's successors may still be able to squeeze some extra growth out of the Soviet agricultural model. But there does not seem to be too much left to squeeze. In May, 1982, Brezhnev proposed a new "Food Program" for the period extending to 1990.[44] As part of this new program, Brezhnev called for the formation of regional agricultural industrial associations whose purpose is presumably to decentralize the allocation of production quotas in more localized regions throughout the country. Unfortunately, there seem to be nothing new in either this or his other agricultural proposals. Much of this had been earlier suggested in the mid-1960's, but then proved to be ineffective. If Soviet agriculture and the economy in general are ever to be more responsive to the average citizen's needs and wants, then Yuri Andropov and his associates must discover how to chip away at the Stalinist economic model, but that of course is likely to set off an avalanche of economic and political chaos. Admittedly, breaking away from the Stalinist model would constitute an ideological retreat. Yet maintaining the status quo entails its own risks. There is good reason to worry about how long Soviet citizens will continue to settle for the same old excuses. As we shall see in the next chapter, sooner or later (and it looks like sooner), unless the leaders of the post-Brezhnev era can find some way to improve conditions, they are very likely to find themselves facing potentially explosive internal unrest.

4. The Soviet Citizen

By decreeing the collectivization of agriculture and forcing through a policy of rapid industrialization, Stalin sought to increase the Soviet Union's economic capabilities as quickly as possible. In that way, he assumed he would be able to broaden the Soviet Union's foreign policy and military options. He also assumed that the initial emphasis on rapid industrial growth of the heavy industrial sector would eventually make possible a significantly improved standard of living and a richer agricultural development. In effect, this was an implicit social contract between Stalin and the Soviet people: sacrifice and suffering now for what was to be a stronger country with abundance later. This forced-draft policy did indeed increase Stalin's foreign and military alternatives, but it did not bring the promised affluence for Soviet consumers. If anything, the Stalinist model seems to be incapable of satisfying consumer needs. Nor does the Stalinist model facilitate structural economic change. Subsequent Soviet leaders have found it all but impossible to make any far-reaching structural changes. For that matter, it has become difficult to make even moderate changes. Moreover, given the Darwinian weeding-out process which has determined the makeup of Soviet leadership over the last several decades, there seems to be little chance that the next generation or two of Soviet leaders will have any interest in attempting a radical restructuring of the economy. Thus if there is to be any significant expansion of Soviet economic capabilities, the Soviet Union will have to find itself a particularly bold leader with a willingness to risk the consequences of upending the firmly entrenched but archaic economic arrangement that has remained essentially the same for five decades. As it stands now, the Stalinist economic and political model does not seem capable of producing such a leader or of tolerating the necessary industrial and agricultural restructuring. At best, there will probably be more of the same, and as we saw in Table II-1, there could not only be a decline in growth rates, but a decline in actual output.

The prospect that there will be no significant improvement in Soviet living conditions cannot be a happy one. In effect, the present-day Soviet Union is paying the price for Stalin's forced industrialization.[1] That is not to say that consumer economic conditions are the same as they were several decades ago; far from it. But while there has undoubtedly been an overall improvement in living standards, conditions actually seem to have deteriorated in certain important areas, such as food, from what they were in the 1950's. This creates the potential for serious morale and discipline problems.

Because the Soviet population is remarkably patient and long-suffering, it seems to endure poor economic performance more readily than other demanding populations. The Soviet leadership, nevertheless, runs a risk that continued poor economic performance will eventually provoke a protest, particularly if Soviet workers come to believe that their implicit "social contract" will not be honored.

The forced-draft type of economic mobilization and the subsequent failure to provide economic abundance has not only increased tensions between the party leadership and the ordinary citizen, it has also increased friction between the Soviet Union's various nationalities. Nationality frictions, of course, predate the revolution, and probably would have continued even if there had been a more gradual economic evolution, but the tensions provoked by Stalin's collectivization and forced saving, and subsequent industrialization, undoubtedly worsened the relationship and increased the resentment and animosity. This was because the Russians were viewed as the ones who benefited most from the industrialization, while those in the outlying republics, particularly in Central Asia and the Caucusus, were viewed as the savers. Most of these problems have been little publicized either in- or outside the Soviet Union. Yet the frictions between rival nationality groups as well as tensions between the have's and the havenot's within the Soviet Union are potentially very serious matters. It should help our understanding of the challenge the Soviet government faces in coping with these difficulties if we first look to see how these differences arose. We shall consider first the frictions between nationalities, and then those between the upper and lower classes.

I.

From the outside, it may look stable, but those in the inside realize that the Soviet Union is an uneasy union at best. Even though formally the country is now called something fancy, like the Union of Soviet Socialist Republics, there has never been much love lost between the Russians who have dominated what is still a Russian empire and the other nationalities and cultures that continue to find themselves within those same borders. Admittedly, the Soviets no longer refer to the entity as "Imperial Russia," but for many who are not of Russian nationality, the country today bears a closer resemblance to the empire of old than to a union of republics, particularly if, by republic, a sense of choice is implied.

The Russian czars actively sought to manifest their destiny in the eighteenth and nineteenth centuries as they extended their dominion outward from Moscow to the west, south, and east. Like others before them who have sought to expand their borders and impose their will over those with a different culture and language, the Russians were not always warmly welcomed. Incorporation into the Russian empire was often a bloody process, which in many instances, required years of subsequent military occupation. When the revolution of 1917 all but dissipated St. Peterburg's and Moscow's control over the periphery, many of the minority nationalities promptly seized the occasion to break away and form their own state. In short order and for a very short time, independent republics were proclaimed in Georgia, Armenia, Azerbaidzhan and the Ukraine.[2]

Some of these nationalists were motivated by a desire to free themselves from the domination of the Russians, and some were opposed to communism. Whatever the motivation, there was more interest in independence than the newly empowered Bolshevik leaders had anticipated. In his exuberance over the prospects for the revolution, Lenin believed the Marxist revolution would put an end to feelings of nationalist oppression and make obsolete the old system of empire. Since this brave new world would not be a Russian dominated state but a socialist one, who would be so shortsighted as to opt out? For that reason, subsequent Soviet constitutions have stipulated that any Soviet republic that chose to, could secede from the republic. Similarly, each republic is purposedly structured so that it borders on some foreign country or waterbody thereby providing it with access to the outer world should that day of secession finally come. Doubtlessly, Lenin did curb some of the extremes of what had been the czarist russification program. Nonetheless, when local nationality groups tried to see if Lenin's pledges were real, they found there was only one answer—no secession. When Stalin acceded to power, he outrussified the Romanovs, the former czars. As if to prove that he, a Georgian, could be a purer Russian than a born Russian, the suppression of minority nationality sentiment during the Stalinist era was greater than it had ever been under the czars.

The imposition of the Stalinist economic model also served to intensify the resentment of the minority nationalities toward the Great Russians. When Stalin embarked on his collectivization and industrialization drives, the effect was to take resources by force from the agricultural regions of the country and transfer them to the centers of the country's industry. That meant that the industrial regions of Leningrad, Moscow, and the Urals in the Russian Soviet Federated Socialistic Republic (RSFSR), and Kiev, Kharkov, and the Donets Basin of the Ukraine were the most favored areas. To some degree, this also represented an intraregional distribution within the RSFSR and the Ukraine, but to the Caucasian and Central Asian republics, this represented an interregional transfer, in which they were the big losers. Subsequently, the flow of resources became somewhat more balanced, and the Soviets did seek to increase industrialization throughout the country. But they did not succeed entirely, and as a result, the earlier resentment of regional exploitation stemming from the imposition of the Stalinist model is the attitude that continues to prevail among the different non-Russian nationalities. In fact, the population of Central Asia seems to be at a disadvantage relative to the rest of the country.[3] This is reflected in income disparity as well as in the level of educational attainment and life expectancy. Nonetheless, it is generally agreed that industrialization and per capita income is considerably more advanced in Uzbekistan than in neighboring Afghanistan. The same comparisons can be made with most of the countries bordering the Soviet Union in the south except for Iran, where the standard of living increased, at least temporarily, with the explosion in petroleum prices. Moreover, as favored as Moscow and Leningrad have been, the fact remains that the Baltic republics of Latvia, Lithuania, and Estonia, aided by their high degree of development before they were absorbed by the Soviet Union, have a level of industrial and economic sophistication that is generally the highest in the country. The Russians have not sought to increase the disparity, but then neither have they sought unduly to eliminate it.

The point is that the Soviets have not significantly exploited their outlying regions, nor treated them merely as raw material colonies. It is probable that on the whole, more has been taken out than has been put in, but the flow is not as one-sided as it is in the usual colonial relationships in the noncommunist world. However, this does not mean that the same perception is always shared by the nonRussian natives. Certainly, there is considerable bitterness in the more sophisticated and economically competent Baltic regions over what they perceive as the milking away of resources that could be utilized more effectively within the region than elsewhere in the Soviet Union, including Moscow. Similarly, signs of regionalism and resentment are ever present in Central Asia over such questions as the shipment of the region's natural gas out of the area to the center and north of the Soviet Union. An energy study prepared in Tashkent and quoted by Leslie Dienes raised, but prudently dropped, the idea of "refusing exports to the Russian Republic at or near the present rate."[4] Similar sentiments exist in Turkmenistan over the region's petroleum and natural gas reserves.[5] The Central Asians also resent the fact that they are inadequately compensated for their very rich harvest of cotton, which not only serves as an important domestic raw material, but as a hard-currency income earner. Such sentiments are not too dissimilar from those increasingly expressed by Scotsmen who feel that England takes their valuable wool, scotch, and oil, and distributes them without sufficient compensation.

In fairness to the Russians, most of Central Asia was poorer than other regions of the U.S.S.R. before they came under Russian control, and the people of the region have not adjusted as rapidly as the European regions to industrialization. Thus there is indeed a serious disparity in income and economic conditions between Moscow and places like Tashkent, but this is due less to exploitation of the periphery by the center than to the fact that Central Asia started out with an economic and vocational handicap.

Exacerbating the tension is the resentment Russians and Central Asians feel for one another. Rightly or wrongly, to the Central Asians, the Russian is an exploiter and an old-fashioned imperialist in a Marxist disguise. Likewise, the Russians do little to hide their almost racist feelings about the Central Asians. To the Russians, the Central Asians as well as the Georgians, Armenians, and Azerbaidzhanis, are profiteers, if not thieves. As the Russians see it, these people have no apparent scruples and delight in exploiting the decent hard-working Russian residents of the north, whose climate makes it impossible to have gardens that produce early season and semitropical fruits and vegetables. As the Central Asian feels exploited by the Russians, the Russians see their resources diverted from the center and north where they would probably be used more productively to more industrially backward southern regions. That the Central Asians and Caucasian regions as a whole may be economically far behind the rest of the country is not what most affects the Great Russian consciousness. Instead, their image of these people from the south is that of a scruffy, shady Georgian or Uzbek sitting behind a counter in the local collective-farm market, charging exorbitant rates for battered apples and melons. These bitter feelings are not allayed by the sight of all these traders running off in the evening with their rubles to the most fashionable and expensive restaurants and nightspots in town. Central Asians and Caucasians describe openly the fights that often occur between Slavs and non-Slavs.

While many of these tensions are fueled by feelings of economic exploitation, they also reflect long held feelings of nationalism. Regardless of what Marx and Lenin may have predicted, nationalism did not die with the coming of the communist revolution. Admittedly, the Soviet Union may not be a fair test, in that it did not have a genuine proletariat revolution. But even when a state begins to take on the trappings of a true worker-state as in Poland, nationalism seems to become stronger rather than weaker. This is also apparent in Yugoslavia, where the much poorer Albanian minorities have already sought to split off. In time, other national groups in Yugoslavia may become just as overt in their demands for secession or separatism.

That the sense of separatism and nationalism should still be so strong after sixty-five years of tight police control must be discouraging for Soviet leaders. Arrests of nationalists and reports of national agitation continue to appear in the underground *samizdat* literature on a regular basis. The police have not been successful in suppressing the growth of nationalist sentiment. It is like pruning a tree: when the state arrests or puts a nationalist in a psychiatric hospital, another equally fervent nationalist materializes to take his place.

The fact that the minority nationalities are growing relative to the

Russian population does nothing to reduce the tension. Moreover, the prospects for the future look even grimmer for a Russia fearful of being overwhelmed by an alien, and as they see it, uncouth horde. Particularly disturbing is the growth of the Moslem portion of the population. While the birth rate among the Slavs and Baltic peoples remains low, the fertility rate of Muslim peoples, although falling slightly, remains at almost triple the level of the Russians.[6] Only Lithuania, a Catholic republic, keeps its relative share of the population. As Table IV-1 indicates, from 1959 to 1979, the Russians' share of the total Soviet population fell from 54.6 per cent to 52.4 per cent. Should that trend continue, and there is every indication that it will, the Russians will continue to be the largest group within the country, but they will no longer constitute over half of the Soviet population by the year 2000 or 2010. As reflected in Table IV-1, the Central Asians and Caucasians combined still represent a small percentage of the population, but the growth of the Uzbeks in particular is striking. Although they still constitute less than 5 per cent

Table IV-1
VARIOUS NATIONALITIES AS A PERCENTAGE OF THE
SOVIET POPULATION

	1959	1970	1979
Russian	54.6	53.3	52.4
Ukrainian	17.8	16.9	16.2
Uzbek	2.9	3.8	4.8
Belorussian	3.8	3.7	3.6
Kazak	1.7	2.2	2.5
Tatar	2.4	2.5	2.4
Azerbaidzhan	1.4	1.8	2.1
Armenian	1.3	1.5	1.6
Georgian	1.3	1.3	1.4
Moldavian	1.1	1.1	1.1
Tadjik	.7	.9	1.1
Lithuanian	1.1	1.1	1.1
Turkmen	.5	.6	.8
Latvian	.7	.6	.5
Estonian	.5	.4	.4

SOURCE: TSU, *Itogi Vsesoiuznoi Perepisi Naseleniia 1959 goda* Moscow, Gosstatizdat, 1962, p. 184; TSU, *Naselenie SSSR,* Moscow, Politizdat, 1980, pp. 23, 24.

of the population, the relative growth from 1959 to 1979 virtually matched the relative drop in the percentage of the Russian population. Collectively, the peoples of Central Asia and the Caucasus grew from 9.8 per cent of the Soviet population in 1959 to 14.3 per cent in 1979. As Lubomyr Hajda has observed, ''in only eleven years, the Turkic-speaking Uzbeks, Kazakhs, Kirgiz, Turkmen, and Azerbaidzhanis and the Iranian Tadzhiks, increased at rates approaching, and even exceeding, 50 per cent.''[7] This tendency is likely to accelerate because it is in the lower age groups that the relative share of Central Asians relative to the Russians is the greatest. Thus as Hajda points out, in the age group 50–59, there were 32.06 Russians for every Uzbek, but in the 0–10 age group, there were only 6.54 Russians to one Uzbek.[8]

The racial concerns of the Russians over such trends are reflected in the statements of several Russian demographers. As one, G.I. Litvinov, a senior researcher at the Institute of State and Law of the U.S.S.R., of the Academy of Sciences, so quaintly put it:

''The state is interested not only in the quantity of its citizens, but also in their quality. The state is not indifferent to which segment of the population, of the labor force, is at issue when it comes to population increase—whether it is a group with high or low qualifications, with a high degree of mobility or, by dint of various circumstances (including large families or a language barrier), one that is bound to a certain region.''[9]

The changing composition of the population has more than racial implications; it also affects the economy. Regardless of whether it was intentional or inadvertent, the fact remains that most industrial activity in the Soviet Union is concentrated in the non-Muslim, and particularly the European region. If it were not for the fact that the number of new entrants into the labor force is falling, this might make little difference, but the fact that the Soviet Union is likely to find itself with an even greater scarcity of labor in the future is certain to have an adverse effect on economic growth. Furthermore, because an increasingly large percentage of the younger population will be central Asian and from the Caucasus, the labor shortage in the European part of the country will be even more acute than might be concluded from looking at the overall national population figures. The Central Asians in particular have generally been reluctant to leave the countryside for the city, and when they do move to the city, it is usually to cities in Central Asia. The move to the European part of the Soviet Union is as traumatic as the first move into the city. It is unlikely that the Central Asians will readily flock to take up the employment slack in the already developed industrial areas. Moreover, since the technical competence of workers from these areas is not as advanced as those from the European part of the country, not only the quantity but also the quality of workers in the west will be limited. Even if the Soviets somehow discover how to utilize their existing Central Asian labor force more productively, the growing importance of Central Asians in the work force will adversely affect growth and technological development. If nothing else, they are likely to complicate communications. Because the Central Asians and people from the Caucasus tend to hold on tenaciously to their native languages, there is likely to be a growing percentage of the Soviet population for whom Russian will not be their first language.[10] There has been a sharp increase at least among the Uzbeks in the number of minorities who have learned Russian as a second language, but based on present trends, there is no doubt that a knowledge of Russian among younger workers will no longer be as extensive as it has been. This inability to speak a common language could affect not only the functioning of the economy, but of the Soviet military force as well.[11] Apparently there have already been some serious problems in the army, especially when Russian officers ordered Uzbek recruits into action in Afghanistan. The recruits could understand and identify more readily with the Afghans than with their Russian officers, and therefore they refused to fight. By the year 2000, Central Asians are expected to account for as much as one-third of those eligible for the annual military draft.

II.

Although the origins of many Soviet problems can be traced back in one way or another to the czarist regime's drive for empire, it would be wrong to blame all of the Soviet Union's current problems on the czars. These problems are not solely a consequence of prerevolutionary nationality problems. Many of the country's current tensions spring as well from the policies of the Stalinist and post-Stalinist era.

A main source of discontent has been the regime's inattention to the needs of its consumers and workers. In part this is one of the more unfortunate consequences of the Stalinist model's emphasis on heavy industry and planning. The consumer's needs have traditionally held the lowest priority—he and she have been expendable. This is a policy that most people may tolerate for a temporary period of time, but are unlikely to tolerate forever. Admittedly, the Soviet standard of living has been increasing over time. The life of the worker is far more comfortable than it was four decades ago, and except for food, it generally improves each year. For example, the number of new apartments and the stock of consumer goods continues to grow every year. Yet periodic shortages, even of goods that are normally in abundant supply, still plague the system. Such basic items as matches, toothbrushes, soap, underwear, toilet paper, socks, eye glasses, and batteries will sometimes disappear from the store shelves.[12] This reflects inefficient, if not chaotic, distribution methods. Thus even when Soviet manufacturers finally do master the production of a new item, the consumer may still not be able to buy it because of an inefficient distribution system. While the distribution of food is also poor, the main problem continues to be an inability to produce, especially when the weather is bad. As we saw in Chapter Three, the shortages of food in recent years have been particularly striking. But given the present structure of Soviet agriculture, there does not seem to be too much that can be done except to import. Moreover, the kinds of crops that the Soviets are best able to produce, such as grain and cotton, are not those which newly affluent Soviet consumers are most interested in buying. If more meats, fruits, and vegetables, and semiprepared foods were available, the Soviets would spend their extra income on them. Unfortunately, as we saw, these are the goods that the Soviets seem least able to produce.

While it is impossible to ascertain just how serious the shortage of various Soviet food items is, there is anecdotal evidence. Visitors to major Soviet cities in the early 1980's have reported long lines of people waiting to buy goods, especially meat. In more provincial areas, there are fewer lines, because in a striking number of instances, there were reports of no cheese, milk, butter, and even no bread in some cities. The Soviet press itself reported that in some cities, store shelves were "completely empty."[13] Even the quality of bread has become a much more serious problem in recent years.[14] Moreover, there were a series of reports in 1981 that rationing had been introduced in twelve cities such as Irkutsk, Kazan, Tbilisi, Volodga, and Naberezhnye Chelny (now called Brezhnev).[15] Another measure of the seriousness of the problem is the sight of shopping buses flocking to cities like Moscow from up to 150 miles away. The passengers on these buses are intent on one thing: buying meat and other prize items that are unavailable outside the capital cities. In turn, the locust-like depletion of food supplies by non-Muscovites embitters the Muscovites. By the time they reach their own stores after work, the shelves are often bare. To cope with this, the government has increased the volume of goods distributed to employees at their place of work. In other words, goods are effectively removed from the normal retail sales-distribution channels, an implicit acknowledgment of the seriousness of the supply problem.

The high prices that prevail on the collective-farm markets, where supply and demand more properly match, is another sign of the shortage of food supplies.[16] Much of the same balancing takes place in the pervasive black market, or second economy as it has come to be called. Unable to find what they want in the state shops, repair centers, or collective-farm markets, and loaded with large, disposable sums of money, Soviet citizens have made the second economy a basic part of their lives. Often the second economy is benign when, for example, Soviet peasants sell their flowers on Moscow street corners rather than on collective-farm markets, or when an automobile mechanic works after-hours repairing cars. In other instances, a substantial portion of the factory's output may be diverted to fill private rather than state plans.[17] This seems to be a perennial problem in the Republic of Georgia and Azerbaidzhan, where in periodic crackdowns, as many as 50,000 people have been arrested in a single sweep. Nor are such activities limited to low-ranking officials. In 1982, Deputy Minister of Culture Nikolai Mokhov, was arrested for smuggling diamonds into the Soviet Union while at about the same time, Vladimir Rytov, the Deputy Minister of Fisheries, was executed, and two other employees of the Ministry of Fisheries were arrested for smuggling millions of dollars worth of caviar out of the Soviet Union. Caviar was hidden in cans that were labeled "smoked herring" in a scheme that lasted for ten years.[18] While most specialists hesitate to apply a precise figure, a reasonable estimate is that such second economy activities account for at least 10 per cent, and maybe as much as 20 per cent of the Soviet gross national product.[19]

Finally, the astonishing growth of savings-bank accounts mentioned in Chapter Two is another sign that Soviet consumers cannot find enough ways to spend their money. A large portion of those savings could also be absorbed if there were more housing available. Most of the housing in Soviet cities is operated by the municipality or the factory of the employee and rented at very low prices. With rents usually amounting to no more than 10 per cent of the family income, more money is available for other purposes. But this is not as advantageous as it may seem. First, we saw that disposable income in the form of savings is already too high. Second, because less money is collected as rent, the housing authorities find it difficult to collect enough money to maintain the housing stock. As a result, Soviet buildings have become notorious for the deplorable state in which they are maintained. For that reason, there is a substantial demand for the considerably more expensive cooperative apartments, which Soviet citizens are now allowed to buy. Such apartments usually cost about $15,000 to $20,000. This is quite cheap by Western standards, but not by Soviet standards. Nonetheless, if such apartments were more readily available, they would be purchased quickly and more of the funds accumulated in Soviet savings accounts would be quickly absorbed. This is because the housing shortage in the Soviet Union is a national scandal. Again, that is a function of the Stalinist model which skimps on the allocation of resources to the consumer sector. Admittedly, shortly after Stalin died, the Soviet Union embarked on an impressive construction effort. Nonetheless, the effort has not kept pace with the need. Thus as of 1981, 20 per cent of Moscow's population still lived in communal apartments; that is they shared the toilet and kitchen facilities with another family living in the same apartment.[20]

The Soviets are also nowhere near satisfying consumer demand for private automobiles. Just as with housing, much has been done to increase production in the last decade. Production rose from 344,000 units a year in 1970 to 1,327,000 in 1980, but 328,000 were set aside for export and between 50 per cent and 75 per cent of the remainder were allocated for official government use. Thus the private demand for automobiles is enormous, and it is usually necessary to wait three and sometimes four years to buy a car. Because the income elasticity for such products is so high, the demand tends to grow even faster as the money incomes increase, as well as the level of anticipation and expectation. Thus despite the increased production in 1977, there was still only about one car for every forty-six Soviet citizens. It certainly must be embarrassing that Polish and Bulgarian drivers have double the number of cars at their disposal. Hungarians have one car for every fourteen people and the East Germans and Czechs have one for every eight or nine people.[21] The disparity with the capitalist world is even greater. The number of cars per citizen in Western Europe is ten times larger, with one car per three or four people. As long as Soviet citizens look only to their past, they have plenty to be grateful for. However, if they look ahead or even sideways to Western Europe, Eastern Europe, or even Asia, then there is likely to be considerable resentment and bitterness. Such differences explain why the Soviet government censors news about economic life in other countries. Although it is much less of a source of tension than it used to be, work conditions also cause discontent among Soviet workers. Generally, conditions are far better than they were two or three decades ago. The work week has been reduced to five days and factory conditions have improved significantly from what they were during the first years of the Five-Year Plan. However, the workers often find themselves forced to do things for which they receive no pay. For example, at least twice a year, the five-day week is converted into a six-day week when most Soviet workers find that they must volunteer for a Saturday effort of unpaid labor. These *subbotniks,* or Saturday volunteer-days as they are called, are supposed to be used for social projects like public cleanups, but just as often, many workers find themselves at their factory bench trying to increase production without pay. Many workers might indeed accept such petty annoyances in exchange for the state policy of guaranteeing the worker a job. Yet apparently that tradeoff is not completely satisfactory to everyone. Whether it is because the full-employment policy is subject to the exceptions we have previously discussed, or because the workers always feel that someone else is deriving more benefit from their work than they are, the fact remains that there is still considerable alienation among substantial sectors of the work force. Furthermore, the importance of worker safety and the control of environmental pollution on the job are still not properly recognized.

All of this has had a very serious impact on labor morale, which in turn affects discipline. This gives rise to very high rates of alcoholism, which along with the poor morale, brings about a sharp drop in productivity.[22] The economist A. Aganbegian finds that alcoholism, which has always been a serious problem, has become even more serious. ''Drunkenness at work time—after work time—this is an extreme level of disrespect for work, an extreme degree of negativism towards it.''[23] That some Soviet authorities are prepared in public to admit that morale, discipline, worker safety, and drunkenness are such problems only seems to confirm how widespread alienation and discontent are.[24]

The seriousness of such problems in the work place, particularly worker safety and alcoholism, has contributed at least in part to the fact that life expectancy rates have been falling. According to the work of Christopher Davis and Murray Feshbach, the age-adjusted death rates of the Soviet population have been rising steadily since the mid-1960's. Whereas the rate was as low as 7.1 per thousand in 1964, it had risen to about 9.4 by 1978.[25] As a consequence, life expectancy at birth for Soviet males has fallen over the decade from 66 to 63 years.[26] Poor medical care is the cause of much of this, but a large part is also probably due to alcoholism, cigarettes, and "bad habits," some of which reflect frustration with the working environment. In addition, poor worker-safety facilities are probably a contributing factor.

Associated with this drop in life expectancy is the rather striking increase in infant mortality. Infant mortality rose by more than one-third between 1971 and 1976. Davis and Feshbach find that the Soviet Union is the world's first developed nation to undergo a "sustained reversal of the normal downward trend."[27] Again such an unusual occurence undoubtedly reflects poor medical care. It is also a result of the Soviet practice of waiting to have a baby until a woman is in her mid-30's and has had several abortions. This postponement is due to the housing shortage, as well as to general economic strains.

If everyone in the Soviet Union were subject to the same kind of deprivation, the sense of struggle might be easier to bear. What is particularly upsetting about the Soviet case is the clearly perceived notion that some, primarily the *nomenklatura* class referred to in Chapter One, are considerably more equal than others. We expect such things in capitalistic society, but not in what is forever described as a workers' state.[28] This is most dramatically reflected in the baronial-type homes provided for state officials. Some of these estates, including the one built by the former Minister of Culture, Madame Ekaterina Furtseva, were financed through the diversion of state funds for their own private housing pleasures. Construction of homes costing as much as 350,000 rubles (about $500,000) have been reported.[29] Nor does it help that those who praise the workers' state the most are almost always those who seem to be spared the rigors of the ordinary life.[30]

Not surprisingly, most factory managers in the Soviet Union are paid substantially more than ordinary workers. Normally, factory managers fall within the *nomenklatura* category. That means that their appointment must be approved by the party, but it also means that they enjoy the benefits associated with being part of the *nomenklatura*. However, most factory managers, unless the factories they manage are large and unless they dominate the area, still find themselves outclassed by senior party, governmental, military officials. Writers, artists, and performers also tend to do better in terms of prestige. Nonetheless, the perquisites that come with being a factory manager make the manager's life considerably more comfortable than an ordinary laborer's. For example, most medium-sized factory managers are assigned the use of an automobile and a chauffeur. The likelihood is that the factory manager will also have preferential treatment in obtaining housing in the apartment complex assigned to the factory. However, given the general housing shortage, it is unlikely that the apartment will be noticeably larger than those of blue-collared workers. The advantage in housing comes, instead, from the fact that the manager's greater access to an automobile means that he and his family will more likely be able to enjoy the pleasures that come with building a country dacha. A dacha not only insures peace and quiet, and an escape from the tension of urban life, but it provides an opportunity for gardening which can make a qualitative difference in diets.

Perhaps the most important power a manager has is his ability to grant favors. He can determine who receives priority delivery of his factory products. On occasion, he may also find it expedient to divert raw materials or components to some particularly deserving user. The implicit assumption is that sooner or later, if not previously, the recipient will provide an equal favor for the factory manager. Such mutual gift giving covers not only the delivery of factory supplies, but of objects intended for personal consumption. As one of my Soviet acquaintances put it after I expressed my astonishment at the wide variety of the goods in his apartment, "It is not what you earn, but whom you know that counts." Moreover, he had paid for none of his normally unavailable luxuries. "To offer to pay when I ask a friend for a favor would be an insult. We both understand that my turn will come and he will have occasion to ask me to reciprocate." While the typical factory manager usually lacks the overall power of a government minister or a party official, the factory manager's command over perquisites and influence more than differentiates his life from that of the worker in his factory.

The resentment of wage and status inequality is by no means unique to the Soviet Union. It exists in every society, noncommunist as well as communist. But the unmitigated hypocrisy that pervades Soviet ideology, and the effort to convey a sense that somehow the Soviet Union, because it is a "workers' state," has eliminated inequality, exacerbates the frustration. It is not just that inequality exists, but that in some ways the lines between classes are even more firmly drawn than they are in the United States. In the U.S., status generally depends on attaining either a prominent position or making a lot of money. By contrast, anyone who makes a lot of money in the Soviet Union, without having a prominent position, is suspect. The likelihood is that the money was probably made illegally. The problem is that as economic growth has slowed, opportunity for advancement and thus access to positions of importance in the Soviet Union, has been sharply curbed so that mobility has been reduced significantly from what it was in the 1920's, 1930's, 1940's, and 1950's.[31]

Given the ever-increasing difficulty of moving up the social and political ladder in the Soviet Union, the difference between groups begins to take on more of a caste- rather than a class-difference. Once you are in, you may well be in for life, and usually for your children's lives. Moreover, the privileges you accrue mark you as a different—somehow superior—human being. You have privileges denied to ordinary Soviet mortals: relative differences that even the powerful in the United States sometimes do not enjoy.

There would probably be violence if we in the United States were suddenly told that every time David Rockefeller or Henry Ford, or a U.S. Senator, went for a drive, the rest of us would have to stop or move aside to let them pass. Yet in Moscow and many other large Soviet cities, the center strip of the main road is set aside for Soviet leaders. This is broadly defined to mean members of the Central Committee, ministers, and chairmen of such organs as Gosbank, and Gosplan. When warned by portable radio of the approach of a dignitary, or a dignitary's spouse, the militia-man on duty will not only insure that the center strip is free, but will halt any traffic coming from the opposite direction if the officials intend to make a left turn. This is necessary because the masses in Moscow are often not allowed to make left turns on major urban highways. Although emergency vehicles are also authorized to use the center strip, it is their use by Central Committee cars that so clearly reveals the Soviet rejection of egalitarianism. Washington traffic also is halted when the President of the United States moves along the highway, but we do not, as a matter of routine, do the same for Senators, the Secretary of State, the Secretary of Commerce, the chairman of the Board of Governors of the Federal Reserve Bank, or the chairman of General Motors or IBM.

As aggravating as it might be, special treatment on the highway is more symbol than substance. Other than pride, little else suffers when traffic is stopped temporarily to permit the passage of some potentate. But there are also important substantive differences between the upper and lower castes. The powerful have government cars and drivers at their disposal. Most even have their own car. This has been the source of considerable resentment. There is a widespread sense that those who are higher-paid and have "connections" have a better chance of obtaining a car than the masses.[32] Nor does the fact that Brezhnev had his own personal fleet of foreign cars, including a Mercedes, Cadillac, Rolls Royce, Lincoln Continental, Monte Carlo, French Matra, and Lancia Beta, do much to generate a sense of equality.[33]

Equally important, the privileged have access to special "closed" stores that are off-limits to over 95 per cent of the population. These stores are specially stocked, not only with foreign goods otherwise not normally available in stores open to the Soviet masses, but also with Soviet goods that are in short supply.[34] This is something completely unheard of in the West. We are not talking about exclusive clubs or vacation resorts reserved only for the elite. After all, such privileges also exist outside the communist world. The system of "closed" stores in the Soviet Union is something different. The best analogy would be if the American government set up a set of elegant stores (say Tiffany's) which were set aside exclusively for members of the Republican National Committee and no one else. Without access to such stores, there is no other way most of the goods sold in such stores can be purchased legally, regardless of price, by the bulk of the population. Moreover, sales are not limited to jewelry and ordinary luxuries, but what most of the rest of the world would consider basic foods such as meat, fruits, and vegetables. To the ordinary Soviet shopper, they are luxuries and more often than not, unavailable most of the year. As the famous Soviet comedian Arkady Raikin put it, "We have everything, of course, but not for everyone."

Similarly, most Russians have almost no chance to travel outside of Soviet borders, even to Eastern Europe. Not that it is assured, but the likelihood of such travel is much greater for a member of the *nomenklatura* elite. The thought of spending a summer vacation working for a Soviet foreign-trade company in New York is an impossible dream, regardless of your ability, unless you happen to be the daughter of the Vice Minister of Foreign Trade or the Chairman of Gosbank, for whom such summers have become a wonderful way to enjoy the vices of capitalism.

Because such abuses are so widespread and so widely perceived, there has not been much serious talk in recent years by either officials or ideologues about when the Soviet Union will approach full communism. Indeed, while teaching at Moscow State University, I was asked by one of my students, "Do you think there are any more communists left in the Soviet Union today?" When asked the same question, he replied, "I doubt it, unless there may be one or two left in some remote corner of Siberia who have no familiarity with what is happening in the country as a whole."

That the day of complete equality and the abolition of the *nomenklatura* class has been postponed seems widely accepted. Even lip service to the ideal seldom appears. Instead, even *Pravda* now carries warnings that inequality, at least for the forseeable future, is here to stay.[35] Lower-ranking Soviet officials go so far as to warn that wage inequality will last longer than a few years. If anything, "vigorous opposition to wage leveling sentiments" are necessary to insure the influence of material incentives.[36]

Admittedly the elite in the United States do have advantages not shared by the masses, but no one pretends that capitalism is supposed to insure equality. But even then, these privileges do not mean that travel and consumer goods are set aside for the use of less than 5 per cent of the population. The continued existence, in the seventh decade after the Revolution, of special stores excluding the masses is a scandal and a source of frustration and bitterness. In times of emergency such as World War II, such steps are sometimes necessary to insure that those who are in most need have these supplies, but such needs no longer exist thirty-five years or more after the war.

For me, one of the most poignant memories I have of Moscow, is watching the reactions of Muscovites to the Berioska Shops, a special set of shops intended for foreigners with hard currency, but also open to well-placed Russians with hard currency. The Berioska Stores sell hard to find goods, but only for convertible, that is, capitalist currencies. One day, while waiting outside the Moscow Berioska set aside for diplomats, I noticed an officer in the police militia attracted to the store. It was clear he was new to the neighborhood and stunned by the large flock of foreign and expensive Soviet cars poised outside awaiting the return of the large number of well-dressed shoppers and their jammed-packed boxes of domestic and foreign exotic items. Puzzled by the smoked-over windows, and his inability to peer in, the young militia lieutenant was clearly consumed by his curiosity and bursting to see what cornucopia was pouring out such forbidden luxuries. After staring but hesitating because of the vaguely decadent scent of the operation, he decided to follow a foreigner into the unmarked door. He was immediately halted by a white-coated pensioner. Seated by the door, the pensioner's function consisted not only of guarding the door from such unauthorized intrusions, but in sweeping up. Awe-struck, the lieutenant stood there in a rush of shame, envy, and embarrassment as the pensioner sought to halt his entry by declaring that entrance to the store was limited to those with foreign currency. The militia man replied that he knew that, but wanted to look around anyway. "No!" asserted the otherwise powerless old man in the white coat. "You have to leave."

By itself the episode was striking enough, but it was made even more so by another incident I had witnessed the day before. This involved another set of militia men. While leaving the American Embassy, I noticed a cluster of militia men paying particularly close attention to a small family group huddled on the corner nearest the embassy entrance. The militia men were primarily responsible for insuring that no unauthorized Soviet citizens walked into the Embassy compound. Given their concern for this family, it became readily apparent to me that this family had been trying to gain entry. After some additional time vainly trying to win permission, the family decided to rush the gate. In the process, two or three of them were badly beaten and arrested by the militia men. The contrast between the two incidents was dramatic. On one day a militia man in full command of his powers attacks a family because it wants to enter the American Embassy, and the next day, another militia man with normally the same power finds that this time he himself is excluded from entering a store reserved only for special Russians and foreigners. How degrading such incidents must be.

If there were signs that this system of privileges amid consumer-goods shortages was being eliminated, it would be cause for high hopes. But industrial and agricultural shortfalls have tended to make the situation worse. Moreover, the inability and unwillingness to cast off the Stalinist model indicates that even with better industrial and agricultural results, the fruits will not be fully shared with the workers and consumers in any far-reaching way. Implicit in the model is the fact that despite the shortages and the welter of abuses and injustices, there is not much an ordinary citizen can do. Many first try to protest and complain through legitimate and established government channels such as the procurator which is the equivalent of our district attorney. Letters to the editors of

Soviet papers often evoke a follow-up story highlighting some particular malpractice. Similarly, just as before the revolution when many Russian citizens petitioned the czar, they now petition Andropov or other high-ranking party and government leaders for help. Some are successful.[37] In addition, some trade unions do stand up for the rights of their members. A recently reported strike at the experimental design plant of the All-Union Scientific Research Institute of the Livestock Breeding Machine-Building Plant in Kiev was led by the Party and Trade Union Committee members.[38] However this is not an ordinary occurrence.

Many simply accept abuse, inefficiency, and inequality in the system as a normal course of events. Once, while waiting thirty minutes in line to collect a five-cent deposit on bottles in a Moscow store, the army officer in front of me had advanced to the front of the line, only to be told by the surly woman in charge that he would have to wait a bit longer while she ran off to do some errand. The soldier simply shrugged his shoulders and said, "Well, that's the system."

It is no wonder that Soviet citizens are abrasive with one another in everyday encounters. The level of shouting in stores, offices, and in the streets strikes even a rather hardened American as unusually abusive. The prevailing attitude seems to be that since you are abrasive to me, I will be equally curt with you. Many cannot stand the pressure and, as we have seen, seek refuge in alcohol. Certainly alcohol is not an escape exclusive to the Soviet Union. Nonetheless, the percentage of the population afflicted with alcoholism is close to the highest, if not the highest, in the world. According to estimates compiled by David Powell, as many as 15 million Soviet citizens may be afflicted with alcoholism in one degree or another.[39] Of course alcoholism was also a problem under the czars and is a common byproduct of urbanization. Still there is something staggering about the extent of alcoholism in the Soviet Union. Moreover, there is little to indicate that alcoholism is being reduced. According to A. Aganbegian, "with the deepest sorrow I notice, for example, drunkenness at the work place more frequently than before. At several enterprises they have even created special brigades for the purpose of preventing drunkenness and keeping workers from machine tools to prevent accidents."[40]

For some, however, alcohol or long-suffering acquiescence do not suffice. Sometimes out of perversity or opportunism, an occasional person persists in his or her cause. But assuming that the legitimate avenues of complaint and rectification are unresponsive, to whom does a person with a grievance turn? Until recently at least, the practice in many countries of the noncommunist world was that those with a grievance who had been either handled inadequately or not at all would often turn to their local communist party. Traditionally it was the communists, particularly in Europe and the Third World, who offered support and encouragement to the oppressed and the aggrieved. On occasion, such as in the case of low wages, the Communist Party in Europe or Asia, through the trade-union movement, still agitates to seek higher wages. In other cases, the party has pursued extra-legal channels, sometimes involving terror and revolution. But what happens when the Communist Party ceases to represent the oppressed, and instead, becomes the oppressor? Then who is there to turn to? Moreover, having learned its lessons well, the Communist Party, once it seizes power, almost always moves to ban all other political parties so that there will be no alternative party around to reach out and represent the aggrieved.

While the Soviet Union no longer has a party devoted to protecting the oppressed, it did not manage to do away with oppression. Consequently, unless the Soviet Community Party or the Soviet government agrees to champion a particular oppressed cause, there is no legitimate forum for pursuing that grievance. By definition then, those who join together or organize to pursue some issue do so illegally. For many, that means that they become dissidents. Although relatively few in number, such dissidents have sought to change both internal and external Soviet policies which they view as wrong, or which the state has refused to alter through normal channels. Many dissidents have been intellectual in bent, and thus have focused on some of the more abstract issues such as human rights, freedom of religion, the invasion of Czechoslovakia or Afghanistan, and the plight of the Chechen-Inguish and Crimean Tatars, people who in World War II were driven from their homes and not allowed to return.

In 1977, the dissident effort was broadened to include more concrete issues such as blue-collar rights at the work place. In the almost mystical way events of this sort occur in the Soviet Union, several frustrated and offended workers joined together to form their own unofficial and unauthorized trade union. Fascinatingly enough, they first came in contact with one another while waiting in the anterooms of such places as the Central Committee of the Communist Party office in Moscow.[41] For the most part, they all arrived there via the same route. In the typical case, a worker would find that he or she had been abused in some way either at work or home. For example, one worker had been disabled because of inadequate safety equipment; another worker had tried to protest unsafe working conditions in a mine; another worker found that she was being made the scapegoat for the restaurant manager's thievery. Rather than tolerate such a situation, the workers sought satisfaction first from higher echelons of the unions, then the government, and then the Party.

Unable to find satisfaction for their petitions at the lower levels, these petitioners, in the old czarist tradition, eventually began to work their way through to Moscow in the hopes of making their appeal directly to Brezhnev or his immediate aides. While waiting in anterooms for a hearing, they began to discover others with similar tales to tell. Eventually in 1977, they decided to unite to pursue their grievances jointly. Led by Vladimir Klebanov, a disabled coal miner from the Donbass, the group decided to hold a press conference for foreign correspondents on November 25, 1977. This brazen act calling the world's attention to the injustices of the system and the unresponsiveness of the trade unions to serious grievances was followed by arrest, psychiatric detention, and ultimately a temporary release for Klebanov and several of his fellow workers. Despite such harassment, the group held two other press conferences resulting in the formal establishment of the AFTU (The Association of Free Trade Unions of Workers in the Soviet Union: Assotsiatsiia Svobodnykh Profsoiuzuov Trudiashchikhsia v Sovetskom Soiuze).[42] This group was small in number, barely exceeding one hundred members, but given the audacity of what it did, and the almost certain consequences, it is remarkable it came into being. Moreover, a year later on October 28, 1978, after most of the leaders of the first union had been dispersed or arrested, a second group formed another union, SMOT, the Free Inter-Professional Association of Workers (Svobodnoe Mezhprofessional'-noe Ob'edinenie Trudiashchikhsia). In turn, the leaders of SMOT were also arrested and hospitalized. They were charged with everything from stealing library books, driving recklessly, committing malicious hooliganism to spreading anti-Soviet propaganda.[43] Its membership was probably under two hundred, but it did win the support of various Western trade union groups and the International Labor Organization (ILO).[44] Even after Vladimir Borisov, a leader in SMOT, was forcibly exiled to the West, other workers formed other union-like groups.[45]

In one instance a group of Donetsk miner activists, led by a miner named Aleksei Nikitin, arranged for Kevin Klose, a correspondent of the *Washington Post*, and David Satter, a correspondent for the *London Financial Times*, to visit other disaffected miners in the Donetsk region in December 1980.[46] His story was a typical one. Nikitin began work in the mines before World War II. After the war he returned to the mines and became a party member. Aggrieved at some of the abuses of Soviet labor laws, worker safety and management corruption he saw in the mines, he sought relief from the Donetsk Oblast Committee of the Communist Party of the Ukraine. Ultimately his protest antagonized the authorities and he was expelled from the party in 1970.[47] Despite being hospitalized several times in psychiatric hospitals, Nikitin continued his protest. After a mine explosion in December, 1971, of the sort he had been warning about, he was arrested for the dissemination of knowingly false information which discredited Soviet political and social power.[48]

It would be a misconception to conclude that such incidents reflect a seething frustration among the country's proletariat. Nonetheless, there is no doubt that there are significant numbers in the Soviet labor force who do feel abused. Unfortunately, the officially authorized trade unions generally refuse to support redress of many work abuses. Not surprisingly, the workers then find their only recourse is to commit some extralegal act. These protests or job actions usually provoked by unresponsive officials or a jacking-up of work norms by an inept manager, take place with surprising regularity. Reportedly such strikes occurred in May, 1976 in Riga; February, 1979 in Kostamuksha near Finland; in Abkhazia in April and October, 1978; and in Baku in January, 1979.[49] These brief episodes, which are usually solved quickly by the replacement of the manager, tend to become more ominous when in addition to the inevitable labor management friction, there develops some more basic economic problem such as the food shortages and price hikes of 1962 and 1963. These also set off strikes, protests, and food riots. Similar tensions began to reappear in the early 1980's in the wake of the four consecutive bad harvests we discussed in Chapter Three. A similar set of circumstances triggered what became the Solidarity Labor Movement in Poland. No wonder Soviet officials were furious when, at its convention in September, 1981, Solidarity officially urged worker groups elsewhere in Eastern Europe and the U.S.S.R. to form their own independent unions and take similar unauthorized actions. Clearly a movement such as Solidarity can have very far-reaching consequences, so it was one that the Soviets were anxious to control. Indeed, there is probably nothing more worrisome or embarrassing for Soviet leaders than to have Soviet workers protest exploitation by the Soviet state, or to have Soviet workers go out on strike. Not surprisingly, the Soviets suppress information about such events. Consequently the workers' demonstrations and strikes of early 1980 within the U.S.S.R. were little publicized, but reports of an unusually large number of incidents nonetheless found their way to the West. Beginning in May, 1980, strikes were reported at several locations in the Soviet Union. The first strike, protesting food shortages, occurred at the Togliatti Auto Plant, where over a two-day period, about 70,000 workers joined in a protest. This was followed by a similar two day stoppage at the auto and truck plant in Gorky. Similar strikes were then reported to have taken place at the Kama River Truck Plant at Naberezhnye Chelny (Brezhnev) and at the tractor plant at Cheboksary, as well as at a tractor factory in Estonia, at a Donetsk coal mine in March 1981, at Kiev in March, April, May, and June, 1981, and Ordzhonikidze in October 1981.[50] There were even reports of a general strike in Odessa in the fall of 1980 provoked as usual by food shortages.

While the vast majority of these protests were sparked by local issues, there is no doubt that coming when they did, they were fueled by some of the same concerns that affected the Polish workers at Gdansk, that is, frustration over the unavailability of foods and difficult working conditions. To head off more extreme reactions, the Soviets moved actively to increase the responsibility and activities of local Soviet trade unions.[51] Toward the same end, efforts to force the trade unions to intervene more actively on behalf of their members were also taken at the Twenty-sixth Communist Party Congress.

Protest is not limited to the work place. Reflecting the festering tensions generated by the imposition of Russian control over distinct ethnic groups, the Soviets have to deal periodically with outbreaks of anti-Russian sentiment. A series of massive demonstrations occurred in 1978 in the Republic of Georgia after proposed revisions in the Georgian Constitution would have dropped Georgian as the official state language. In response to this protest, the Georgian language was retained.[52] Within Georgia itself, there was a similar type of protest by an ethnic group called the Abkhazians. Just as the Georgians resented attempts to Russify their culture, so the Abkhazians resented attempts to Georgify Abkhazia. Similar manifestations of nationalism occurred in Estonia in October, 1980. The protests were triggered by the cancellation of a pop singing group's performance at a soccer match in Tallin.[53] Before long the protest spread and took on an anti-Soviet character. Since Estonia was so close to Poland and since there was such turmoil in Poland at the time, the Soviets regarded the Estonian protests as particularly menacing. Nor could they have felt assured when an attempt was made to organize work stoppages in all three Baltic republics on December 1, 1981.[54]

Some labor or nationality protests have taken a violent turn. Although little publicized, the Soviets have had to deal with assassination attempts, bombings, and terrorism. In 1969, for example, an army lieutenant fired at automobiles carrying Brezhnev and some Soviet astronauts.[55] Brezhnev was not hit, but a driver was shot and an astronaut was hit by flying glass. In 1978, a Russian representing what he called "The Russian Liberation Army" tried to take over the Finnair Office in downtown Moscow, and force Finnair officials to provide him with a plane.[56] That same year a prison official in Azerbaidzhan assassinated the interior minister of the Republic, and in 1981, there was an unconfirmed report that a KGB colonel was killed in a Moscow bomb blast.[57] Arson was reportedly the cause of a fire on Moscow's Rossia Hotel in February, 1977, and there was also arson in Tbilisi, Georgia, in May, 1973.[58] While it is difficult in each instance to determine how if at all the violence relates to some broader issue, there is reason to believe the fire in Georgia was set by a Georgian nationalist, as were bomb blasts in Sukhumi in 1975–76.[59] Similarly, a group seeking Armenian secession from the Soviet Union set off a bomb blast in Moscow's Pervomaiskaia metro station on January 8, 1977, which killed at least seven people and wounded thirty-seven.[60] Apparently the same group was caught just before they were to bomb the Kursk Railroad Station in Moscow in October of the same year. Subsequently, the Soviet Union's Office of Information in Paris was bombed in February, 1980, in reprisal for the execution of three Armenians charged with the bombing of the subway and attempted bombing of the railroad station. The Paris attack was reportedly carried out by a group calling itself the New Armenian Resistance.[61] Just as the Armenian nationalists have expanded their attacks on Turkish property and personnel in the West, so they may someday decide to extend their campaign to include attacks on Russians and Russia. If this happens, such attacks will not be easy to control, and they may well be imitated by other ethnic groups.

III.

Clearly Soviet authorities have cause for concern. Given the discontent with the results of the Stalinist model and the continuing abuse of power and privilege, there is need for surveillance and control. The difficulty is of course that the pervasiveness of control in the Soviet Union increases the tension and stimulates attacks on that control. There is much to attack, since police and government control pervades all aspects of Soviet life. For example, every Soviet citizen sixteen years or older is required to have an internal passport.[62] Unlike the United States, this passport is not intended for foreign travel, it is solely to provide identification inside the Soviet Union. It is impossible to move from city to city in the Soviet Union, or within a city, for more than a day or two without that passport. To keep the peasants on the farm, the government until 1974 did not issue internal passports to the peasantry except by special request. Soviet citizens take it as a matter of course that they may be stopped at any time to have their papers checked, whether it be at the library when they take out a book, when they buy a train or airplane ticket, or when some Soviet policeman decides to ask. This holds especially for automobile drivers. It is all but impossible to drive more than five miles in Moscow without seeing at least one or two drivers stopped for questioning. In most instances, there has been no traffic violation; the police are simply checking to see if the drivers' papers are in order. Militia men are stationed at every major road intersection, so that it is virtually impossible to travel any significant distance without being observed by a militia man in a little booth. Police are similarly located at all important highway intersections surrounding the city so that it is difficult for any driver to enter or leave the city without being observed. In part, this is to keep a lid on plotting, but even more important, it is to discourage economic free-lancing or theft of state property. With time, the increase in the availability of automobiles increases the likelihood of such thievery or misappropriation, and thus the strain on the state sector of the economy.

However, the constant harassment and surveillance not only affects morale, but it also gives rise to all kinds of graft and bribery. Like policemen all over the world, Soviet police are underpaid. Moreover, a large number of them are recent arrivals from the countryside who quickly find themselves dismayed by the sinful ways of the city, but easily succumb to the temptations open to them. Thus in addition to carrying out the wishes of the state, Soviet policemen have their own personal reasons for stopping motor vehicles so frequently. Similarly Soviet custom officials have become particularly noted for their willingness to accept and demand a bribe now and then.[63] Even border guards have been arrested for smuggling. That is not to say that a member of the KGB is as susceptible as an ordinary policeman, but it is frankly disquieting to see such corruption in what continues to pass as a communist society.

Yet Russian leaders are reluctant to relax their controls. Given Russian history, they recognize that beneath the surface there is continual ferment. While there have been many instances of organized conspiracy and rebellion in Russian history, what makes control so difficult in the Soviet Union is that sometimes rebellion is set off without any evident leader or group in charge. Both the 1905 and March 1917 revolutions seemed to have occurred spontaneously. There apparently was no single guiding or conspiring individual or revolutionary band. When pressed beyond a certain point, Russian workers have the capacity to lash out in anger. If the grievances are widespread enough, particularly when there is a shortage of food, large numbers join in spontaneously. There is then a dangerous potential of a chain explosion. With the sudden development in the late 1970's and early 1980's of what to an outsider could pass as a series of remarkably similar protests, it is clear that economic and social conditions have been the source of enormous tension. Given these underlying conditions, there is a good chance that future generations of Soviet leaders will have to deal more and more with such manifestations. Certainly the Soviets will try everything they can to contain such worker protests. As we saw, in the wake of the Polish unrest, they have even begun to nudge the officially established but usually unresponsive unions towards greater sensitivity.[64] However, given the magnitude of the grievances and the fact that adherence to the Stalinist model prevents any far reaching reforms, it is unlikely that such steps alone will remedy the problem. In one way or another, future Soviet leaders will have to pay heed to legitimate worker grievances. Failure to do so invites unrest.

Watching a group of ten or so workers leaving their job site near a Moscow hotel, it became clear to me how threatening such a group could be. Ignoring a single policeman's order to obey a traffic light, the group simply surged out into the street. Emboldened by the size and spirit of their group, the workers were profane and intimidating in a way that somehow was more menacing than similar groups of workers in similar high spirits in the United States. The Moscow policeman wisely decided to ignore the whole episode.

Because Soviet leaders know the routine so well, an organized conspiratorial revolution is, for many reasons, probably less likely to occur in the Soviet Union than one that appears to be leaderless and spontaneous. Not surprisingly, present Soviet leaders have taken extra precautions to insure that they are not surprised by organized groups, especially since they—the leaders—would be the displaced this time, not the displacers. Not only are Soviet police particularly sensitive to unauthorized gatherings, they keep close control over copying machines and even typewriters. When I used the copying machine of an office of an American corporation in Moscow to copy some letters and classroom materials for my Soviet students, the KGB knew about it almost immediately. During long holiday weekends, office typewriters and copying machines in Soviet offices are locked up not so much for fear that they will be stolen, but out of concern that they might be used for antistate purposes. For that matter, I was required to return my Moscow Rent-A-Car during the week of the anniversary of the Bolshevik Revolution. All such cars were ostensibly called in for servicing at holiday time, which really meant that such cars were taken off the streets to reduce the likelihood of some antistate act.

IV.

Given the continuing sense of frustration at the distortions produced by the Stalinist model and the general unpredictability of the Soviet worker and peasant, the continuing need for such surveillance and suspicion so long after the revolution is only to be expected. Will Andropov and those of the post-Brezhnev era be able to usher in a more relaxed, more tolerant relationship, or will the tension continue or even grow?

There is a serious danger of overdramatizing the problem. Foreign observers of the Soviet scene tend to emphasize its pathological aspects. They focus on the seamier, but not necessarily the representative side of Soviet life. After all, no one disputes the fierce chauvinism that the Russians in particular, but even many minorities, have for the Soviet Union, especially when it is the Soviet Union against some foreign country. Few peoples of the world are so loyal in such circumstances. But even taking such deep-seated patriotism into account, for the Soviets to relax internal police and political controls will be difficult. Until something is done to improve the production and distribution of consumer goods and abolish the caste system, there will be a large oppressed class, some of whose members are not happy with the status quo. There are numerous others in the society who are determined to collect the debts they feel are owed them by those in power. Yet as we saw in earlier chapters, one reform leads to demands for another. Relaxation could set off a rise in expectations which would quickly become uncontrollable. That, perhaps more than anything else, explains why there has been so little loosening of political controls. The Stalinist model's legacy remains to haunt not only the economy, but society.

Assuming the best, that is that Soviet leaders do manage to control ethnic groups, marshal the resources needed to satisfy consumer demands, outpace the rising level of expectation, and balance off the solidifying and splintering forces associated with the new technology, they still may encounter problems, although of a different sort. Satisfying consumer demands may give rise to a new set of disruptive pressures. Materialism can be very seductive. The French used to refer to it derisively as "americanization," at least until they also became seduced. There is a chance that materialism may similarly weaken and corrupt Soviet citizens so that they will find even less reason to tolerate the police controls and the constant mobilization that are required of a state which has acted as if it were under siege for the last sixty-five years. Already more and more Soviet citizens are beginning to complain about how disruptive the need for Spartan controls can be. In other words, Soviet leaders may find to their dismay that once they yield to pressure to improve living conditions in the U.S.S.R., they will have inadvertently set in motion forces which may result in a weakening, if not the debilitation, of the country's external readiness.

5. Soviet Trade, Aid, and Technology Transfer

While foreign analysts may be justifiably skeptical about Soviet economic capabilities, few dispute the fact that the Soviet Union is a formidable power on the international scene. Considering that before World War II, no one paid much attention to the Soviet Union when dealing with international matters, the emergence of the U.S.S.R. as a main force in international matters is a remarkable accomplishment. Yet despite Soviet military strength, it is still beset by weaknesses, and Soviet leaders now and in the future will have some critical decisions to make which will affect Soviet capabilities in the international arena. These choices will not be easy to make, because like everything else we have examined so far, such choices—if improperly made—may set off far-reaching changes which could alter the basic character of the Soviet Union and carry the country far beyond where its present leaders want to go. The Stalinist model has even left a legacy in international relations.

Even when it was militarily, economically, and politically weak, the Soviet Union, just because of its size and location, could never be completely ignored. In the nineteenth century, for example, when its industry was one of the most backward in the West, Russia was called the gendarme of Europe, a reactionary sentinel guarding against revolutionary forces. It was Russia that halted Napoleon's drive and forced him into a retreat from which he never recovered. Subsequently, Russia also quashed a revolution in Hungary in 1848. Ironically, a century later, after having had its own revolutionary fling, the Soviet Union reemerged as the gendarme of Europe and once more put down revolutions in East Germany, Poland, Hungary, and Czechoslovakia.

Because of its magnitude, there is little that can take place in Europe, particularly in the Eastern part, that does not involve the Soviet Union in some way. More than that, there are some who have argued that given the key location of the Soviet Union, he who controls Eastern Europe and the Soviet Union, controls Europe, which in turn makes it possible to control Africa, which then makes it possible to control the world.[1] Those adhering to this Mackinder school of geopolitics thought it only natural, therefore, that early on, Hitler would send his troops off to conquer the Soviet Union. They warned that if Hitler were successful, there would be no stopping his takeover of the whole world.

What Mackinder's followers somehow never seemed to ask, however, was why the communists themselves had not conquered the world? After all, they were already in control of the Soviet Union. They had been in possession of the heartland for twenty years, and were not able to do more with it—at least prior to 1945. There are many explanations, including the one that the theory is meaningless, but for those who accept the theory, the answer is that when Russia is weak, control of the European heartland is meaningless. Control of that territory does not necessarily guarantee strength. In fact, over the course of history, Russia has more often been weak than strong. This holds not only for the first four and a half decades of the twentieth century, but the late nineteenth century. When it is simply a question of the quantity of manpower and simple technology, the Russians usually do relatively well (unless of course they have to deal with the Chinese or Mongol manpower). But if a more advanced technology is involved, then the Russians are likely to suffer. The gendarme proved to be a paper tiger, not only during the Crimean War of 1854 which followed shortly after the putdown of the Hungarians, but also during the war with Japan in 1905, and with Finland as late as 1940. So heartland or no heartland, just because they have a large number of people and a large territory at their disposal, the Russians have not always been able to push their way around. To be effective, they must also have an economic and technical competency that allows them to stand up to their challengers.

Thus the international role of the Soviet Union in the future is very much dependent on whether or not Brezhnev's successors can reshape the Soviet economy. As things stand now, there is little doubt that the present Soviet system is well suited for maintaining and even increasing the Soviet international presence. Granted that the Soviet economy may be ill-suited for the Soviet consumer, it is nonetheless well-suited for equipping a conventional military force. In particular, the economy produces just the right product-mix for infantry, tanks, artillery, and the navy. What concerns Soviet military leaders, however, is that someday the Soviet people will discover, just as Soviet planners before them, that the rest of the world has gone off to run a different kind of world-power race, and that its economic and military establishment is ill-designed to duplicate what the rest of the world is doing. It is necessary therefore for the Soviets to seek Western technology and resources to insure that the Soviet Union maintains the competitiveness of its military technology. However, bringing in foreign technology and technicians sets in motion other forces that potentially may be a threat to the Soviet Union's goal of increasing its international strength.

I.

Given the world today, the Soviet Union finds itself especially well-positioned to increase its relative world strength. Indeed, it would be difficult to design a system better structured for catering to the needs of a military establishment. The Stalinist model fails miserably when it comes to satisfying consumers, but those very failures turn out to be strengths when it comes to supplying the needs of the military-industrial complex. For example, the emphasis on heavy industry and steel is made to order for a conventional army and navy. The nature of the Soviet-type command economy insures that a large percentage of the country's GNP is devoted to the military sector. Just as there is little an individual can do to protest the very large share of the GNP devoted to investment, so there is little that can be done to reduce the military sector's share. Not surprisingly, therefore, Soviet officials have had no trouble setting aside as much as 10 and maybe as much as 16 per cent of the country's GNP each year for military expenditures.[2]

Some economists such as Franklyn D. Holzman have argued that the actual percentage is lower than 10 to 12 per cent. In part, their argument is predicated on the way the United States estimates of Soviet military expenditures are calculated. Because the Soviets do not release reliable figures about their defense expenditures, estimates must be drawn up using reasonable approximations. Most of these estimates involve an effort to determine how much it would cost the Soviets to buy the same amount of manpower and weapons in the United States with American dollars at American prices. To Holzman, this is an unfair comparison because he insists that actual Soviet costs are much cheaper. But while a dollar figure and even the precise percentage of GNP devoted to military expenditures may be uncertain, most observers do agree that the Soviet stock of weapons and manpower is awesome, and has grown at 5 to 6 per cent, a year over the last decade or so.[3] As long as the population seems to be so passive, who is there to prevent similar increases in the future?

The United States, particularly during the Vietnamese War, was criticized frequently and loudly because of the way its military-industrial complex ran the country. There is no doubt that the United States has a military-industrial complex, but its power relative to the total GNP pales compared to its Soviet counterpart. Moreover, the military-industrial complex in the United States does not always get its way. Admittedly it took several years, but the United States eventually withdrew from the war in Vietnam when a substantial portion of the nonmilitary industrial complex establishment concluded the war was hurting the country, and communicated that concern to the President and Congress. It was a long, hard, sometimes desperate, and even violent struggle, but with loud and effective protests from the left and middle spectrums of the country, the military-industrial complex in the United States was finally overruled. Eventually, there were enough people in the United States who came to realize that if the war were to continue, the country's economy would be weakened by inflation and chaos, which in turn might set off a revolution. While undoubtedly the left played a very important role in generating an awareness of the problem, the nonmilitary components of the military-industrial complex ultimately provided the nudge which brought about an end to the whole sorry mess.

In contrast, the Soviet military-industrial complex seems all but immune to almost all comparable pressures. There are several reasons for this. First, the sense of Soviet paranoia and patriotism have traditionally insured a significant level of support for Soviet military activities. The Soviets find fulfillment when they are asked to rally around the flag. Second, the industrial ministries, managers, and planners have a remarkable commonality of interest with the military sector. There are very few at the upper levels of the industrial hierarchy who are in favor of reducing the allocation to the military. Indeed, if the military sector was not there, where else would all that steel be sent?

It is hard for some Westerners to appreciate just how favored and powerful the military-industrial complex has become in the Soviet Union. They are bona fide members of the upper or *nomenklatura* caste. Their cars also have the right to traverse the center lane, and they too have their own system of shops. True the United States military has its own PX network (Post Exchange), but the analogy between the two types of stores hardly conveys the flavor of what it is like to have access to the special stores in the Soviet Union. In the United States, the main advantage of the PX is the absence of excise taxes and thus the assurance of lower prices. In the Soviet Union, access to special shops makes possible access to goods that are unlikely to be found anywhere else. To the extent that a comparison between Soviet special shops and an American PX is meaningful, it would only be if the PX's sold goods unavailable in civilian stores such as was done during World War II.

Because they are so powerful, it is remarkable that Soviet military officers have so seldom interfered overtly in internal Soviet political life. Once in June, 1957, when he was in trouble with some of his rivals in the Politburo Khrushchev found it expedient to call in his minister of defense, Marshal Zhukov, for some political and logistical support, but otherwise Soviet generals have been content to take a back seat. But in determining military matters, the military tends to dominate the scene, even to the point of excluding those in the civilian sector.

An often-told story illustrates how secretive the Soviet military officials are. During one session of the strategic arms limitation talks (SALT), the American side was enumerating what it thought to be the exact size of the Soviet and U.S. missile forces. During the next break in the talks, Nikolai Vasil'evich Ogarkov, one of the senior Soviet military men present, immediately pulled one of the American participants aside, "Please," he pleaded, "do not discuss data about the size of our forces; the civilian members of our delegation are not supposed to have access to this information."[4]

Such stories accurately reflect the unquestioned dominance of the military-industrial complex in Soviet military matters in a way not matched by the American military. Similarly, when Khrushchev tried to cut back the size of the Soviet armed forces in the late 1950's, he met with bitter resistance from his officers, who protested all efforts to shrink the size of their dominion. Thereafter, they did little to support Khrushchev against his internal opposition.

The power of the military-industrial complex has been enhanced even more since it has begun to pay at least part of its own way. For years, the Soviet Union offered large quantities of military equipment at subsidized prices for soft currencies to virtually anyone who would take it. But that did nothing to help the U.S.S.R. with the hard currency problems. It was therefore an unexpected stroke of luck when the price of oil suddenly soared in 1973, and large numbers of Soviet customers from the Third World became rich overnight. Loaded with hard currency, these countries found that they could pay hard currency for almost all the weaponry they dreamed of—they no longer had to beg or borrow. Moreover, since many of them, especially Iraq, Libya, and Algeria, had, for a time at least, broken relations with the United States, the Soviet Union became their main source of supply. This not only provided a hard currency windfall for the Soviet Union, but it allowed the Soviet Union to capitalize on what had become its comparative advantage. In fact by 1979, Soviet arm sales to the rest of the world as estimated by our intelligence agencies totaled approximately $10 billion a year.[5] What makes this figure even more impressive is that, according to some estimates, this exceeded American arm sales from 1979 to 1981. Given a GNP that is not quite 60 per cent of that of the United States, the fact that the Soviet Union can support such arm sales with its smaller economic base is a further indication of the formidable size of the Soviet military-industrial complex. Somehow the world still regards the United States as the world's largest arms merchant, and by a significant amount. That the Soviet Union has come to outsell the United States emphasizes not only the strength of its military-industrial complex, but that military arms production is one of the few things that Soviet industry does well.

Not only does the Soviet Union produce large quantities of traditional heavy arms equipment, but unlike the civilian industry, it generally produces good quality, and often innovative, military products as well. Many Soviet specialists find it difficult to explain how the Soviet Union can be so innovative with its military equipment while it has such difficulties in the civilian sector. In part, the difference is explained by the high priority assigned to the military sector. Managers in the military industry, unlike their counterparts in the civilian world, are provided with more flexibility, more capital and more skilled labor. The Soviets seem to gather together the best specialists and engineers and assign them to special military factories and provide them with special housing and other material privileges. For such favored groups, achievement, not cost, is paramount. As a result, innovation is facilitated. As we saw in Lebanon, this is not to say that Soviet military equipment is the most advanced or sophisticated in the world or that it has no shortcomings; far from it. Soviet military equipment tends to be considerably less sophisticated and more bulky than comparable Western military products—but compared to the Soviet civilian sector, Soviet military production is much closer to the world standard. The question arises, therefore, as to why the Soviets cannot be equally innovative in the civilian sector. The answer is that the Soviets can establish only so many priorities. Therefore, the bulk of what is produced must be handled in a routine manner which means that it is subject to the planning and inefficiency we have spent so much time considering in Chapter Two. Illustrative of the problem is the fact that most factories producing military equipment also produce consumer goods within the same facility. While the military goods may be reasonably sophisticated and advanced, the consumer goods produced in those same factories tend to be unsophisticated and not designed with the consumer in mind. Somehow, crossing the line from the military to the civilian portion of the factory results in a loss of economic responsiveness and flexibility. This helps explain why it is that, contrary to the pattern in the United States when something innovative is produced in the military sector, the chances are quite remote that there will be any spinoff into the Soviet civilian sector. To permit the necessary managerial flexibility and decentralization of capital all over the economy would spell the end of the centrally planned and controlled economic system. Evidently, to Soviet planners the benefits that might result from improved product-quality are not worth the risks of losing control over the economy.

Soviet successes in the military production field no doubt look as good as they do because since the end of World War II, most of the rest of the world including the United States has devoted relatively more of its attention to the civilian than to the military sectors. Partly this is a reaction to the waste and destruction that resulted from World War II. This tendency became even more pronounced in the United States after Vietnam. This in turn has fostered the emphasis on consumerism that marks our age of materialism. It also reflects the fact that many Europeans and some Asians have concluded that there is no chance of holding off the Soviets, so why bother with any serious defense activity? This reluctance to spend money on armaments even in the NATO countries serves by default to make the Soviets look relatively stronger. Yet, continual warnings by Western specialists that the Soviet Union is continuing to build up its military sector, while we in the West and the United States do not, has probably become counterproductive, at least in some countries. Instead of frightening the listener into action, those who issue such warnings have begun to convince a large number of people that there is little that can be done against all that Soviet might. Those who feel this way are further swayed by the argument that another twenty or fifty ICBM's more or less hardly makes any difference. There are already enough missiles on both sides to destroy each other several times over. The determination of the Reagan administration to counter these trends by increasing the spending in both the United States and the rest of the world is an attempt to halt this apparent and real shift in relative power before it is indeed too late. To do this, however, requires a de-emphasis on consumerism and a willingness to increase the power of the military—a difficult task in a democratic and unplanned society.

II.

The impression prevails that the Soviets have done quite well on the international scene. For a time, those who argued this way, especially the liberals, sometimes insisted that this was inevitable since history was on the Soviet side, by which they meant that the collapse of capitalism and the expansion of communism was inevitable. A more careful look suggests, however, that such a Marxist interpretation of history is a poor guide, and that the Soviet Union has not always been a steamroller, flattening all opposition in its way.

Soviet failings have pretty well balanced off their successes. This does not mean that the relative strength of the United States and the Western alliance is as great as it was a decade or two ago. Nor does it deny that there has been a drop in the number of countries which unquestionably accept American views on communism and world questions. But this does not automatically mean that those who decide to reject American leadership have necessarily become Soviet satellites. Instead the number of "intermediary" countries has grown.[6] While this is hardly an indication of a successful American foreign policy, it is not necessarily a sign of Soviet success. For example, Tito's break with Stalin in 1948 was one of the monumental developments of the postwar era. Those who recognized that the break was more than an internal squabble had ample proof that history was not on the Soviet side. Similarly, given its size, China's breakaway in 1960 was even more of a rupture. Because so few anticipated the break, it took observers several years before they came to accept the split for what it was, and not just some deceptive maneuver to mislead American and Western policy makers. And unlike Yugoslavia which tried to seek out a neutral ground, China moved quickly from being a staunch supporter of the Soviet Union to being its harshest critic. Measured simply in terms of numbers, China's defection reduced the size of the Soviet bloc to about a third of what it had been.

Yugoslavia's and China's break away was in part made possible by the fact that each country was situated on the fringe of the Soviet sphere of influence. Only a portion of their borders adjoin the Soviet Union or its other satellites. In the years since Yugoslavia broke away, it has become clear that were it not for the geographical facts of life, China and Yugoslavia would have been joined at least by Poland, Hungary, and Czechoslovakia, and possibly Rumania. Only Bulgaria seems to have been steadfast. However, during the prosecution and trials of East European officials which followed Tito's breakaway, even the Vice Premier of Bulgaria was purged for harboring anti-Soviet and nationalistic sentiments.[7] We shall consider Eastern Europe in greater detail in Chapter Six.

Soviet adventurism outside of Eastern Europe and China has also had its failures. Despite having provided hundreds of millions of dollars of foreign aid, the Soviets nonetheless eventually found themselves thrown out of such countries as Indonesia, Ghana, Egypt, Somalia, and Chile. Occasionally, the Soviet fall from glory has been facilitated by a little push from the United States, but mostly the decision to throw the Soviets out reflects disillusionment with Soviet help and fear of Soviet intervention. Even in Cuba, Afghanistan, and Ethiopia, where the Soviet Union is still the dominant influence, the Soviets have encountered serious problems. Afghanistan has proven to be an enormous headache in which the cost to the Soviet Union is measured, not only in rubles, but in Soviet lives. In the case of Cuba and Ethiopia, the cost has been more in terms of rubles, and in the clash of personalities. During the early 1960's, Castro in particular sometimes took an independent and even hostile stand when dealing with the Soviet Union. Sooner or later, the Soviets may realize that the burden of empire is a heavy one. Like Rome, Spain, France, England, and the United States before it, the U.S.S.R. will ultimately discover that empire is expensive, and probably not worth the cost and aggravation. In its earliest "manifest destiny'' stage, Soviet foreign expansion was exciting and gratifying, especially since each new convert to communism or to Soviet policy usually came at the expense of American foreign policy. Moreover, the initial costs of military and economic aid were justified because it was assumed that once the revolution had taken place and these countries were no longer being exploited, they would shortly become self-sufficient if not profitable producers. Castro and Khrushchev were convinced that once Cuba could free itself of its overdependence on sugar, as well as American domination, Cuba would become industrialized and serve as a model for other countries seeking to free themselves from colonial servitude. After Castro's victory in 1959, the Soviet Union soon began to pour over $400 million a year into Cuba. Yet economically there has been very little to show for it, particularly since the cost has soared to $3 billion a year. While there is a higher literacy rate than before, and income distribution is probably much more equitable, Cuba's economic condition is not much improved over what it was in 1959, the time of Castro's takeover. In some ways it is worse off—it is forced to ration consumer goods, for example. And while Cuba rid itself from the dominance of American colonial servitude, it found itself with a new colonial master, the Soviet Union; not much of an improvement. The story is much the same in Vietnam and Ethiopia, each of which costs the Soviet Union $150–450 million a year in economic aid alone.

Given their own limited circumstances, many Soviet citizens seem distressed at the diversion of such sums to the Third World. Few of them are mollified by the explanation that their sacrifice is in the tradition of true socialism. This skepticism and resentment becomes all the more pronounced when as so often happens, the recipients such as Indonesia, Egypt, and Ghana then turn their backs on the Soviet Union and become hostile and indifferent. If the Soviet is ever to prevent the cost of its empire from becoming impossibly burdensome, the least it should do is avoid the basket cases it now seems to attract and focus instead on more prosperous countries such as Saudi Arabia and Libya.

Equally embarrassing is the discovery that many of the Third World countries are beginning to lump the Soviet Union and Eastern Europe together with the richer countries of the OECD (Organization for Economic Cooperation and Development) as exploiters of the Third World. Despite Soviet protestations that it is a socialist country, and therefore not capable of exploiting poor countries, the Third World leaders point to the Soviet Union's own pronouncements about its economic success as proof that the Soviet Union is "a have" nation.[8] Thus the Soviet Union is being asked to pay for the costs of Third-World exploitation without having, at least until recently, been able to enjoy the full benefits.

Furthermore, the Soviet Union finds its image is no longer as enticing as it once was, at least in the Third World and amongst radical communists. Now that the United States is out of Vietnam, the U.S.S.R. is much more a classic colonial power today, and a nasty one, as its behavior in Afghanistan indicates. That is not to say that there are no revolutionaries in the world who would appeal to the Soviet Union for help to free themselves from their local right- and sometimes left-wings. But because Soviet problems, particularly its economic ones, are so serious, there are not many revolutionaries who can find much to emulate in the Soviet Union.

Even foreign-aid advisors from the Soviet Union have become suspect. For years the Soviets belittled American efforts to concentrate on agricultural reform and growth. The Soviet Union insisted that was the American way of keeping its aid recipients economically backward and in bondage. Concentrate instead, the Soviet Union argued, on heavy industrial growth—à la the Stalinist model. Given subsequent Soviet agricultural disasters and its inflexible industrial responsiveness, the Soviets are no longer so insistent that theirs is the only true way. Such failures, particularly when contrasted with the recent economic miracles in East Asia, have led most leaders of the emerging world to look to the Japanese or Taiwanese for economic guidance, rather than to the Soviet Union. The fact that Soviet economic growth has slowed, that the Soviet Union has difficulty innovating, and that it must import millions of tons of grain each year is an enormous embarrassment. Indeed, the Soviet Union has lost its allure. Who wants to grow up to have an economy like the Soviet Union's? Even to the Soviet Union, the world-march towards communism no longer looks as inevitable as it once did.

III.

In the past two decades, the Soviets have found that dealing with the outside world requires a much more sophisticated policy, one whose consequences are not easy to predict. We in the West have long been frustrated by the complications we confront in foreign policy. We believe that unlike ourselves the Soviets have had it easier. What we realize now is that, for them as well, the issues of international life are not black and white. Thus it is true that we are distressed by the fact that the West Europeans are not uniformly hostile to the Soviet Union. Yet the strong neutralist strains affecting German foreign policy have done little to alleviate basic Russian anxieties that West German militarism will again come to haunt them. Moreover, while it is true that the United States has to contend with growing neutralist sentiment among some of its most important allies, the Soviets have also to cope with outright hostility if not insurrection from some of its most important allies such as Poland and Rumania. There have even been antinuclear demonstrations in Rumania and East Germany. The Soviets now recognize that encouraging further neutralization and involvement with Western Europe entails a cost, both to it and to its allies, that some nationalists in the Soviet Union do not regard as worth the benefit.

In Stalin's day, Soviet foreign political and economic policy was uncomplicated. Basically, Stalin wanted as little contact with the outside world as possible, and what contact there was had to be on his own terms. After Stalin's death, Khrushchev moved away from the more rigid aspects of the Stalinist model of foreign conduct. Khrushchev accepted invitations to visit outside the Soviet bloc and invited noncommunist leaders to Moscow. Trade and travel by foreigners to Moscow increased as the Soviet Union sought to woo the Third World to its cause, an effort previously all but ignored by Stalin. Yet most of this contact and activity involved a very thin strata of the Soviet population. Most Soviet citizens remained, as under Stalin, fenced off from foreigners and travel. Similarly, Soviet foreign and military policy makers have never fully relaxed their vigilance or abandoned their antagonism to all that was foreign. In other words, while the Stalinist model of international intercourse has been modified from what it once was, many of the controls and concepts instituted by Stalin have remained in place. Soviet leaders still fear that too much contact will trigger demands for ever more relaxation. However, Soviet leaders also seem reluctant to go back to the more extreme forms of the model. Conceivably, Brezhnev and his successors could go back to the more rigid Stalinist stance, but the cost of autarchy and isolation would probably be too high. For better or worse, by adopting a somewhat more relaxed international relations model, the Soviet Union seems, even if hesitantly, to have become a part of the world community. Thus even though many of the strict Stalinist restraints remain, the Soviets have also implied, by acknowledging their interdependence with the rest of the world, that the capitalist world, in particular the United States, is not evil incarnate. Certainly there is something bittersweet about the way Soviet leaders so warmly welcome and hobnob with a Rockefeller, Harriman, or the chairmen of Pepsi Cola or Coca Cola, the very symbols of what once stood for the evils of capitalism.

To some extent, Soviet leaders have had little choice in the matter. Modern technology has caused the world to shrink. Today New York is closer to Moscow in terms of travel time than it was to Chicago forty years ago. Moreover, the telephone makes it theoretically possible to talk with someone in Moscow almost as quickly as with someone in Chicago. Technology has also shrunk time and distance within Moscow itself; news now travels much faster than it used to. Despite state censorship, broadcasts by Western correspondents to the West about happenings in Moscow today are transmitted by shortwave radio back to Moscow informing Muscovites of events that formerly might not have been reported at all.

While teaching at Moscow State University in 1977, I was asked to make a broadcast for the Voice of America about what I was teaching. For three weeks after the program was broadcast, students, strangers, and friends from all over Moscow told me they had heard me on the Voice of America. Upon my return home, I made another Voice of America broadcast in which I commented about the large number of my students and faculty colleagues who listened to the Voice of America. Having heard me themselves, senior university and party officials soon after called a special meeting to warn my former students and colleagues to stop listening to such broadcasts.

Such widespread interest in foreign radio broadcasts has provoked the Soviet media into being more informative and timely about broadcasting events than formerly. If the Soviets do not provide their version of such events, Soviet citizens may accept the facts as presented by the West and Soviet media will find it harder to sustain what little credibility it has. Of course, the Soviet Union could resume the jamming of foreign broadcasts, but that works imperfectly, particularly outside the cities where the jamming centers are located. In any event, jamming undermines the Soviet Union's effort to depict itself as a reasonable member of the international community in a technologically shrunken world.

Another force causing the Soviet Union to interact with the West is its need for economic help. In Chapters Two and Three, we saw that the Soviet Union was unable to provide for its own basic needs. Imports of grain in a bad harvest year amount to as much as 35 per cent of the Soviet grain harvest. Grain imports, which cost the Soviet Union $5 to $6 billion in 1981, about a quarter of its total hard-currency import bill, are not the only commodities the Soviets must seek outside their country. Because they lack enough high-grade deposits of their own, they have also become dependent on foreign suppliers for about 40 to 50 per cent of their bauxite and alumina.[9] Similarly, they have also begun to import huge quantities of phosphates and phosphoric acid. As large as the Soviet Union is, the likelihood is that with time it will need increasing amounts of various minerals as its own deposits are depleted.

In addition to the raw materials, the Soviet Union in the late 1950's also began to purchase substantial quantities of technology. To some this seemed to be a departure from the Stalinist model. However, Stalin had also brought in foreign technology in the 1920's and mid-1940's. Compared to normal technology trade between countries in the West, these late-1950's Soviet purchases were not large, but compared to what the Soviet Union imported from the West in the late 1940's and early 1950's, the amounts were substantial.[10] This too increased the Soviet Union's vulnerability to outside influences, as it discovered when the United States embargoed technology as well as grain in protest against the Soviet invasion of Afghanistan. Neither the grain nor the technology embargo crippled the Soviet economy, but it did cause considerable inconvenience.[11] Some factories had to do without some essential spare parts and the Soviets had to scurry around to buy more grain from other countries. As a measure of how vulnerable the Soviet Union has become, the economist O. Bogomolov reports that the Soviet Union now imports over 11 per cent of all the raw materials it uses in production.[12] By Western, particularly West European standards, that is still a relatively small figure. But when measured against the past autarkic practices of Stalin, where imports seldom totaled more than a few hundred million dollars, the vulnerability of the economy has increased significantly.

From the Soviet view, not all imports, especially the technological ones, have been that helpful. On occasion, Soviet appetites have been bigger than their abilities. Because of the huge size of the country and its leaders' aspirations, Soviet planners often do things on a larger scale than elsewhere. In addition to satisfying their sense of power, theoretically this emphasis on largeness of scale should also make possible economies of scale. Thus the Kama River Truck Plant has the largest capacity of any diesel engine plant in the world, and Soviet ammonia plants, unlike the standard plants in the West which are designed to produce one thousand tons a day, are designed to produce fifteen hundred tons a day. Unfortunately, just because a plant is large brings no automatic guarantee of efficiency. In fact it can be counterproductive, particularly when a technological process is implanted without regard to the context of the existing technological capacity of the Soviet Union. As in Poland, there are factories in the U.S.S.R. that have proven to be unsuited, ill-equipped, poorly designed, and uneconomic to operate.[13] Under the circumstances, instead of trying to catch up with the world in a gigantic leap, the Soviets might have done much better if they had imported technology that was much more modest in scale and scope. It would have made more sense if they had started slower and then upgraded what they had. That is the Japanese strategy. They import technology and upgrade it by what has come to be called enhancement engineering. In contrast, the Soviets frequently are unable to go much beyond what they bought in the first place. With some notable exceptions like electrical transmission and welding, they often seem to have difficulty merely reproducing what they purchased.[14] In fact, most American businessmen find that when their technology is installed in the U.S.S.R., it normally operates at only 60 per cent of the efficiency it operates at in the United States.[15] In contrast to Japan, there is relatively little likelihood that Soviet purchases will be upgraded and then exported to other countries.

Although the Soviets may not be able to use their newly purchased technology as effectively as it could be, some of their technological imports are absolutely crucial for the Soviet Union.[16] For example, until they brought in foreign equipment, the Soviets had no offshore drilling capacity. More importantly, the Soviets have had particular difficulty in developing their own computers for everyday industrial use. Thus, without foreign computers, the Soviets would have had a very difficult time working out such complex tasks as scheduling production at a plant as large as the Kama River Truck Plant or integrating air traffic-control operations. Similarly, a surprisingly large percentage of their chemical industry depends almost entirely on the importation of foreign machinery.[17] And as might be expected, this equipment operates below its rated capacity.

At the same time, there have been some outright disasters. Some foreign imports have been used very poorly and some not at all. In several cases, Soviet officials would have been pleased to have attained productivity that was even 60 per cent of U.S. levels. All too often, foreign equipment has been left outdoors for months at a time, where it is then subject not only to the weather, but to cannibalization by Soviet workers who cut out parts and divert them to makeshift uses.[18] As of January 1, 1981, the Ministry of Ferrous Metallurgy had 1.5 billion rubles worth of equipment from hard currency countries sitting around waiting to be installed. In late 1981, the Deputy Minister of the Petroleum Industry was fired because he had let about $50 million worth of imported secondary recovery equipment and materials lie idle for months with no sign that it would be used.[19] Such practices are a frequent occurrence in the Soviet planning system. Responsibility for building new factories and installing equipment is fragmented and so construction normally takes years longer than it should to complete. What is noteworthy here is that Soviet workers and managers treat imported machinery just as carelessly as domestic machinery.

But it is not only a matter of an absence of clear lines of authority. Sometimes the technology is just ill-suited. It was because of inappropriate technology that the fifteen hundred ton a day ammonia plants referred to earlier turned out to be a particularly serious failure. Shopping for the cheapest bidder they could find, the Ministry of Trade Officials finally signed a contract with an American company which, despite its expectations, found it could not scale up the ammonia operation from the thousand-ton standard model to fifteen-hundred tons in the way the Soviets wanted. As a result, the Soviets found they had spent tens of millions of dollars on four plants, but that none of them could be made to realize their potential.

Allowing for both successes and failures, several Western observers have tried to calculate just how much Western technology has contributed to Soviet economic growth. According to the estimates of Padma Desai, the overall increase in productivity from Western imports, on the average, has been small and not worth the cost. In contrast, estimates by Donald Green and Herbert Levine indicate that the return was much higher. These latter authors subsequently concluded, however, that their initial results were overly optimistic.[20]

Despite the fact that in specific instances foreign technology has been very important, some Soviet leaders have appropriately concluded that the overall gains have not measured up to their expectations. This in part probably accounts for the fact that, beginning in 1981, Brezhnev seems to have become more critical of imports. "We must examine why we sometimes forget our priorities and spend large sums of money to purchase equipment and technology from foreign countries that we are fully capable of producing ourselves, and often at a higher quality."[21] That is a decidedly different tone than Brezhnev has used in the past.

Not surprisingly, such sentiments are not restricted to Brezhnev alone. For example, academician A. P. Aleksandrov, President of the Soviet Academy of Sciences, complained that "We must actively develop our national techniques and technology. We must not create gaps in our technological development by unjustifiably relying too extensively on foreign techniques."[22] In the same vein, but in a much more ominous way, S. Tsvigun, First Deputy Chairman of the KGB, warns that undue reliance on foreign technicians may sometimes lead to supervision and sabotage. He charges that late in 1980, a representative of the Burroughs Corporation was found to be purposely preventing the proper start-up of imported American computers. Soviet citizens, Tsvigun warns, should be vigilant because some foreign businessmen have sabotaged Soviet equipment.[23] This is a remarkable throwback to the 1920's and 1930's, when Stalin used to blame foreign engineers for many of the shortcomings in the Soviet economy.

The combined effect of such thinking helps explain the drop in Soviet machinery and technology imports in the late 1970's and early 1980's. Thus according to Soviet data, machinery imports from England, France, Germany, Italy, Japan, and the United States, which amounted to $3.7 billion in 1975, rose to a peak of $5.3 billion in 1978 and then dropped off to $5 billion in 1979. They increased slightly to $5.1 billion in 1980, but then dropped sharply in 1981 to $3.7 billion, back to where they were in 1975. Moreover, since these figures are in current, not real, dollars, that this was a significant drop. Philip Hanson has attempted to measure machinery exports from countries of the Organization for Economic Cooperation and Development (OECD) to the Soviet Union in 1975 prices; he found that 1975 exports were $4,576 million, rose to $4,785 million in 1976, and then fell steadily to $3,400 million in 1979.[24]

Were it not for such incidents and the occasional arrest of foreign businessmen such as Jay Crawford of International Harvester in the summer of 1978, the Soviet Union in many ways would be an ideal trading partner for the OECD countries. It buys technology and exports raw materials. In those few instances where Soviet products are competitive on world markets, the competition focuses primarily on price—not on quality or performance. The Soviets set their prices so low that the buyers are tempted to forgo the higher-quality foreign goods in exchange for lower quality but lower-priced Soviet goods.[25] Their competitors tend to view this as a form of dumping. The Soviets can engage in such practices because Soviet workers are paid in soft currency or nonconvertible rubles, and because most Soviet products do not incorporate many if any foreign components or manufacturing costs. This, plus the fact that the Soviet economy is owned by the state and run like one giant company, where profits from the export of one product can be used to subsidize the cost of another export, means that the Soviets can cut their prices to almost any level they want. Such price cutting is particularly important if a lower price will bring them foreign hard currency which in turn will allow them to import products with a higher productivity than comparable goods found at home. While potentially this form of price-cutting could be a source of tension, for the time being, the Soviets have been unable to generate a large enough volume of exports, even at distress prices, to pose any widespread disruption. So far 83 per cent of what the Soviet Union exports to the hard currency world still consists of raw materials, whereas about 41 per cent of what it imports from Western Europe consists of machinery (53 per cent if pipe and rolled steel are included). By most definitions, this makes an ideal trading partner for industrially developed countries.[26]

But while this may make an ideal customer for the OECD countries, it is a much more threatening posture to the low cost technology and raw material exporters of the Third World. In fact, the substantial increase in the low cost exports of Soviet petroleum in the late 1950's was a major factor in provoking the oil producing countries into forming OPEC. Similarly, today some raw material producers continue to view the U.S.S.R. as a rival holding down various raw material and semiprocessed product prices. It turns out therefore that in many ways, the Soviet Union is actually more of a competitive threat to countries like Brazil and the Philippines with their low technology items than to the OECD countries with their more sophisticated products.

Will the Soviet Union someday pose the same kind of competitive threat to manufacturers of more highly fabricated goods? Because they seek to catch up with the world of high technology, Brezhnev's successors will certainly try their best. However, to do so means that they must abandon the Stalinist model and open up the Soviet economy to more internal and external competition and innovation. Yet even if they maintain the status quo, the likelihood is that the Soviet Union in the future should be able to upgrade its raw material exports, particularly where the Soviet Union has either a comparative or geographical advantage. As one example, rather than remain content with just exporting natural gas, the Soviet Union decided to process that gas into ammonia and then export it. That of course upset ammonia manufacturers in the importing countries, but capturing the value added for itself this way is a natural progression for the Soviet Union. Soviet petrochemical producers are also likely to increase their degree of sophistication and their export earnings. Here is where the large endowment of Soviet raw materials should prove to be helpful.

The Soviets also seem to do well in international markets where a large concentration of capital is required to compete. Because it can muster capital resources so effectively, the Soviets have bid successfully on several massive dam and hydroelectric construction projects. They have also been able to put together very competitive fishing and merchant marine fleets. It helps that the Soviets are not constrained by labor costs in the same way that private merchant marines or fishermen are. This allows Soviet authorities to cut their rates, particularly in the shipping industry. This is also regarded as a form of dumping.[27]

Soviet involvement with foreign markets is a complex one. In principle, Soviet economic planners seek to manipulate foreign trade for their own specific purposes. They are not interested in the promotion of world trade as a general principle. If there were no other constraints, Gosplan would make a determination as to what it needs to import and then gather together enough exports to pay for it. The goods selected for export would have to meet at least two criteria. There would have to be a demand for them in foreign markets, and presumably the diversion of such goods from the Soviet economy would be more than compensated for by the productivity of the imports they make possible. If planning were done properly, the goods selected for both export and import should be placed in two separate columns and rank-ordered. The goods highest on the import list would be those goods that are the most essential and provide the Soviet Union with the most productivity. The goods highest on the export list would be those with the lowest productivity whose export would affect the Soviet Union the least. It would be ideal if those Soviet goods which were most in demand in the outside world were also those least needed in the Soviet Union, i.e., those at the top of the export pile. Soviet planners and exporters should then work their way down the export list until they have exported enough goods to earn the hard currency they need to pay for the imports they want at the top of the import list. The importers should then begin to work their way down the rank order of imports to those with successively lower productivities. However, there is a danger they may import too much. Soviet planners should never allow the importers to bring in so many imports that they work themselves down the rank order of productivity to a point where, in order to pay for those imports, they have to export so much that they lose more productivity from exports than they gain from those imports.

Unfortunately, life seldom conforms with the ideal. Frequently the Soviets have had to import more than they wanted or expected to. In addition, they have had to export items they would have preferred to retain, but were forced to export because most other Soviet products were unsellable in foreign markets. More than anything else, the recurring poor harvests in the Soviet Union have forced Soviet planners to lose control of their import plans and therefore of their export destinies as well. Since 1972, the need to dip into foreign grain elevators for food and feed grains has become a normal part of Soviet economic life. What has been more of a surprise is that the Soviet Union has also found itself caught up in capitalist business cycles. It discovered, for example, that contrary to expectations, the capitalist recession of 1975 hurt the U.S.S.R. badly. For a time, the Soviets thought they could have their pick of the bargains from capitalist suppliers whose fellow capitalist customers had stopped buying. Initially, Soviet importers went on a spending spree. (See Table V-1.) However, they quickly realized that when the capitalists stopped buying, they stopped buying from everyone, including noncapitalists. Thus while Soviet imports in 1975 soared by almost $5 billion, almost doubling from what they had been in 1974, exports according to Soviet data, at least, actually dropped. This left the Soviet Union with a trade deficit of $4 to $5 billion, one of the largest in its history. In order to reduce the size of that trade deficit and pay off some of the past debt, the Soviet Union stepped up its exports in a massive way. As Table V-1 indicates, according to Soviet data, Soviet imports from 1975 to 1977 barely increased while Soviet exports rose sharply by $3 to $4 billion. In 1976, almost $1.7 billion of that export increase consisted solely of petroleum exports and was diverted by Gosplan intentionally to reduce the Soviet debt. During the two year

Table V-1

SOVIET TRADE BALANCES WITH HARD-CURRENCY COUNTRIES (millions of dollars)

	1971	1972	1973	1974	1975	1976	1977	1978
Capitalist data								
Imports from USSR	2,553	2,915	4,561	6,839	7,166	8,803	10,548	12,387
Exports to USSR	2,251	3,338	4,892	6,258	11,086	12,106	12,112	13,862
Balance for USSR	+302	−413	−333	+581	−3,920	−3,303	−1,564	−1,475
Soviet data								
Exports to West	2,319	2,491	4,327	6,739	6,346	8,420	10,187	11,145
Imports from West	2,429	3,565	5,254	6,910	11,419	12,574	11,845	14,413
Balance	−110	−1,074	−927	−171	−5,073	−4,154	−1,658	−3,268

Exchange rates: 1971   1 ruble = $1.11
             1972   1 ruble = $1.21
             1973   1 ruble = $1.34
             1974   1 ruble = $1.34
             1974   1 ruble = $1.32
             1976   1 ruble = $1.34
             1977   1 ruble = $1.37
             1978   1 ruble = $1.50

period, the value of petroleum exports practically doubled from $3 billion to $5.3 billion, so that petroleum made up considerably more than half of the increase in export earnings.[28]

The Soviet Union found itself in almost the same predicament during the recession of 1981 and 1982. As in the earlier period, the Soviets also had a poor grain harvest and thus had to increase grain imports more than anticipated. At the same time, the price of raw materials, especially petroleum, began to fall. By the end of the second quarter of 1981, the Soviet Union had built up a trade deficit of about $4.5 billion. At that rate, the deficit for the year would have totaled close to $10 billion, twice the size of the 1976 deficit. In a throwback to 1976, however, the Soviet Union sharply increased the export of petroleum. For example, exports to the Netherlands, the site of the spot-market for petroleum, abruptly and atypically increased by about $500 million in the fourth quarter of 1981. At the same time, there was a sharp drop in imports from countries like Brazil.

In addition to using exports to balance off imports, the Soviets use foreign trade, particularly exports, as a way of winning and keeping friends and threatening and intimidating potential and real enemies. Thus just like OPEC the Soviet Union has used the oil weapon in an effort to keep some of its friends in line. One of the first to experience this Soviet weapon was Yugoslavia. In 1948 Yugoslavia found its oil imports from the Soviet Union had been cut by one-half. They were terminated completely when Tito broke away from Soviet domination. In similar fashion, the Soviets suspended oil shipments to Israel after it invaded the Sinai in 1956. China, which from 1955 to 1961 was the Soviet Union's largest purchaser of petroleum, found its imports cut back sharply in 1964 and all but severed entirely in 1965 as the Soviet and Chinese feud broke into the open. Oil shipments to Castro in 1968 were held back when he became too independent. Similarly, oil shipments to Finland were halted in late 1958 until the Finns came up with a President more to Soviet liking. Since the Soviets made the same kind of threat to Finland in November, 1981, there is every reason to expect the U.S.S.R. will behave the same way in the future. In fact, there are several analysts who expect the Soviets will try to exert similar leverage in the sale of what has become known as strategic raw materials.[29] In particular, because there are only one or two other producers in the world, some Western strategists, such as Daniel Fine of MIT, see the Soviets trying to manipulate sales of chromium, titanium, lead, and platinum for political purposes. Certainly there is nothing in the Soviet Constitution or the Soviet code of ethics that would stop them from trying to impose such a stranglehold. The Soviets may have such intentions, but in fairness, it should be pointed out that it sometimes appears as if nothing the Soviet Union does is right and that the U.S.S.R. will be criticized no matter how it behaves. For example, when the Soviets tried to break into the petroleum market and found that the only way they could uo so was to cut prices, they were accused of dumping. Now when it seems that they might hold back some of their raw materials from export, they are accused of being highwaymen. Undoubtedly there is an element of truth in both accusations, but it is understandable how a Soviet trader might conclude that whether they sell or they hold back their sales, they will be criticized.

Whether or not they are able to use trade as a weapon depends on whether or not Brezhnev's successors can exercise enough control over their particular market to make such a move meaningful. It also depends on whether or not the Soviets can find enough goods to export to pay their bills. Much as they might like to hold back vital raw materials from sales to foreigners, they have to find something to export if they want to import. Oil is the supreme strategic weapon, but the Soviets nonetheless have been forced to export much larger amounts than many in the Soviet Union think advisable. The main reason for the large export of petroleum is that oil is their most lucrative product. Petroleum provides them with over 56 per cent of their hard currency exports; nothing else including gold comes close. If they are able to increase the amount of natural gas they can ship to the West, then it is likely that they will substitute natural gas for petroleum, but in the meantime, they have little choice. They might want to hold onto particular raw materials, but they have found that they may not always have an option in the matter.

The Soviets have discovered that foreign trade is addictive. They start with one import and before long they find themselves importing and of necessity exporting much more than they ever anticipated or desired. Indeed, there is a school of thought in the Soviet Union which argues that the Soviet Union should not export its raw materials at all but instead should hold on to them for future generations when those raw materials will be even more valuable. The most outspoken of such statements have come from Soviet dissidents like Alexander Solzhenitsyn and Boris Komarov. In Solzhenitsyn's words, ''We, a great industrial superpower, behave like the most backward country, by inviting foreigners to dig our earth and raw materials and then offer them in exchange our priceless treasure—Siberian natural gas.''[30] Similarly, Boris Komarov, a pseudonym for a Russian with an obviously keen knowledge of Soviet environmental problems, complains that raw materials are being exported to pay for the inefficient operation of the economy, which is no sin in itself, but unfortunately those "resources can be used only one time."[31] Certainly neither Solzhenitsyn nor Komarov qualify as official spokesmen, but there are others including senior officials in the Ministry of Petroleum whose views are not too much different. Even Brezhnev now speaks of the need to husband exhaustible supplies of the Soviet Union's raw materials. Whereas once he spoke of the Soviet Union's "inexhaustible opportunities," he subsequently changed his attitude: "The Soviet Union's demand for energy and raw materials grows increasingly and therefore production becomes all the more costly . . . it is necessary to use raw materials more effectively."[32]

Yet whether it be Brezhnev or a dissident, the decision to export is not entirely a matter of free choice. Obviously the Soviets would prefer to export machinery and other products typical of an industrial nation. But given the obsolete nature of the preponderant portion of Soviet industry, they have to fall back on oil, gas, and raw materials, including some like titanium, chromium, lead, platinum, and even enriched uranium, all of which have important military or industrial uses. Because they need the money, the Soviets may have no other option. To coin a phrase, the Soviet Union at times has been so eager to earn hard currency, that it has sold us the proverbial rope (titanium) which we have then used to fashion a noose (military aircraft) just in case there should be a hanging. This makes for a certain amount of irony. Thus at the same time that American authorities restrict the sale of the strategic metal titanium to the Soviet Union for fear it might be used in the Soviets' aerospace arsenal, the Soviets export their own titanium to the United States at a cheaper price. In 1977, 33 per cent of the titanium used in the United States was imported from the Soviet Union.[33] As long as the Soviets have such raw materials to export, as long as they find they need imports for food and technology, and as long as they have virtually nothing else but raw materials that can be converted into currency in world markets, they are likely to continue to sell us that "rope."

IV.

As attractive as a return to "fortress Russia" might be for some Soviet leaders, it represents a vision of the past not the present. That is not to say that Soviet political and economic behavior in the international field will always be a model of deportment. The Soviets will continue to press their influence wherever and in whatever way they can, but their influence has more to do with Great Russian imperialism than with the effort to spread communism. Nor will the scenario of Soviet behavior be entirely under the control of future Soviet leaders. More and more, they are likely to find that they have become the victims of the very system they are trying to master and manipulate. Participation in an interdependent world brings with it some degree of freedom, but it also takes some away. After a time, it becomes difficult to tell who is manipulating whom. One of the reasons why the Soviets advocated detente was because they realized that it would contribute to the general relaxation of tension in Europe. This in turn has helped to weaken support for NATO so that in the extreme, Finland has been, and even Norway may become, Finlandized—that is, neutralized. However, détente is a two-way street. Just as there has been erosion in the NATO alliance, so there is an echo effect in the East, where the Russians now find themselves also having to contend with antinuclear protests in Rumania and East Germany. In the extreme, Poland has already, and it appears Rumania may soon, become Polandized. Thus each side finds that it is forced to yield up hostages to the other.[34]

The Soviet goal is to neutralize or intimidate the noncommunist bloc, while holding on to the bloc East European countries comprising the Council for Mutual Economic Assistance (CMEA). Whereas Stalin used the threats and bluster of the Cold War, recent Soviet leaders have apparently concluded that propaganda and the trade opportunities associated with détente are a more fruitful way of pursuing that goal. However, such a policy entails enormous risks for the Soviet Union which must be considered by future Soviet leaders. The Soviets have learned that the same technology they bring in to strengthen their military forces may also tend to subvert if not debilitate the moral resoluteness of the population. It may change one day if the West allows itself to become overly dependent on Soviet raw materials and natural gas, but so far, increased involvement with the outside world has increased Soviet vulnerability to foreign pressures and leverage more than Western vulnerability has been increased by Soviet pressure and leverage.

Rather than risk confrontation or dangerous experiments, future Soviet leaders will probably continue their existing foreign, economic, and political policies. This would mean that the Soviet Union will probably continue to win and lose a few struggles each year. The world map is not likely to change much, at least in the short run. But in the long run, simply maintaining the status quo entails serious risks. Moreover, it does nothing to prevent the Soviet economy and its technology from falling further and further behind. Yet increased and even continued contact with the West will increase the country's exposure to uncontrollable and corrupting influences. Such concerns are not frivolous. These are issues which have troubled members of the Soviet intelligentsia since at least the nineteenth century.[35] In the past, Russian leaders have been able to control such foreign contacts in order to maximize the benefits of such arrangements. They took what they wanted and cut off the flow when they felt such contacts were no longer to their net advantage. However, given the new age of interdependence for both agriculture and technology, future Soviet leaders may find that it is impossible to break off all relations without serious damage to their economy.

In the same way as the population becomes accustomed to the economic and political relaxation brought on by détente, it is likely to begin questioning the need for a continuing garrison-state mentality. There could be an increase in pressure for even more relaxation and even better material conditions. Why, Soviet citizens are now beginning to ask, should we worry about encirclement and invasion by the West when Western Presidents and Prime Ministers parade through Moscow constantly with their agreements, trade contracts, and symphony orchestras? Likewise, Soviet leaders go on similar missions and send the ballet to the West. If the leaders can be so friendly and intimate with one another, why can't the masses share in that sense of rapport, relaxation, and friendship? Similarly, why should they spend so much on defense and heavy industry? Indeed, what purpose does a Stalinist model serve in the last two decades of the twentieth century? Economically and politically, it is no longer necessary in this age of détente. If anything, the Stalinist model has become a fetter. If carried to the extreme, such questions could threaten the very roots of the Soviet system. This is no idle worry. Just such enticements have seduced and demoralized Eastern Europe. What has happened in Eastern Europe suggests the type of shoals that lie ahead in the Soviet Union itself.

6. Eastern Europe: A Bane or a Blessing

Politically, Stalin's idea of an iron curtain and a cold war separating East and West seemed to make good sense. Considering the sacrifices the Soviets were being forced to make, it was clear that the Soviet people would have to be kept ignorant of the improving economic conditions in the noncommunist world. Therefore, Stalin set out to create a buffer zone between The Soviet Union and Western Europe, especially Germany. On the assumption that the regimes in Eastern Europe would be reasonably stable, this Stalinist belt of East European countries was to serve several functions. First, it was to act as a trip wire signaling an invasion from the West. With East Europe as the first line of defense, there would be no surprise invasion of the Soviet Union as there was in June, 1941. These countries would serve not only as a battleground before the gates of the Soviet Union, but they would also have armies that could be added to Soviet forces in any major East–West confrontation, or conceivably East-East confrontation within the bloc. Second, the band of East European countries would serve to insulate the Soviet Union from the unsettling winds and radio waves of the outside Western world. Third, a loyal set of buffer countries could also act as compliant trading partners and thus broaden Soviet trading opportunities. Fourth, the East Europeans could also serve as arms suppliers and as military advisers and mercenaries when the direct involvement of Soviet supplies and troops would be awkward and embarrassing, if not provocative. Finally, with the East Europeans as allies, the Soviets would not be so isolated in world forums.

For the most part, Eastern Europe has functioned as it was designed to do. Nonetheless, it has also proven to be a major headache for the Soviet Union because Eastern Europe is not always an unsullied and true adherent of the faith. Since the Soviets exercise tight control over Eastern Europe, the slightest deviation from the Soviet line is viewed both from inside and outside as apostasy, if not a fundamental crisis. Thus whenever any Eastern European country shows signs of being more tolerant of Western ways or of adopting some Western reforms, the Soviets fear that a part of their empire has been subverted. Tito's declaration of independence in 1948 and China's disaffection in 1960 seemed to confirm these anxieties. Perhaps if the Soviet Union had been guaranteed that such experiments with deviation would advance to a certain point and no farther, they would not have been so nervous. But all along the Soviets have been fearful that the dynamics of the process might eventually carry some of the more venturesome beyond the pale into the Western camp. From the vantage point of the Soviet leaders, therefore, the ideal East European countries were to be replicas of the Soviet Union; there were to be no variations. What may have originally been intended as a buffer zone, quickly became transformed into a front line against the West. It is impossible to seal off a buffer zone completely from its neighbors. Moreover, with time, particularly with the relaxation of cold war tensions, contact with, and hence contamination from, the West has become inevitable. To the extent that the East Europeans then passed on those ideas into the Soviet Union, or to the extent that some East European countries began to work out an ideology or a political framework for themselves, Eastern Europe no longer served as the safe buffer zone it once had been. Instead, some East Europeans have become a burden for the empire as a whole. Indeed, over the years, as the East Europeans have become more and more nettlesome, there must be at least a few in the Soviet Union who have wondered if the advantages of an East European buffer system really outweigh the disadvantages.

I.

Following the end of World War II, there seemed to be general agreement that the benefits of the East European states to the Soviet Union far exceeded the costs. They were referred to as satellites because they did little that did not reflect their center and sun—Stalin and the Soviet

Union. Although Tito's deviation and the unmasking of some unrequited nationalists in the ministries of Eastern Europe did serve to dim some of the luster and to diminish Stalin's pride in the system, Eastern Europe seemed, on the whole, to suit Soviet needs quite well. In addition to the advantages mentioned earlier, once it had virtually unrestricted access to Eastern Europe, the Soviet Union was able to claim and then confiscate large quantities of industrial equipment as reparations from those countries that had fought on the Axis side in world War II. There are no precise figures as to just how much was taken, but some estimates suggest that Soviet officials sent home to the Soviet Union several billion dollars worth of merchandise from countries that, by the end of World War II, had become just as needy as the Soviet Union. Such shabby treatment could hardly be expected to generate good will, especially since almost all of these countries became members of the communist bloc soon after they were occupied by the Soviet army.[1]

The Soviets also used their strength to extract concessions even from those countries such as Poland and Czechoslovakia which had been attacked and victimized by the Axis. This the Russians did by insisting on favorable trade terms for such valuable items as Polish coal and Czech uranium. In addition, the Soviets opened up joint stock companies on the territory of most of their new allies. Although the profits of these companies were shared equally, the capital contribution came almost entirely from the host countries. The Soviet contribution, nominally 50 per cent of the operation, consisted in fact of confiscated German property found in the host country. The Soviet Union claimed this property and what were once German companies for themselves. Instead of shipping these assets back to the Soviet Union along with the other reparations, the Soviets left them in place and used them as their capital contribution in the newly formed joint stock companies.

Soviet economic policies in Eastern Europe went beyond the removal of capital equipment and the establishment of joint stock companies. Whereas before World War II, Western Europe and particularly Germany, were the chief trading partners of almost all of the East European countries, the Soviets after 1945 ordered that virtually all economic activity in Eastern Europe be reoriented from the West to the East and that the East Europeans make the Soviet Union their chief customer and supplier. Thus before World War II, Soviet exports and imports to Eastern Europe constituted 20 to 30 per cent of all Soviet trade; by 1950,

Eastern Europe accounted for close to 60 per cent of the total.[2] As part of this reorientation, the East Europeans were induced to redirect their purchases of raw materials from outside the communist bloc to within it. Since the Soviet Union was the largest producer of raw materials in the bloc, that made the Soviet Union the chief supplier. Western observers, and some Eastern critics as well, viewed this redirection as an effort to make the East Europeans economically dependent on the Soviet Union. For example, steel mills in Eastern Europe were frequently built near the Soviet border to be more accessible to Soviet suppliers of iron ore and coal. Once they were located inland and toward the East, it became very difficult and costly to supply them with other than Soviet raw materials. Thus a Soviet cutoff of raw materials supplies could bring economic chaos to the economies of virtually all these countries.

The Western powers saw what was happening but there was little they could do to stop the Soviets from manipulating and exploiting the economies of Eastern Europe. Despite periodic threats from the Western powers that they would not tolerate such exploitation, the West was not prepared to use military force, so the Soviets exploited at will. Some Western economists have documented the complaints about these conditions that began to emerge from both emigrés and dissident sources within Eastern Europe. Comparing the export prices of raw material exports, the economist Horst Mendershausen found that Soviet export prices to Eastern Europe systematically exceeded the export prices of comparable goods to the noncommunist world.[3] This, he argued, followed inevitably from the way the Soviets set up their joint stock companies and from Soviet exploitation of its satellites.

Taking issue with Mendershausen, Franklyn Holzman argued that because of the peculiarities of the Soviet and East European trading systems, the relationship was not so exploitative.[4] According to Holzman, if Mendershausen had only looked at the other side of the equation, that is, at the exports of East European goods to the Soviet Union, he would have found that the East Europeans were playing the same game as the Soviets; they were charging the Soviets higher prices than they were charging noncommunists for the same goods. It would have been equally correct for the Soviets to have complained that they were being exploited by the East Europeans. The reason for all this, according to Holzman, was that the East European and Soviet trading network was, in effect, a customs union in which the members of the union treat each other differently than they treat those on the outside. Admittedly, each participant within the East European bloc was charging the other a higher price than that charged to those outside the bloc. Yet since each was treating the other communist partner the same way as they themselves were being treated, the impact was neutralized, so that in fact there was no undue discrimination.

Given the way the Soviets laid claim to such large quantities of reparations, Holzman's findings were treated skeptically by many East Europeans who instinctively felt that they were being abused. Moreover, before too long, Soviet authorities also began to take issue with the idea that no one was being discriminated against in the bloc. As they saw it, there was discrimination all right, but it was Eastern Europe that was doing the discriminating, and it was the Soviet Union that was being abused.[5]

Forcing the East Europeans to become dependent on Soviet raw materials seemed like a good idea in the beginning, but after a time, the Soviets began to realize that they were in danger of being turned into a raw material producing colony of the East European countries. They were exchanging their raw materials for East European machinery—the usual subordinate function of a colony. Granted that they were also selling machinery to Eastern Europe, the Soviet were nonetheless quick to point out that there was a larger share of machinery in the East European trade-mix that moved east than in the Soviet trade package that moved west. Moreover, the East Europeans were generally building more sophisticated equipment. In addition, as the East European appetite for raw materials continued to expand, the Soviets found that they were being forced to move further and further east within the Soviet Union in order to find enough new sources of raw material supplies. Not only were some of their richest and most accessible deposits being depleted, but of necessity, this meant higher costs for both transportation and exploitation, and therefore lower profits, as well as increased costs of manufacturing for the Soviet Union itself. Thus in the process of satisfying East European raw material demands, the Soviets found that their own production costs were rising faster than they would have otherwise, and that their profits on exports to Eastern Europe were falling. By some measurements, it even appeared as if the Soviets were losing money on their East European sales—thus the cry of exploitation.

The charges and countercharges were all part of a ritual which preceded the price-setting decision which was made once every five years.

Each side tried to generate pressure for a revision of prices in its favor. Given the artificial and complicated way in which prices were set, it was difficult to sort out who, if anyone, was being adversely affected. Thus, while there was some legitimacy to the Soviet charge, there was also no doubt that the East Europeans were paying higher prices than other noncommunist purchasers of Soviet raw materials. But it soon became irrelevant whether these prices were high enough to cover Soviet costs or whether the customs union effect meant that no one in the bloc was exploiting anyone else. The existing pricing relationship within the bloc and between the Soviet Union and the noncommunist world was thrown out of alignment by the 1973 jump in petroleum prices. Prices paid by noncommunist buyers for the purchase of Soviet petroleum jumped almost immediately. But, as just mentioned, the price agreement with the members of CMEA was based not on a shipment by shipment or a one year basis, but on a five year basis. In 1971, the price for Soviet petroleum to be paid by CMEA members for the period January, 1971, to December, 1975, was set at a fixed level for the ensuing five years. As was the tradition, this price was determined by equating it to the world price of petroleum that existed in 1970. Because of this agreement, the Russians in 1974 found themselves selling petroleum to their East European allies at pre-1973 prices of about $3 per barrel while charging some West European customers as much as $17 or $18 per barrel. Moreover, most of the West European customers were paying in hard currency while the members of CMEA were in effect bartering their goods in exchange for the bargain-priced Soviet petroleum.

In this topsy-turvy world, all the old arguments and theories had become meaningless. Whatever the validity of Soviet or East European complaints about exploitation prior to October, 1973, there was no doubt that subsequently the Soviet Union did find itself exploited by the East Europeans. As the world price continued to increase, eventually the Soviets decided that holding to the pre-1973 price was too much of a burden for them to bear. Thus, despite their contractual commitment, in January, 1975, a year before their contracts expired, the Soviets unilaterally altered the way in which the CMEA bloc determined prices so that the Soviet Union could raise its prices. Therefore, effective January, 1975, the Soviet price of petroleum for members of CMEA was adjusted to correspond with the average price of petroleum in the world market for the immediately preceding three years. That meant that prices were changed every year instead of once every five years and that the base period had been reduced from three to five years. That allowed the Soviet Union to take advantage of the higher prices of 1974 and late 1973, but it also included the low prices of 1972 and early 1973. Beginning in 1976, the system was changed again so that the price base was once again extended to a five-year term. However, it was also decided to make the base period a movable one, so that since then, prices have been adjusted each year, based on a moving average year by year of world prices for the immediately preceding five years. Of course, that meant that as long as world prices were heading upward, the prices the East Europeans would have to pay the Soviet Union for petroleum would continue to be below what the Soviet Union charges in the noncommunist world. Since prices did rise in the noncommunist world throughout much of this period, there has been a real opportunity cost for the Soviet Union, because it has not sold all its petroleum to the noncommunist world. Thus even allowing for the "customs-union" effect, there is no doubt that as of late 1973, the East Europeans did exploit the Soviet Union. This is because even though the price of the machinery the East Europeans sell to the Soviet Union is adjusted on the basis of the rolling five-year average of world machinery prices, machinery prices at least until 1982 have lagged behind the increase in energy prices. Thus the East Europeans have not been able to raise their prices as fast as the Soviets have. Moreover, it was much easier for the Soviets to sell their oil outside the bloc than it was for the East Europeans to do the same thing with their machinery. The Soviets were really passing up sales opportunities. Thus the Soviets complained they were being exploited not just because the Soviets did not collect as much from the sale of their petroleum to East Europe as the increase in the relative scarcity of petroleum in the world market would have allowed, but because the Soviets were also forced to pass up the opportunity to earn substantial quantities of hard currency in the process.

Whether the East Europeans will admit it or not, there is little doubt that since 1973, the Soviets have been subsidizing the East Europeans. Admittedly the East Europeans have been forced to provide loans to the U.S.S.R. now and then, but that does not compensate for the lost petroleum sales. In effect, supplying Eastern Europe with oil has become one cost of having an empire. Some estimates indicate that the combined cost of subsidies and outright economic and military loans totaled over $20 billion in 1980.[6] However, if the Soviets want to have an empire, there is not much they can do about it. Without Soviet support, the East Europeans would not be able to finance the raw materials and other imports they need. If they had to import from the hard-currency world, costs in Eastern Europe would increase and lead to inflation. If these countries could not afford to import what they need, that could lead to a breakdown of their economies, which in turn would likely ignite political protests. Thus far, the Soviets have little choice but to continue to subsidize raw material, especially petroleum exports to Eastern Europe. But to an economist, it is sinful to underprice raw materials, particularly energy raw materials. By charging below market prices, the Soviets are in effect (no matter how reluctantly) subsidizing petroleum usage in Eastern Europe and therefore stimulating greater use than there would otherwise be. Under the circumstances, there is no reason for the East Europeans to seek petroleum outside the CMEA bloc. It is too expensive. Unless such Middle East petroleum can be obtained on a barter basis, in almost all cases it will require hard currency, which of course will only increase the size of the hard currency debt of the East Europeans. To the extent that the Soviet Union finds it necessary to be a guarantor of last resort for the debts of its East European allies, that would merely mean tossing the problem back into Soviet hands again.

The costs of this Stalinist empire go beyond having to backstop East European economic debt. The Soviets also have military obligations in Eastern Europe. Of course the East Europeans maintain their own large armies in the area and also apparently sustain a share of the cost of maintaining Soviet troops on their territory, but there are still substantial costs which the Russians must bear as well. Moreover, no one knows just how reliable troops in Eastern Europe would be in any showdown within one of the East European countries. Although they do seem willing to put down protest in a neighboring country, as the use of troops from almost all of Eastern Europe in Czechoslovakia in 1968 demonstrated, most of the East European armies cannot be counted upon to suppress protest amongst their own people. Not surprisingly, troops from Cuba, since they have no border contact with the Soviet Union, seem to be the most trustworthy and the most willing to carry the battle beyond their own circumscribed borders. In effect, they have become the mercenaries of the communist world. Soldiers from the German Democratic Republic seem almost as willing to go off in the service of empire, and therefore they have joined the Cubans and Soviets in Ethiopia, Angola, and reportedly in Afghanistan as well.

Soviet units have been used regularly within the East European bloc, and military advisers of one sort or another have appeared in many parts of the world, but the Soviets were always careful to avoid any indication that the Soviet troops were engaged in fighting on foreign territory outside of Eastern Europe. The appearance of Soviet fighting units in Third World countries marks a new departure. For the Russians, this must have been a particularly difficult decision for a variety of reasons. First, the Russians have been very careful to avoid the loss of Russian soldiers' lives in outside countries. Second, there is no way they can avoid the impression of being the aggressor. Third, the Russians have tried to keep their soldiers within the borders of communist countries for fear of ideological contamination. Such fears can be traced back to the Napoleonic Wars when Russian soldiers returned from the West and, in 1825, participated in the Decembrist Revolution. Stalin in particular seemed to fear such contamination. In his eyes, Soviet soldiers who somehow found their way behind enemy lines were automatically suspect. Apparently some of the troops later sent to put down the unrest in Hungary and Czechoslovakia were also thought to have become contaminated by their experience, and therefore they were also judged to be in need of a purge. Fortunately in more recent years there seems to be less concern about the need for decontamination. This relaxation suggests that the pressures generated by the Stalinist model may no longer generate the paranoia they once did, at least when it comes to tolerating exposure to outside corrupting influences. Yet the juggling around of the first batches of Soviet soldiers sent to Afghanistan suggests that, even now, the model generates fears and constraints that have not yet been abandoned completely.

II.

Whereas in the past, Soviet leaders were most concerned with the perimeter of the communist bloc, increasingly they have had to devote more and more of their attention to the maintenance of control within the bloc, that is, within the boundaries of a given member of CMEA. In large part, this is a reflection of the resurgence of nationalism. Marx to the contrary, nationalism never really disappeared in Eastern Europe. All things considered, it is remarkable that nationalism was so dormant after World War II. After all, Eastern Europe has historically been a hotbed of nationalism. The Soviet bloc covers a major portion of what

at one time was better known as the Balkans, where regional nationalism was the spark that set off World War I. And in the non-Balkan
areas of the communist bloc, many of the nationalist tensions, such as
those between the Rumanians and Hungarians, the Czechs and Germans, and the Germans and Poles, reflect passions formed over the
course of several centuries. In addition, almost every one of the East
European countries except Bulgaria has an historic grudge against the
Russians.

The coming of détente was like fanning the nationalistic sparks that
the Soviets and their viceroys in Eastern Europe had tried to smother.
Détente called into question the very need for two hostile military blocs.
If there was no need for the two blocs, there was no need to be so
dependent on the Soviet Union. Admittedly, détente has given rise to
some serious fissures in the Western alliance as well. But for those in
Eastern Europe, the impact both inside and outside the bloc has been
even more far-reaching. With Soviet leaders shuttling back and forth,
bear-hugging Western leaders, what was the point of preparing and sac-
rificing as if invasion might occur at any time? Even the strident cry of
encirclement began to lose some of its urgency. Despite very skilled
propaganda, after a time it became harder and harder to generate enthusiasm for continuing military expenditures and a garrison-state readiness when the expected enemy was having lunch and drinking with
one's own leaders and generals. The Stalinist model for controlling
Eastern Europe became more and more inappropriate.

Yearnings for a more open society were further nourished by the
Helsinki Agreements. These called for a freer flow of ideas and information and increased contacts between East and West. Moreover, the
Helsinki Agreement helped set in motion intellectual movements
throughout Eastern Europe which sought to further human rights.
Crackdowns by local authorities did not cease, but they were made more
awkward by the fact that the governments of Eastern Europe had signed
the agreement. This awkwardness became all the more upsetting when
dissidents in most of the CMEA countries formed Helsinki Watch Committees, which undertook on their own to check for violations of human
rights, at least as spelled out in the Helsinki Agreements. Certainly no
one in Eastern Europe or the Soviet Union had ever envisaged the formation of such watchdog committees when the Agreement was first
proposed. Admittedly the Communist side won some potentially far-

reaching concessions on trade as well as the recognition of existing boundaries, but in the long run, it is likely that the human rights clauses will have the most lasting impact. Even without détente, the very passing of time has made it more difficult for the Soviets to maintain control over Eastern Europe. As those who had lived through World War II began to pass from the scene, there were fewer and fewer who had reason to be grateful to the Soviets for their efforts in expelling the Nazis. Whatever good will the Soviets had engendered was gradually dissipated by the growing awareness of how disadvantageous the association with the Soviet Union had become. Almost everyone in Eastern Europe had a sense that history—at least economic history—was on the other side. Being closer to Western Europe and being able to see more clearly through the rusting iron curtain, the East Europeans perceived better than the Soviets how far behind the West they had slipped. With the growing availability of television, the East Germans, Czechs, and Hungarians could see West German and Austrian television, and the Poles could see Scandinavian programs. Ironically, it had been feared originally that television would be the perfect tool for insuring ideological control in a totalitarian state, whereas in fact, television had become an insidious influence in undermining control. Radio reception, while not as dramatic in its impact, makes it possible to reach out even further. And as much as East European and Soviet authorities may have wanted to jam or block the air and television waves, it has become all but impossible to do that in the age of détente. Jamming the air waves would show little commitment to détente. Therefore, despite their subversive nature, these stations have been allowed to beam news from the West to the East. In the process, Eastern Europe learned of the exceptional economic progress made by the non-communist world in the 1960's and 1970's. Inevitably, such contrasts have highlighted what the East Europeans might have been able to do under a different system.

No doubt part of the East European discontent was a natural consequence of disliking what they have, and ideologizing (sic) what they haven't. The shortcomings of the planned economy were all too apparent for everyone in Eastern Europe to see. Not surprisingly, therefore, support for the market system frequently seems to be greater in Eastern Europe than it is in Western Europe and the United States. And vice versa, having seen the shortcomings of the market system, critics in

Western Europe and the United States often appear to be much warmer advocates of a centrally planned economy than those who know it best within Eastern Europe.

III.

It was all but inevitable that once set loose, these forces would generate turmoil and eventual confrontation within Eastern Europe, which in turn would spark an effort to break out of the Stalinist model. Though Poland's Solidarity movement in 1980 will probably prove to be the most far-reaching challenge to the communist system and the Stalinist model, it was not the first time an effort has been made to change the economic and political systems within Eastern Europe. Frustrated over the years by the failure to improve economic and political conditions, clashes with state and party authorities occurred in East Germany in 1953, in Poland and Hungary in 1956, in Czechoslovakia in 1968, and Poland again in 1970. There were many causes of these outbursts. Often they were set off by shortages of food, or price hikes, or by the unrest following the death or denunciation of Stalin, or by protests over what came to be regarded as undue Soviet interference in local affairs. Nevertheless, the events in Poland which began in September, 1980, no matter what their eventual resolution, will be much more momentous. The formation of an independent trade union challenges the supremacy of the Communist Party, the authority of the Soviet Union, and in turn the viability of the Stalinist model. Turning Marx on his head, Solidarity sought to capture the country's surplus value rather than leave it with the Communist Party to plow back into capital formation and perquisites for the privileged. Once allowed to circulate in Poland, these ideas are likely to spread throughout the block and thus make all the East European countries much more difficult for the Soviets to deal with.

In large part, the Polish events are a consequence of the policy of détente. However, in the late 1960's when the era of détente in Europe began to take shape, it was unlikely that many in the East, or for that matter the West, realized how disruptive détente would be for the Communist bloc. Opponents of détente in the United States, for example, feared that the Soviets would use détente to build up their military technology and capabilities and then threaten the United States. Such a buildup would be more threatening than usual because, in the mood of peace and friendship, that would prevail, it was feared that our West

European allies would relax their vigil and military preparedness. Under the beguilement of détente, they would become so interested in making money in the short run that they would neglect to maintain their security in the long run. Many hard-line critics of détente argued that the same malaise would probably infect the United States.

Most of these fears have indeed been realized. However, few proponents of détente ever dreamed that it would be the cause of an even more fundamental fissure in the Communist world. Most proponents focused their attention on the prospects for relaxed international tension between the blocs, not on the likelihood of demands for more democratic procedures within the bloc. In the years to come, when historians draw up a cost-benefit analysis of détente, they may conclude that the gains in military strength that détente made possible for Eastern Europe were in no way commensurate with the erosion of party control and Soviet influence within the bloc. The move toward democratization in Poland attacked the very heart of the communist system, whereas the transfer of Western technology to the east, while militarily significant and potentially dangerous in the short run, does not threaten the essence of the Western system in such a fundamental way.

Many East Europeans saw détente as a form of deliverance. First it meant that war was less likely. Second, it meant that there would be less pressure from the Soviet Union. There was not as much need to maintain discipline in the ranks when the enemy suddenly becomes transformed into a competitor, which is a much less threatening stance than that of a potential aggressor. Third, all the members of the bloc viewed détente as a way of improving their technology. But the Poles saw détente and trade with the West as more than that—it was a way of nudging their economy away from the East toward the West. By purchasing large quantities of Western technology, the hope was that Polish industry would be brought up to the competitive standards of the West. This would allow it to increase the amount of its economic interaction with the West and gradually allow it to evolve away from the Stalinist model.

To some extent, this strategy was pursued by all the countries of Eastern Europe, but the Poles were the most ambitious. Beginning in 1971, Poland embarked on a new economic strategy. Largely due to protest over the economic situation in Poland, Wladyslaw Gomulka had just fallen from power. Determined to improve the economy and win worker support, Edward Gierek, his successor, concluded that the quickest and probably least threatening way to break out of the confines of the Stalinist model was to turn to the West and purchase large quantities of Western technology and equipment. Given the peculiarities of the Stalinist model, the Poles realized that innovation would not come from within; thus they turned to the outside world.

However, turning to the West for technology required a lot of money and the Poles found it necessary to borrow substantial sums. This was easy to arrange for a variety of reasons. First, it was assumed that the imported technology would quickly pay for itself. The increased production the new machinery was to make possible would be exported for hard currency which would then service the debt. Second, in 1971, the Poles had no debt to speak of. The size of their hard-currency net debt that year (their total debt, less the hard currency held by the Poles in Western banks) was less than $800 million, a paltry sum given Poland's gross national product and earning capability. (See Table VI-1.) Third, it was widely assumed in the Western banking community that if an East European borrower like Poland found itself faced with financial difficulties, the Soviet Union would ultimately step in and redeem the debt. The Soviet Union, it was agreed, would never jeopardize its own or its allies' credit rating by allowing an East European country to default.

Admittedly, there were dangers to borrowing Western funds with which to import technology, but how else could Poland evolve out of its Stalinist economic model into the modern industrial world? Failure to act quickly would surely set off more workers' protests. The flow of Western investment imports rose rapidly. From 1971 to 1980, the total of investment imports amounted to about $13 billion, of which only about $5 billion was paid for by Polish exports.[7] Unfortunately, not all those exports were newly created as a result of the investment program. Thus, traditional exports had to be diverted for this purpose. The original expectation was that both new and old exports would increase. But as the Polish economist Bronislaw Sulimierski points out, these expectations were not realized.[8] The rate of growth of exports actually declined. Unfortunately, in contrast the annual rate of growth of all imports rose from 9.1 per cent in 1958–1970 to over 18 per cent in 1971–1974. This is the opposite of what was supposed to happen. To pay for all this, the Poles had to fall back on foreign credits. As Table VI-1 indicates, the size of the Polish hard currency debt began to increase at a rate of 50 per cent to almost 100 per cent a year. Whereas until 1971, under Gomulka's very conservative administration, Poland had

Table VI-1
EASTERN EUROPE: GROSS AND NET HARD CURRENCY DEBT TO THE WEST
(millions of U.S. dollars)

	1971	1972	1973	1974	1975	1976	1977	1978	1979	1980
Total										
Gross	6,072	7,398	9,762	15,352	23,033	29,351	36,695	46,901	57,633	62,524
Net	4,927	5,723	7,950	12,732	18,657	25,297	32,860	42,267	51,220	56,200
Bulgaria										
Gross	743	1,009	1,020	1,703	2,640	3,198	3,707	4,263	4,415	3,774
Net	723	909	997	1,360	2,257	2,756	3,169	3,710	3,700	3,000
Czechoslovakia										
Gross	485	630	757	1,048	1,132	1,862	2,616	3,206	4,099	4,557
Net	160	176	273	640	827	1,434	2,121	2,513	3,070	3,300
East Germany										
Gross	1,408	1,554	2,136	3,136	5,188	5,856	7,145	8,894	10,912	11,736
Net	1,205	1,229	1,876	2,592	3,548	5,047	6,159	7,548	8,950	9,700
Hungary										
Gross	1,071	1,392	1,442	2,129	3,135	4,049	5,655	7,473	8,529	8,476
Net	848	1,055	1,096	1,537	2,195	2,852	4,491	6,532	7,300	7,100
Poland										
Gross	1,138	1,564	2,796	4,643	8,014	11,483	13,967	17,844	22,669	25,120
Net	764	1,150	2,213	4,120	7,381	10,680	13,532	16,972	21,500	24,500
Romania										
Gross	1,227	1,249	1,611	2,693	2,924	2,903	3,605	5,221	7,009	8,861
Net	1,227	1,204	1,495	2,483	2,449	2,528	3,388	4,992	6,700	8,600

SOURCE: CIA, *Handbook of Economic Statistics, 1981* (Washington, D.C.: U.S. Government Printing Office, November, 1981, NFHES81-001), p. 41.

one of the smallest hard currency debts of all the East European countries (only Bulgaria and Czechoslovakia had net debts that were smaller), by 1973 under the free spending regime of Gierek, Poland's debt was larger than any other country in Eastern Europe and was growing. According to Sulimierski, the reason that Polish exports did not rise as expected was that Poland was unable to handle the influx of such sophisticated equipment. Here was the conundrum. The capital-import program was designed to help Poland break out of its Stalinist mode, but the rigidity of that model all but guaranteed that any such effort, particularly one that was intended for prompt action, would fail. The infrastructure was not developed enough to provide the extra transportation and energy resources needed to put these extra imports to work. Moreover, many of these new factories were poorly located in relation to the infrastructure that did exist. Because Polish planners and workers lacked the necessary flexibility and skill to incorporate western technology and industrial methods, the importers were not able to build their factories and put the plants on stream soon enough. In addition, American suppliers noted that Polish labor seemed to lack the training, skills, and enthusiasm needed to run the new factories efficiently. Apparently, Polish workers had been so alienated by the traditional way Polish factories were operated that Polish authorities were unable to motivate Polish workers to learn how to operate the more sophisticated Western-equipped plants. Nor did it help when they discovered that the planners had not carefully thought through the investment program. A surprisingly large number of the new factories were designed to operate on imported inputs. Consequently, each product produced added to the hard currency deficit. To the extent that factory output was exported and sold for hard currency that posed no problem, although even under the best of circumstances, that meant that the hard currency earnings would never be as high as might have been anticipated initially. But to make matters worse, almost all the imported factories suffered a delay of several years before they were able to begin operations. By then, as the managers of the RCA-Corning Glass–Polkolor color television tube plant discovered, the markets these plants were expected to satisfy had been preempted by other manufacturers.[9] Nor did most factories even reach their rated capacities. For example, Polkolor's production was scheduled to reach 600,000 sets in 1981. But a combination of inadequate provisions for producing the necessary number of component parts and final products, plus a host of managerial mistakes, held production to about 50,000 sets, less than one-tenth of what had been scheduled.[10]

Trying to graft Western-designed factories onto the Polish economic system, with its Stalinist model, was like trying to transplant a heart. The body of the recipient reacts to the alien intrusion by setting in motion all kinds of mechanisms intended to reject this foreign body. Extra steps have to be taken, therefore, to insure that the implanted heart is properly assimilated into the differently oriented system. Unfortunately, such efforts proved to be inadequate and for the most part unavailing in Poland. The net effect of all this was that the expected flow of export earnings was delayed or, in some cases, not forthcoming at all. At the same time, the costs of inputs together with the funds needed to service the foreign debt rose rapidly. Polish planners found that by the mid-1970's, their borrowings were going mainly for raw materials, imported components, consumer imports, and debt servicing. The amount going for new investment projects fell off drastically, which of course meant a collapse of the whole strategy. Unfortunately, while there seemed to be little chance that the export earning ability of the country would increase significantly, the size of the import and debt service bill kept growing because of compound interest. Even in 1970, before Gierek took over two-thirds of all Poland's hard currency earnings had to be set aside to pay for component imports in order to sustain production.[11] By 1975–77, the collapse of Poland's strategy was predestined when it became apparent that Poland's hard currency earnings were no longer sufficient even to pay for the imports needed to sustain production.

In fairness to the Polish planners, their failure was in part due to circumstances beyond their control. Like debtors all over the world, they had concluded that it paid to borrow to import, because with time inflation would reduce the real costs of their repayments. Moreover, borrowing seemed to be so easy. With enormous sums at their disposal to invest, Western bankers were literally throwing themselves and their money at the Poles. It seemed to be poor business not to loan. This was vividly illustrated to me when one of the largest banks in the midwest asked me to present my views about the credit-worthiness of the East European countries. They were dismayed when I provided them with figures for each of the East European countries showing the size of their hard currency debt and their annual trade deficits, which of course would mean a further growth in future debt. In the hope that conditions might have improved, they invited me back the next year and heard essentially the same story, except that the deficits and debts had increased even more in the interim. This left the bank in an awkward position. It was as if Dun and Bradstreet had been asked for a credit reference and the bank decided to make a loan, even though Dun and Bradstreet had warned that the situation was not only bad, but deteriorating rapidly. Yet the midwestern bank felt itself under competitive pressure from its rivals, which were making loans to Eastern Europe and attracting new customers who needed financing for their exports to Eastern Europe. Not surprisingly, therefore, the bank decided that if it were to make such loans, it would have to avoid hearing such advice, and so they ended the consultation.

Although Poland's debt had already soared to $10.7 billion by 1975, double that of any other East European country, and its purchase of new investment capability had all but ceased, it is remotely possible that Poland might still have been able to muddle through if not for external events. Because they were coal exporters and because their petroleum imports were in part subsidized by the Soviet Union, they were not hurt as badly in 1973 as many others were, but nonetheless their economic expectations suffered. If for no other reason, the 1973 energy crisis precipitated the 1975 recession, which made it more difficult for the Poles to export. In addition, the Poles found themselves victimized by the huge increase in interest rates that took place in the late 1970's. When the Poles proved to be slower in repaying their debts than they had expected, Western bankers insisted that future loans be tied to a floating or a variable, rather than a fixed, interest rate, which the banks originally used. This loan rate was tied to the London Interbank rate or LIBOR. This would have presented no problem if interest rates had remained constant or fallen. But by the late 1970's, interest rates were at a record high, and the Poles considered themselves fortunate if they could only export enough simply to pay the interest rates due on their debt. Moreover, the unanticipated high interest rates also meant that the real cost of repaying the debt had not been inflated away. After a time, the interest rates became so high that the real cost of repaying the debt in some instances actually increased. Finally, just as in the Soviet Union, a succession of bad weather and poor harvests aggravated what had always been an inefficient food-supply system. Communism had also converted Poland from a net food exporter to a net food importer, and unfortunately, food shortages invariably heightened tempers. Issues which in a condition of adequate food supply will cause anger, but little else, will precipitate action in a condition of shortage. It is unlikely that the strikes in Poland in 1980–81 would have taken place in the midst of a good harvest and general prosperity. Given the seriousness of their plight and the inability of the Polish system to respond appropriately, the poor harvests were, despite the pun, the final straw. Certainly the crisis would not have occurred as early as it did if interest rates had been lower and harvests higher. Yet because the Poles were having such a difficult time absorbing their foreign technology, even if the weather and the bankers had been more amenable, there was probably no way in the long run that Poland could have avoided the workers' protests that ultimately took place.

Admittedly Poland had never followed the Stalinist model as faithfully as the Soviet Union. For example, unlike the Soviets, the Poles pulled back early from collectivization and allowed the peasants to reclaim their private farms. Moreover, the Polish Catholic Church unlike the Russian Orthodox Church has remained a strong religious and even cultural and nationalist force. Consumer goods at least in the 1960's were relatively more abundant in Poland than in the U.S.S.R. Nonetheless, Gierek may have set himself an impossible task. Yet what else could he have done? Instead of emphasizing heavy industry, conceivably he could have tried in the 1970's to provide more of an immediate return for the consumer in the hope of generating more support and productivity. This might have reduced worker alienation and increased support for the system. Americans from the Pullman Corporation who were installing a foundry in Poland were shocked to see the resentment Polish workers felt towards the reindustrialization effort and the abuse the workers took pride in inflicting on the new equipment. Presumably this reflected their bitterness at not deriving any benefit from such programs. Providing the workers with more of the rewards earlier in the process might have solved the investment and savings effort. It should be clear by now that no growth in productivity will take place without the voluntary enthusiasm and participation of the workers. The Poles have discovered how hard it is to escape the legacy of the Stalinist model.

IV.

While the Polish problem is not the direct responsibility of the Soviet Union, there is no way that Soviet leaders can ignore it. It is amazing that the Soviet regime was patient as long as it was during the early months of the troubles. The Polish upheaval was as serious a matter for the Soviet leaders as yet another crop failure. In both instances, the

Soviets found themselves beset with political headaches and economic costs.

The Polish crisis has basically been a no-win situation for the Soviet Union. Unless Soviet leaders are more ingenious than they appear to have been, there is virtually no way they can restore control in Poland without incurring enormous costs. The very fact that the Polish events of 1980 and 1981 took place at all is an embarrassment. The spectacle of Polish workers striking and trying to determine their own fate will profoundly affect the future course of events in Eastern Europe. The Polish protests do not suggest that history is on the communist side (at least as defined by Moscow).

Probably the least costly solution for the Soviets was to pressure the Polish government and army to put their own economic and political house in order. Certainly, that is what the Soviets have tried to do with mixed success. Alternatively, a Soviet invasion would probably have been a bloody and unfortunate affair. Even if there were no bloodshed, the economy would be left in such poor shape, and workers' resistance such that the Soviets would find themselves faced with the very expensive task of having to supplement a very large percentage of the Polish GNP. But if there were an invasion, it is unlikely that the economic bill would be the only one that the Soviet Union would have to pay. Being the romantics they are, the Poles would probably fight. Even more importantly, Poland, unlike Afghanistan, is much closer to the Western world, so that news coverage of the fighting would likely be more extensive. The Soviets would also risk another grain embargo and an end to discussions about building a natural gas pipeline. This is not to deny that, after a time, any Russian invasion of Poland would be forgotten in the same way that similar intervention in Hungary and Czechoslovakia was also forgotten. Nonetheless, because the Poles have been so outspoken and have gone so far, it will probably take longer to forget, and the resulting costs will probably be greater.

Yet unless Poland can solve its economic and political ills, the cost is likely to be just as high as, if not higher than it would be if the Soviets ultimately do decide to invade. Like the Mediterranean fruit fly, the contagion could spread everywhere in the bloc, both in Eastern Europe and possibly even within the Soviet Union itself. The discontent and difficulties are much the same throughout Eastern Europe, and as we saw, there is similar tension within the Soviet Union. Short of some substantial improvement in living conditions, the fire of a protest could be ignited at any time. Nor did it do much to cool passions when in September, 1981, the leadership of Solidarity offered their help to other workers elsewhere in Eastern Europe who might want to set up their own independent unions. Rumania, for example, has already had some serious labor problems in its coal mines. A worker strike there in 1977 lasted several weeks, and another strike accompanied by violence erupted in October-November, 1981. Work stoppages also took place in Bucharest itself in 1980 at the August 23rd factory.[12] In East Germany, an underground group reportedly has circulated leaflets demanding free elections, freedom of speech, and freedom to organize.[13] East German workers were urged by their colleagues to do no less than their Polish comrades. As we noted in Chapter Four, echoes of the Polish events were even heard in the Soviet Union itself, especially the Ukraine, and there were reports of attempts to set up independent unions and strikes in the U.S.S.R., Rumania, and Hungary.[14]

Just how explosive the Polish events are is perhaps best illustrated by one of the dilemmas of the Polish newspaper *Trybuna Ludu*. One of the conditions of the settlement of the Gdansk shipyard strike in 1980 was that the Polish newspapers would agree to publish the text of the settlement. Virtually all the newspapers did, except *Trybuna Ludu,* which published most but not all of the agreement. In anger, the leaders of the union Solidarity demanded to know why *Trybuna Ludu* had not honored its pledge. Highly embarrassed and apologetic, the editors pleaded for understanding. They conceded their failure to adhere to the agreement, but pointed out that being the main newspaper of the country, *Trybuna Ludu* was widely read inside the Soviet Union. It would not do, they pointed out, to have Soviet readers learn that the leaders of the Polish Communist Party had agreed that henceforth they would give up their special privilege stores and estates. That would be too inflammatory.

Certainly the possibility of a true workers' state in the middle of Eastern Europe, with the workers demanding an increased share in the country's surplus value, made the leaders of the various neighboring parties quite nervous. It was just possible that Marx might prove to be correct after all, and that the true communist revolution would indeed come to states with a large proletarian class. After a series of false starts, almost all of Eastern Europe is now qualified for such a revolution. Certainly it would only be poetic justice if the first and probably truest socialist workers' state were to emerge out of a revolution led by workers in a communist country like Poland, rather than out of a revolution led by intellectuals in a feudal country like Russia in 1917.

What is particularly distressing for other leaders in Eastern Europe is that once the Polish events occurred, there was no way to limit the Polish problem to Poland. Even where the workers in other East European countries such as Hungary and Czechoslovakia had been quiescent and had been kept within the bounds of the official communist unions, the economies of these countries were inevitably affected by the events in Poland in one way or another. We used to speak of the ''domino effect'' in Southeast Asia. But today it is probably even more meaningfully applied to Eastern Europe. For example, the disruption of production within Poland has meant that exports from Poland were similarly disrupted. For years there had been intense discussion about the meager interrelationships between members of CMEA, but even if meager, the cessation of this flow was important enough to cause severe problems elsewhere in the bloc. The Poles produced components for use in various products assembled in the Soviet Union. Some of their parts were intended for use at the Fiat-built automobile plant in Togliatti and at the Kama River Truck plant. Until the production disruptions, 50 per cent of the truck brake systems used at Kama were made in Poland. Polish components were also being used in Czechoslovakia, Hungary, and East Germany. Almost all the countries of the bloc were dependent on Polish coal and sulphur. Without these components and this coal, the assembly lines could not operate at full capacity. As a result, production has lagged elsewhere in the bloc as well. When this happens, there is no way of knowing how far reaching the consequences may be. Thus the fact that Polish coal exports in 1981 were half of what they had been the year before undoubtedly contributed to the reduced generation of electricity in Rumania. For Czechoslovakia, this meant not only a shortfall in Polish coal deliveries, but a drop in electricity exported by Rumania.[15] The curtailment of such vital deliveries has of necessity forced Poland's allies to go into the world market to make up for the missed Polish deliveries. This in turn has intensified the hard currency shortage throughout the bloc.

Similarly, after Poland's default on its debt, Western bankers took a closer look at the credit status of the other members of CMEA. As is usually the case when one customer defaults, banks begin to reevaluate the credit worthiness of their other creditors who are in comparable positions, to insure that the banks will not again become victims of a similar default. This led to a tightening of credit to all members of the bloc. As a result, even though other members of the bloc may have been in good financial health, this tightening of credit has tended to precipitate other defaults that, in a more normal climate, might not otherwise have occurred. For example, Rumania was denied an $80 million loan for a nuclear plant because of rumors that Rumania was unable to pay off some of its other debts which had fallen due. Even Hungary, supposedly the most sophisticated and best credit risk in the bloc, has had some of its short term credit loans recalled.[16] Although most East European members of CMEA have been more restrained in their borrowing than the Poles, there is nonetheless some legitimate cause for alarm. By 1980, a few of them had indeed built up net foreign debts that were too large for comfort. None of the other East Europeans had debt exceeding $10 billion, but the German Democratic Republic, Rumania, and Hungary were close to it, and on a per capita basis, their debt may have exceeded the Polish per capita debt. Moreover, the higher interest rates that had so badly hurt the Poles were also causing a severe strain in the other countries of Eastern Europe. In part, these factors were the cause of the almost $2 billion jump in the Rumanian debt in 1980, along with the $1.3 billion increase in the East German debt.

The defaults by Poland and Rumania have been very unsettling for Western bankers, particularly those in West Germany. The Germans have provided over half of the credits for Eastern Europe. The problem is so serious that some banks in Germany may become insolvent if there is not a substantial recoupment of their Polish loans. Some of them have foolishly extended loans to Poland which exceed their capital. The Commerzbank was forced to omit the payments of its dividend for two years in a row, 1980 and 1981, in large part because of its $400 million Polish loan.[17] The much smaller Bank Für Gemeinwirtschaft has $418 million in Polish loans which is a very large amount for a bank its size.[18] Indeed, there is now some reason to question the impressive trade surpluses West Germany used to report. It now looks as if German exports, to a larger extent than realized, were made possible by loans from German banks, which the bank's stockholders and Hermes, the German Export and Import Bank, will ultimately have to pay for. To the extent that Hermes, a bank run by the German Republic, receives its funds from the government budget, this means that the German taxpayer will be the ultimate bearer of the burden.

All of this was not supposed to happen. The universal assumption was that the Soviet Union would underwrite the credit worthiness of all of Eastern Europe, the so-called umbrella effect. Rather than an umbrella, however, the Soviets seemed to have been using a leaky rainhat instead. The Soviets only protected a limited portion of the Polish debt. Between August, 1980 and August, 1981, the Soviets extended about $4 billion of extra credits which was made up of about $2 billion in hard currency and the rest in merchandise and a deferral of the Soviet debt to Poland. But this was not nearly enough. In effect, the Soviets have allowed Poland to go bankrupt. It was called a moratorium and a fancy rescheduling package was more or less agreed to, but no one was fooled. If this could happen to Poland, it could happen elsewhere in Eastern Europe. This caused at least some Western bankers to hold back and reconsider their other loans to Eastern Europe. Without the easy credit the others in Eastern Europe were accustomed to, their chances for economic recovery became much less promising.

Given their resources, the Soviets could have done more to avoid such defaults. With a net foreign debt of their own that had fallen to about $10 billion in 1980, the covering of a loan or two would probably not have been too much of a strain. However, the Polish default has set off other defaults and a tightening of credit from West European lenders that undoubtedly will generate considerable strain on the Soviet Union. The need to support Poland came at a bad time for the Soviets. In 1981, the deficit in the Soviet balance of trade climbed to over $5 billion for one year alone. As we saw in Table V-1, that equals the largest previous deficit of $5 billion in 1975. The 1981 deficit reflected a bad harvest, the falling price of petroleum exports, and the need for increased assistance to Eastern Europe.

Given the enormity of these problems and the sparsity of the resources at their disposal, the Hungarians, the Poles, and presumably the Russians decided that Hungary and Poland had best apply for membership in the International Monetary Fund. Hungary was admitted in May, 1982. Were Poland also to be admitted, that would mean that according to IMF rules, both countries would have to open their financial books to Western eyes, and more importantly, they would also have to agree to IMF imposed financial constraints and changes in operating procedures. In exchange, the IMF would make available its financial support for the Hungarian and Polish economies. The implications of such an arrangement are mind-boggling. Should the IMF, which was originally intended to provide short-term loans for countries with temporary currency disproportions, be used for what will surely be long-term credits to provide structural changes? For that matter, can Poland's problems be solved by anything short of the complete abandonment of the Stalinist model and, by implication, the withdrawal of the Polish economy from the Soviet dominated bloc?

Some bankers are not that pessimistic. They correctly point out that Poland is not the first country to have defaulted on its debt and to have experienced economic problems. For example, Turkey has not only accumulated enormous foreign debts, but like Poland, it was preoccupied with internal unrest and strife. A team from the IMF, however, recommended some basic economic reforms. They noted in particular that the connection between money and command over goods had been severed. Money had lost its value. Smuggling had become the most productive part of the Turkish economy and farmers and workers were spending more time bartering their services for goods than working for money which had lost much of its value. While the Turkish economy is still in serious trouble Turkish economic regulations were rewritten under IMF prodding so that the incentive to smuggle disappeared and money regained its value.

Obviously, the hope is that the same kind of change can be implemented in Poland where money has also lost its value and where the farmer would rather barter than sell his goods for paper currency. Indicative of the problem faced by Polish economic authorities is that until 1982, when prices were increased, their pricing system had become so distorted that it was cheaper for Polish peasants to buy subsidized bread from the official state stores and use it to feed their livestock than to grow or buy unprocessed grain for the same purpose. In 1981, for example, Radio Warsaw reported that the government spent approximately $3.75 billion on food subsidies.[19] Without the proper incentives, Poland has become only 80 to 85 per cent self-sufficient in food (remember it used to be a net exporter of grain), and it must import up to 30 per cent of the feed grains needed to feed its livestock.[20]

But the example of Turkey has limited relevance for Poland. The reforms in Turkey could be made because Turkey was an independent country responsible only to itself, and in this case, the IMF. Poland is not a free agent. If it were to make the economic reforms needed, the changes would be so far-reaching that they would undoubtedly upset and even threaten the Soviet Union. To make the "second economy" a part of the first economy would require a significant upgrading of the market and probably a substantial increase in the role of private enterprise, more so than has thus far occurred in Hungary. Even more intriguing, if membership in the IMF ultimately means fundamental structural reforms for Poland, will similar medicine be necessary for Hungary, Rumania, and the other members of CMEA? By allowing these two countries to join the IMF, does the Soviet Union realize the consequences of such a decision or has it found that it is unable to finance the economic needs of its East European allies in any other way? As noted earlier, the cost of empire has indeed proven to be more expensive than the Soviets ever anticipated.

V.

Eastern Europe will become even more of a headache for Soviet leaders than it has been in the past. The tensions are now more acute and more deeply felt. Admittedly, because conditions in Poland have deteriorated so, the other East European countries may decide it is saner and safer to follow a more traditional, slower moving course. But that will mean that the economic gap between East and West will continue to grow. Yet if the Polish road brings nothing but chaos and anarchy, the old Stalinist model may still be preferable. Granted that it is out of date, but at least the Stalinist model is steady and avoids chaos and anarchy.

Seemingly the one exception to all of this is Hungary. Ever since they learned their lesson in 1956, they have become increasingly pragmatic. Somehow they have managed to straddle the political and economic mine-traps with an incredible degree of discipline and finesse. They absorbed price hikes in a way no other East European country seems to have done. In large part, this is because the political and economic leadership has moved very cautiously, consulted with its trade unions and signaled its moves well in advance. Not only has it prepared the way for price hikes, but for lower rates of economic growth. This has had the effect of holding levels of aspirations in check.

Yet as adept as the Hungarians have been, they may find themselves swept up in the vortex of the Polish collapse. Their debt of $7 billion in 1980, as we saw, could cause them more problems than originally thought. Moreover, while the Hungarians seem to be well along the road to making their currency convertible and their economy more flexible and adaptive, at least when compared to those of their East European neighbors, the fact remains that, despite appearances, the Hungarians have never completely freed themselves from the legacies of the Stalinist model. Thus the Hungarians have also had their difficulties in integrating their factories imported from the noncommunist world. For example, Professor Tibor Erdos, a Hungarian economist, reports that it takes twice as long for Hungary to integrate an imported factory as it would a Western country.[21] Just as in Poland, this means that the products eventually produced in these factories are, often as not, obsolete by the time they finally leave the production floor. In addition, much of the existing industrial capital stock is woefully out of date.[22] Logically therefore, just as happened in Poland, Hungary is likely to encounter increasing difficulty in generating the exports needed to pay off its industrial credits. Even Hungary has found it difficult to rid itself of the Stalinist economic influence.

In sum, the situation in Eastern Europe poses serious headaches for Brezhnev's successors. Even if they somehow manage to dampen the unrest in Poland, history and the odds suggest that Andropov and his comrades will still have their hands full. A change in Soviet leadership in the past invariably has set off uncertainty and unrest in Eastern Europe. The trouble may not follow immediately, but it does seem to follow with a disturbing regularity. Thus after Stalin's death in 1953, there were riots soon after in East Germany and in Hungary in 1956. After Khrushchev was shunted aside in 1964, Soviet troops had to be sent to Czechoslovakia in 1968. In a sense, the Polish events may have anticipated Brezhnev's departure. However, it is unlikely that this will be the only trouble. If anything, the events in Poland might serve as a jumping-off point for reactions elsewhere. In the absence of some good economic and agricultural news, these reactions when they come may be the most far-reaching and forboding that any Soviet leadership has had to face.

7. He Who Rides a Tiger is Afraid to Dismount[1]

The legacy of the first sixty-five years of Soviet rule imposes an enormous burden on Soviet leadership, both present and future. In some respects, the Stalinist model has been modified, but the basic character of the model is little changed. Thus the regime still holds together more from inertia and fear than from momentum and hope. The sense of radical change and experiment has long since passed. Now there seems to be general agreement that even a minor change might trigger an uncontrollable avalanche.

In the political sphere, the Communist Party continues to rule according to the whims of a small leadership group. Admittedly, considerably less terror is used than was the case under Stalin, but the power of the police is still awesome and there remains a lack of responsiveness to the feelings of the masses. Control is more relaxed than it was under Stalin but it is still firmer than it was in the late 1950's under Khrushchev. In other words, there does not seem to be a consistent trend toward gradual liberalization. Periods of relative relaxation have been and are likely to be followed by periods of increased restraint, but even in the more relaxed part of the cycle, the police continue to maintain tight control over expressions of protest and popular concern.

One of the most pressing issues the Soviet Union has to deal with is the problem of succession. Since all change, and particularly major change, is feared, changes in leadership, one of the more important changes a nation has to make are avoided as long as possible, regardless of the consequences. Unfortunately, or fortunately depending upon your point of view, there is no way the replacement of leadership can be postponed forever. But because it has been put off for such a long time, the replacement process is likely to set in motion all kinds of unanticipated reactions. Just how uncontrollable even minor changes may become has been well documented in the past. The recent intolerable events in Poland, at least in Soviet eyes, are a reminder, if one is needed. Once they started challenging the existing regime, Polish workers eventually moved so far that they even sought to circumscribe the Communist Party's power. For a time, the Poles had established regulations, unparalleled in Eastern Europe, that actually prescribed the terms of office and procedures for leadership transition. But in the process, they have also created what to the Soviets and orthodox Polish communists appeared as anarchy. Ultimately, the army was called upon to restore order, and it responded by instituting a strict regime of martial law.

Because the prospect of setting off something similar to what happened in Poland is so traumatic for them, the Soviets cannot even bring themselves to set out any systematic and institutionalized process for the implementation of change. As we have seen, the reigning leaders tend to put off and even oppose such steps for fear that someone or some group may prematurely utilize such procedures in order to attempt a leadership change. As a consequence, change when it comes tends to be ad hoc.

Conditions in the economic sphere are not much cheerier. While there is virtually no unemployment, at least for those who are not political dissidents, almost all other economic indicators are discouraging. Except for natural gas production, actual production, not just the rate of growth, of most of the basic industrial commodities is beginning to fall or at least level off. That is not much different from having a recession. It is unlikely that in the mid-1980's there will be the precipitous drop in oil production that the CIA had at one time predicted, but output of machine tools and steel, not to mention agriculture, has already dropped. Such a drop is all the more striking, since high rates of growth have heretofore been a hallmark of the Soviet economic model. Does this mean the Soviets can no longer count on increasing the production of these basic commodities? What has happened to the nation of steel eaters? They cannot even do that well any more. Will the economy and the populace be able to come to terms with no growth, or at least a low rate of growth, which the Soviet Union will most likely endure in the next few years? In addition, the Soviets will have to deal with a diminishing labor supply and a falling level of capital productivity. There is also nothing to indicate that the Soviets will soon be able to increase their rate of innovation, which has always been disappointing. As raw material supplies in the world become more limited, the Soviets will probably find that their existing supplies, while perhaps more expensive to produce, will nonetheless become relatively more valuable. However if that is all the Soviet Union has to show for itself, there are bound to be some skeptics who will demand to know if that is what the Communist Revolution was fought for. Did the Russian people endure nationalization and the five-year plans merely in order to turn their country into a raw material colony for the industrialized countries of the capitalist world? Such a future does not provide much to look forward to.

Nor does Soviet agriculture offer much promise. Why, after such massive sums of investment were diverted to agriculture, is there not more to show for it? In part investment funds have been misdirected to the wrong kind of projects. For that matter there is reason to suspect that instead of focusing on agricultural investment, Soviet planners would have been better off if they had concentrated on revamping agricultural institutions. Indicative of that realization, some Soviet specialists have begun to concede that it is not just the weather which accounts for the dismal achievements in agriculture.[2] Presumably, more could have been done to increase peasant prerogatives and incentives. However, this would have had to come at the expense of the collectivized sector. Consequently, if such steps had been taken, they might have been just the first step in the unraveling process that the Soviets seemed to fear, and thus it is a step that the Soviets would only take with extreme caution.

Given the dismal results and dim prospects in industry and agriculture, there is little likelihood of much substantial improvement in the Soviet standard of living. If anything, there will likely be a decrease of production and an increase in shortages and frustration. Food supplies may be even tighter than they have been in the past, as the Soviets find it necessary to draw down more of their stocks to compensate for the poor harvests that are likely to continue. Under the circumstances, it is unlikely that the quantity and the quality of nonfood goods will be much improved. The inability to improve the standard of living will do little to bolster morale or reduce the underlying conditions. If living conditions do not improve soon, the Soviet government runs an enormous risk; it may end up violating its implicit social contract with its population. In exchange for a high rate of savings and investment the Stalinist model offered a world of abundance in the future. That was a long-run promise. In the short run, conditions would be Spartan, but these would nonetheless provide a slow but sure improvement in the country's material well-being. But with the food shortages of recent years, the Soviet government has had difficulty in keeping its side of the bargain. Not surprisingly, the Soviet populace in turn takes its commitment to work less seriously; the result is poorer morale, poorer work discipline, poorer productivity, and equally serious, if not more serious, production problems in the future, all of which will, of course, just prolong the cycle.

Failure to improve economic conditions is also likely to increase caste and nationality differences. Frictions within such groups will probably never disappear entirely, but when economic conditions for everyone are good, there are usually fewer problems. In an environment of prosperity, there is less concern over who is taking what share of the pie when everyone is able to enjoy a larger piece.

In addition to worrying about dampening rivalries between groups within the Soviet Union, the Soviet leaders also have to worry about what is happening in Eastern Europe and in the Soviet Union's other dominions. While the tendency is to refer to the countries under Soviet influence as the Soviet bloc, it is more appropriate to refer to it as the Soviet empire. But like everything else, an empire becomes more of a burden when economic conditions in the home country are strained. If in addition the empire itself proves to be economically costly, then the offsetting benefits of the empire become less and less attractive. After a while even the unsophisticated come to realize that smaller commitments overseas would mean more goods available at home. In times of economic difficulty, the opposition to foreign aid and involvement is particularly keen. For example, after it was announced that there would be a third bad harvest in 1981, one Muscovite was heard to complain that ''the reason we have such a problem is that we are feeding one-half of the world.'' That happened not to be the case. If anything, it is the rest of the world, particularly Argentina, Canada, Australia, and the United States which provide the Soviet Union with as much as 25 per cent of the grain it consumes. In sum, against this background of both internal and external problems, even the most expansive Soviet leader must feel a good deal of trepidation about the prospects for economic growth and political stability.

I.

It is hard for most outsiders to be objective about Soviet prospects. When looking at the Soviet Union, many of us tend to highlight the weaknesses and ignore the strengths. Certainly, we should not forget that some critics have been predicting the imminent collapse of the U.S.S.R. since the early 1930's. At the other extreme, there are some foreigners who neglect the Soviet Union's internal contradictions and concentrate on the very real evidence of Soviet military might and expansionism. How can the Soviet Union be both on the verge of economic collapse and world expansion at the same time? The Soviets seem to be able to handle this paradox because ordinary Soviet citizens seem willing to endure poor conditions at home and they allow their leaders to divert so much to defense and heavy industry with a minimum of protest. The Russian people have a higher tolerance for deprivation and suffering than most other peoples of the developed world. Not many could have endured the collectivization and purges of the 1930's and World War II and its aftermath the way the Russians have. Indeed, many specialists confidently predicted in the past that, when conditions became particularly onerous, the Soviet people would rebel. But they did not. Indeed, maybe it would have been better if the Russian masses had been less accepting and less tolerant; then their government might have been more responsive. But the Soviet people are patient and stoic.

The question is how long will the Soviet people be patient, especially now that they have seen some East Europeans arise in protest. The fact that the Polish protests were forcibly repressed with such efficiency is certain to give pause to those in the Soviet Union who might have thought about doing the same thing. After all, the typical Russian's initial reaction to such protests is that the East Europeans, and Poles in particular, are ingrates with no appreciation of the sacrifices that the Soviet Union has made on their behalf. However, after a time, particularly as the Soviet economy continues to deteriorate, a larger number of Soviet citizens have begun to wonder whether or not they should continue to be so passive.

To head off protests, a far-sighted Soviet leader might therefore begin to experiment with reform on the Hungarian model. Of all the countries in Eastern Europe, the Hungarians seem to have been the most skillful in negotiating between the trap of moving too close to the capitalist

world, which would upset the Russians, and the other trap of not moving far enough away from the Stalinist model, a movement which is
necessary if the government is to be more responsive to the populace
and thus able to reduce alienation. However, the Hungarians come from
a different tradition than the Russians and have different economic skills.
More living Hungarians remember their experience with the market system before the communist takeover in 1945. Fewer and fewer living
Russians experienced the market system which ended in the late 1920's.
Hungary has also developed a greater consensus for its political and
economic goals than any other country in Eastern Europe. There seems
to be less polarization in the country. That is, after all, somewhat of a
surprise, given the uprising of 1956 and the tensions that developed at
the time. But according to Janos Kornai, a Hungarian economist, the
very intensity of the uprising and the loss of life that ensued served to
bring the Hungarians together in a resolve that such a tragedy must
never be allowed to occur in Hungary again. Somehow, a consensus
was created and almost everyone agreed to limit their demands and
accept a compromise. In that spirit, Janos Kadar, the head of the Hungarian Communist Party since then, has devoted a substantial portion of
his efforts towards healing the wounds caused by the uprising and
developing a unity of purpose. That unity has undoubtedly been facilitated by the fact that the Soviet Union is looking over Hungary's shoul-
der and checking on any undue deviation from the Soviet line.

Whatever the explanation, the Hungarians have learned how to tighten
their belts and enjoy it—and if not in an absolute way, certainly better
than their other neighbors in Eastern Europe. They also seem less
addicted to what has come to serve as the opiate of the people in Eastern
Europe, economic growth, at least heavy industrial economic growth.
By de-emphasizing economic growth, the Hungarian leaders have tried
to dampen expectations and focus more on day-to-day needs and
improvements. They realize that promises about a better future will wear
thin if there is not some immediate manifestation of that future. All
future and no present, certainly as in the U.S.S.R. after six decades,
begins to appear after a while more like a long-term confidence game
than a meaningful program of economic development. By not trying to
deceive their workers, the Hungarians seem to have won what for Eastern Europe is a good deal of trust and a willingness to work and reform.
By contrast, Soviet leaders have built up little trust and confidence. The

record of past Soviet attempts at reform is not a good one. Despite countless promises and plans, there have been only brief periods where the leaders have demonstrated a sincere effort at reform and a real trust in the people.

Nor is it only a question of mutual suspicion and mistrust. It turns out that Marxism is ill-suited for the kinds of needs the Soviet Union presently has. Without doubt, Marxism-Leninism is a powerful force for change and revolution—at least when pitted against the non-Marxist economic and social system. However, while it may be a revolutionary force before the revolution, Marxism-Leninism after the revolution tends to become a conservative if not reactionary restraint. For a time it appeared that only when Marxism-Leninism was applied in the peculiar context of Russian history and culture did it transform itself into such a reactionary instrument. However, as more and more countries have been subjected to what has been called a Marxist-Leninist revolution, it has become increasingly apparent that after the initial upheaval, Marxism-Leninism becomes a rigidifying and conservative force. After a short time, revolution and change ceases and upheaval is no longer an ongoing process. A communist revolution tends to preclude evolution. Given this transformation from radical change to reactionary repression, the populace ultimately becomes skeptical of new promises and reform.

Yet some change in Communist systems is necessary if for no other reason than that tastes, availability of raw materials, technology, world power, and governing techniques also change. If a society is to endure in the long run, it must find some way to adjust and cope. Moreover, many of the most important and dynamic changes are unpredictable.

Ironically, the industrialized countries of the noncommunist world seem to handle ongoing and evolutionary change better than the so-called revolutionary communist world. In the West, it is often called "muddling through," but however unromantic the description, the process does allow for change and accommodation. In part, this is a result of the democratic system—when new ideas become popular, the proponents of those ideas are generally voted into office. In the economic sphere, the bearers of attractive ideas increase their profits while the unpopular go bankrupt. The absence of democracy and periodic referenda on the merit of various government practices and the distaste for and unwillingness to face economic bankruptcy (here the United States may not be all that different) lessen the opportunity for change in the communist world. Yet just like the human body, in which old cells continually die and new cells continually develop, there must be death and life at the state level as well. If anything, communism tends to freeze political and economic life. That is not to say that communism has lost its role as an ideology. However, once the revolution has taken place, instead of an ideology of change, communism transforms itself into an ideology of the status quo. In other words, communism seems to work best when it is challenging capitalism rather than when it is the prevailing ideology.

This predilection to oppose change is yet another obstacle confronting any Soviet leader who decides to face up to the reforms that must be introduced if the system is to continue to develop. Those who do recognize that something must be done would be well advised, therefore, to proceed slowly and modestly. They will also have to earn the trust and support of the masses since the process of change will not be smooth or easy. A reformer's first priority, then, should be to increase the quantity and quality of goods going to the consumer. Since the Eleventh Five-Year Plan specifies that the output of consumer goods (production of Type B goods) is to increase at a faster rate than the output of producer goods (Type A goods), even the nonreformist leaders seem to agree that in theory, at least, something should be done to help the consumer. It remains to be seen, however, how long Soviet leadership, present and future, will adhere to this commitment. If the past is any precedent, as long as the planners continue to use the "material balance" method of planning rather than the market system, the planners are likely to revert to an emphasis on producer goods for fear that if they do otherwise, economic output will fall even further behind target.

But even if the planners do decide to switch resource allocation in favor of consumer goods, that will not be enough. It is not only a question of producing more and better food and manufactured goods for the consumer, but also of ensuring that such goods are delivered to the consumer in a more efficient and pleasant way. That will require both an increase in funds allocated to services and a change in attitude. Soviet planners have traditionally held down investment in services. Reflecting Marxist ideology, services are generally regarded as nonproductive—or almost unclean. Most services are even omitted from Soviet calculations of the GNP. It always has seemed to be ideologically more satisfying to devote resources to production rather than to fancy warehouses,

stores, or restaurants. The effect of curbing outlays on services, however, does not necessarily mean that the real costs of distribution are as
low as they apparently seem. What happens is that the cost of obtaining
consumer goods is absorbed, instead, by the consumer in the form of
time spent standing in line, searching from store to store for scarce
merchandise, and preparing food and clothing at home that in a non-
Communist society are available in the form of frozen or semiprepared
foods and ready made clothing.

The long lines contribute to a surly attitude in Soviet sales personnel.
It is hard for even the most altruistic sales clerk to be courteous when
he senses that his customer must either take what the sales clerk has to
offer or do without. As a minimum, those who provide services need
some extra incentive, or some extra competitive spur. Taking a leaf
from Yugoslavia and Hungary, one possible step would be to legitimize
the creation of some privately owned service institutions. This seems to
have stimulated a noticeable improvement in the way services are provided in those countries. The owners of these institutions tend to be
more eager to offer better service than the employees of state-owned
firms, who are little more than civil servants. Since such a step has
already been taken elsewhere within the CMEA bloc, Soviet ideological
purists may not feel quite as threatened by such an experiment. In any
event, such privately owned restaurants, retail shops, hotels, and repair
services would be most likely limited as to the number of people they
might employ. In the same spirit, private operations in agriculture might
be similarly encouraged. We saw in Chapter Three how the precedent
for such action in the Soviet Union itself has already been established.
Conceivably, private operations might even be extended to small-scale
industry, but clearly this would be a much more controversial and
threatening step.

Even if such actions were found to be acceptable ideologically, they
would be potentially risky. They could set off an unraveling process
which could not be controlled. Ideally, the basic system would remain
in governmental hands. In effect, the Soviets would continue to "command the heights" of the economy and simply release the fringes to
private control. To some, this might come to resemble the New Economic Policy (NEP) of Lenin. Since NEP was Lenin's idea, that would
mean that such a step should be ideologically permissible. However,
such a move raises the specter of a great reduction in state control, if

not anarchy. Similarly, allowing the workers more say in factory operations through workers' council and worker management, as in Yugoslavia, and permitting more freedom for importers and exporters would
also seem to be steps that will have to be taken to bring about the
remolding and reindustrialization of the economy. Merely to revive steel
and simple machine-tool production hardly constitutes a long-term solution to Soviet economic problems. Somehow the Soviet economy will
also have to learn how to compete in the arena of both industrial and
consumer high technology. But it is difficult to see how industry can be
set loose without at the same time setting loose the political and social
furies that have been pent up during the past six decades of repression.

Yet Andropov cannot wait forever to make the necessary changes.
Indeed as we saw, the longer they are postponed, the greater the magnitude of the change required, and thus the more traumatic the transition
is likely to be. Moreover, even though the relatively modest reform of
the type just spelled out would help to ameliorate some of the most
abrasive aspects of Soviet life, there is a very real gamble involved.
Even a modest change is sure to set off rising expectations that there
will be greater improvement in the future. Thus while there is no guarantee that reform will make is possible to realize long-run solutions,
there is almost near certainty that reform will bring about some short-
run unrest.

Perhaps one of the most tragic but enduring shortcomings of Russia
and its culture is that historically Russian leaders have found it very
difficult to implement change. So little that came to Russia and now
comes from the Soviet Union has been evolutionary or gradual. This is
reflected not only by the relatively large number of revolutions and
attempted revolutions the country has endured, but by the way non-
revolutionary change must today be introduced. Soviet leaders learned
long ago that if they wanted change, they would probably have to lead
a massive campaign to bestir the actual implementers of these changes.
Given the nature of this system and the penalties usually imposed on
those who show too much initiative, there is normally great hesitancy
to move on one's own. This attitude, as well as the incentive system,
tends to militate against any disruption of existing procedures. Consequently, when the leaders decide to take some new step, they must
exhort and cajole the intermediary layer of ministers, managers, and
planners. That was why it was not enough for Khrushchev to announce

that he wanted to increase production of corn, fertilizer, or chemicals, nor for Brezhnev simply to order an increase in the amount of land put under cultivation in the non-black-soil regions of the country. In each instance, Khrushchev and Brezhnev had to go beyond the use of ordinary economic incentives and launch a nationwide campaign.

II.

Given the durability of the Soviet system all these years—and the fact that, despite what for others would be impossible conditions, major changes have been avoided—there is nonetheless a reasonable possibility that present and future Soviet leaders will continue to hold onto their power without any major trouble. Whatever unrest may surface will be easily diffused or intimidated. At the same time, there is also a good chance that the time is riper than ever for some kind of explosion. Four successive crop failures will undoubtedly intensify food supply shortages that were already severe after two bad harvests. It is worth noting that this is the first time since World War II that the Soviet Union has had three or four bad grain harvests in a row. In fact, there have not been that many instances in which there have been two bad harvests in a row. Those years were 1953–54, 1959–60, and 1974–75.[3] While digging into reserves and increasing food imports may have alleviated conditions somewhat, the record string of poor harvests has sorely depleted the food pipeline for years to come. It is not like missing four nights of sleep and trying to make it up with one good night's sleep on the fifth day. A succession of good harvests will be required to insure a steady and improved flow of food throughout the country. But good harvests alone will not be enough. Remember that even in good harvest years, the Russian consumer has to contend with food shortages and supply disruptions. The point is that just as food is likely to be in shorter supply than usual, at least until the mid-1980's, so popular morale will correspondingly be very low. Ordinary tensions may easily escalate, and therefore violent outbursts might occur during this period.

Admittedly change and attempts at change come infrequently to the Soviet Union. But they do come. Defining exactly what constitutes a change is a bit of a problem, but the last major change or attempted change in Russian government came in 1917, over six decades ago. That change came a decade after the 1905 Revolution, and two decades after the attempted assassination of the czar in 1881. Five and a half decades earlier the Decembrist Movement of 1825 took place. Thus the current system has gone longer without an attempted radical change than any time within the last two centuries. This is not meant to say that a change or an attempt at one will of necessity occur, but it does suggest the magnitude of the pressures for change which have been held back over all these years.

Finally, change in Soviet leadership in the past has often proven to be unsettling, both within the Soviet Union and in Eastern Europe.[4] It may be that the present Soviet leadership in agreeing to Andropov's assertion of power has found a way to break out of the traditional mold and transfer power without giving rise to the confusion and uncertainty that followed Lenin's death or the rioting and turmoil that followed Stalin's death and Khrushchev's replacement, particularly in Eastern Europe. But if so, thus far there is no hint of how that process has been institutionalized so that it can be repeated in the future. Nor should Soviet leaders be lulled by the absence of immediate unrest. In some instances, these outbursts took a number of years after the transition to materialize, but in every case, the uncertainty set off by the change in leadership added to the already existing discontent. After all, even in the noncommunist world, a leadership change can sometimes be very unsettling; thus we should not be surprised by a similar sort of reaction in the communist world.

If Sovietologists used seismographic tools, the growing rumbling of the Soviet political and economic system would serve as a strong indicator that the Soviet Union is ripe, if not overdue, for a change. But there is a danger of relying too heavily on such logic. In the same way, if Western Sovietologists were logicians, they might have concluded that, like the bumble bee, the Soviet Union should have fallen long ago of its own weight. By most standards, the Soviet Union should have crashed at least five decades ago and at least once a decade since then. But the U.S.S.R. has survived. This should constitute a lesson in humility for anyone tempted to conclude that the Soviet Union is on the verge of collapse. Yet the fact does remain that, in one way or other, the Soviet system has some enormous problems to overcome and that it will have to adapt and reform if it is to make it intact to the year 2000.

Assuming that future Soviet leaders ultimately conclude that they must reform to survive, they must still decide which type of reform they should make. Piecemeal reform is not likely to assuage over six decades of pent-up frustration. Unless administered with more skill than most

Soviet leaders have heretofore demonstrated, piecemeal or gradual change is more likely to whet demands for ever more relaxation, and the system may give way as it has in Poland. Alternatively, Soviet leaders will have to oversee such a fundamental reform that it would mean a fundamental change in the system. But while such a complete aboutface may satisfy one set of demands, it would undoubtedly give rise to another. Those displaced in the upheaval or those who cannot cope with spontaneity or excessive freedom will do all they can to seek a return to the order of the previous regime. There is always the chance that, once set in motion, the pendulum will swing so far that it excites pressure for a reaction and another need for change.

Thus the challenge facing Soviet leaders, both present and future, is not an easy one. There is general agreement both within and outside of the Soviet bloc that the existing economic system is not performing as it should. More importantly, there is little to hope for in the future. If anything, the economic conditions are likely to deteriorate even more in the years ahead. It is not only that there seems to be little hope of introducing such things as high technology into the civilian sector; there is now even pessimism about the ability of the state to bring the traditional sectors of heavy industry and agriculture up to their former levels of production. A few years ago, Soviet citizens used to console themselves with the thought that it may have been bad in the past, but conditions had improved and would be even better in the future. Now there is a sense that economic life may actually have been better in the past and that the future may be even worse.

But as we have seen, attempts to introduce economic and industrial reform to revitalize the economy could set off uncontrollable political and economic forces. This then is the Soviet dilemma. It may be inappropriate in the Soviet context, but this dilemma brings to mind an old Chinese proverb: "He who rides a tiger is afraid to dismount." The present situation is bad, but the consequences of a reform may be even worse. The need then is for leadership that is prepared to face the tiger and find the treacherous road that runs between the extremes of no change and too-radical change. Based on how previous leaders have handled change, there is not much room for optimism. To find a balanced compromise will be a sizable challenge.

Notes

1.

1. For a good description of the Stalinist model, see Abram Bergson, "Towards a New Growth Model," *Problems of Communism*, March–April, 1973, p. 1.

2. Zbigniew Brzezinski, *The Permanent Purge* (Cambridge: Harvard University Press, 1956).

3. There is even a report that the Soviets are trying to draw up a plan for the period, 1990 to 2000. RFE-RL Radio Liberty 255 / 81, June 24, 1981, p. 2.

4. *Pravda*, May 8, 1981, p. 2.

5. *Pravda*, May 8, 1981, pp. 2–3.

6. Seweryn Bialer, *Stalin's Successors* (Cambridge: Cambridge University Press, 1980), p. 83, Table I-2.

7. Charles A. Beard, Mary R. Beard, *The Rise of American Civilization* (New York: MacMillan, 1927), pp. 114–115, 142–143, 162–163.

13. Thomas Sowell, *Race and Economics* (New York: David McKay Co., Inc., 1975), pp. 51, 53.

9. Michael T. Florinsky, *Russia: History and Interpretation* (New York: MacMillan, 1955), II, 784.

10. Alexander Gerschenkron, *Economic Backwardness in Historical Perspective* (Cambridge: The Belknap Press of the Harvard University Press, 1962), p. 5.

11. *Ibid.*, p. 18. See also Robert C. Tucker, "Swollen State, Spent Society: Stalin's Legacy to Brezhnev's Russia," *Foreign Affairs*, Winter, 1981–82, p. 420.

12. Bailer, *op. cit.*, p. 89.

13. Keenan, "Russian Political Culture," U.S. Department of State, Contract No. 1722-420119 (Cambridge: Russian Research Center, Harvard University, July, 1976), p. 77, mimeograph.

14. Aleksandr I. Solzhenitsyn, *"The Gulag Archipelago* (New York: Harper and Row, 1973), p. 27.

15. Edward Kuznetsov, "The Status of the Soviet Political Prisoners," *Crossroads,* Winter-Spring, 1981, No. 7, p. 191.

16. Winston Churchill, *The Hinge of Fate* (Boston: Houghton, Mifflin, 1950), pp. 498–499.

17. Franklyn Holzman, *Soviet Taxation* (Cambridge: Harvard University Press, 1955), p. 153.

18. See Janet Chapman, *Real Wages in Soviet Russia Since 1928* (Cambridge: Harvard University Press, 1963).

19. Henry W. Morton, "The Soviet Quest for Better Housing—Impossible Dream?" *The Soviet Union in a Time of Change* the Joint Economic Committee (Washington: U.S. Government Printing Office, October 10, 1979). p. 794. Hereafter Joint Economic Committee publications will be referred to as JEC, with the appropriate years.

20. Tsentral'noe statisticheskoe upravlenie (hereafter TSU), *Narodnoe Khoziaistvo SSSR v 1956 Godu,* Moscow, Gosstatizdat, 1957, p. 42. (Hereafter referred to as *Nar Khoz* with the appropriate statistical year.)

21. *Ibid.*

22. *Ibid.,* p. 60.

23. Abram Bergson, *Productivity and the Social System—the USSR and the West* (Cambridge: Harvard University Press, 1978), p. 122.

24. Gerschenkron, *op. cit.;* Paul Rosenstein-Rodan, "Problems of Industrialization of Eastern and Southeastern Europe," *Economic Journal,* June-September, 1943, p. 202; R. Nurkse, *Problems of Capital Formation in Underdeveloped Countries,* (New York: Oxford University Press, 1953); Walter Rostow, *Stages of Economic Growth,* (Cambridge: Cambridge University Press, 1960).

25. *Nash Sovremennik,* January, 1981, pp. 187–191.

26. *Ibid.* The word in square brackets is added. While no doubt the state's intent was to be authoritative, it usually ended up being authoritarian.

2.

1. Alexander Erlich, *The Soviet Industrialization Debate: 1924–1928* (Cambridge: Harvard University Press, 1960), p. 10.

2. Central Intelligence Agency, *Economic Statistics* (Washington, D.C.: ER80-10452, October, 1980), p. 24.

3. *Ibid.,* pp. 124–191.

4. *Pravda,* November 20, 1962, p. 4.

5. Paul Hare, Hugo Radice, and Nigel Swain, eds., *Hungary: A Decade of Economic Reform* (London: George Allen & Unwin, 1981), p. 117; Joseph

Berliner, *The Innovation Decision in Soviet Industry* (Cambridge: MIT Press, 1976), p. 33.
6. Igor Birman, "Who is stronger and why?" *Crossroads*, Winter-Spring, 1981, p. 121.
7. *Lesnaya Promyslennost'*, July 13, 1961, p. 3. See also Philip Hanson, RFE-R.L. *Radio Liberty Dispatch*, "USSR Gosplan and the Matching of Production with Demand," RL-250/81, June 23, 1981, p. 2.
8. A. Savin, "Tsenoobrazovanie kak ekonomicheskii rychag povysheniia effektivnosti obshchestvennogo proizvodstva," *Planovoe khoziaistvo*, November, 1979, p. 103.
9. T. Khachaturov, "Prirodnye resursy i planirovanie narodnogo khoziaistva," *Voprosy ekonomiki*, August, 1973, pp. 20–21; RFE-RL RL324/81, August 18, 1981, p. 3.
10. January 27, 1978, p. 2.
11. Marshall I. Goldman, *The Enigma of Soviet Petroleum: Half Empty or Half Full* (Boston: Allen & Unwin, 1980), pp. 46–47.
12. *Pravda*, January 18, 1981, p. 2.
13. *Pravda*, February 15, 1978, p. 3.
14. *Nar Khoz*, 1980, p. 345.
15. *Nar Khoz*, 1970, p. 490.
16. *Pravda*, December 10, 1963, p. 6.
17. *Pravda*, November 28, 1978, p. 1; *New York Times*, December 14, 1972, p. 1.
18. I. I. Konnik, "Proportsional'nost' v narodnom khoziaistve i denezhnoe obrashchenie," *Dengi i kredit*, December, 1976, p. 49; *Sotsialisticheskaia industriia*, January 20, 1973, pp. 2–3; Joseph Berliner, p. 211, 351; *Izvestiia*, September 19, 1981, p. 6.
19. I. A. Orlov, "Nekotorye voprosy povysheniia kachestva tovarov narodnogo potrebleniia," *Voprosy ekonomiki*, May, 1964, pp. 45–46; *Sovetskaia torgovlia*, October, 1961, p. 9.
20. *Nar Khoz*, 1979, p. 538.
21. Murray Feshbach, "Population and Labor Force," paper prepared for Conference on Soviet Energy Toward the Year 2000, Airlie House, Virginia, October 24, 1980, p. 1.
22. Joseph Berliner, p. 518.
23. Seymour E. Goodman, "Computers and the Development of the Soviet Economy," JEC, 1979, I, 524; E. Rakovskii, "Tekhnicheskii progress i faktor vremeni," *Planovoe khoziaistvo*, July, 1966, p. 16.
24. Emanuel Bobrov, "Applied Computer Science in the USSR: A Personal Account," Papers on Soviet Science and Technology (Cambridge: Russian Research Center, Harvard University, May, 1981), p. 12.
25. Sutton, *Western Technology and Soviet Economic Development, 1917–*

1930 (Stanford: Hoover Institution Publications, 1968); Sutton, *Western Technology and Soviet Economic Development 1930–1945* (Stanford: Hoover Institution Press, 1971).

26. *Trud,* August 31, 1978, p. 2; *Pravda,* June 11, 1974, p. 6; John Kiser, "Soviet Technology: The Perception Gap," *Mechanical Engineering,* April, 1979, p. 29; *The Wall Street Journal,* September 3, 1982, p. 1.

27. Robert H. Hayes and William J. Abernathy, "Managing our Way to Economic Decline," *The Harvard Business Review,* July–August, 1980, p. 67.

28. *Pravda,* June 9, 1981, p. 2.

29. Abram Bergson, p. 24.

30. Bergson, p. 24.

31. Egon Neuburger, *Central Planning and its Legacies* (Santa Monica: The Rand Corporation, December, 1966), p. 6.

32. *Ibid.,* p. 16.

33. Marshall I. Goldman, "Economic Controversy in the Soviet Union," *Foreign Affairs,* April, 1963, p. 498.

34. Hare, Radice, and Swain, pp. 93, 99.

35. *Pravda,* January 29, 1970, p. 1.

36. *Soviet News,* October 21, 1969, p. 28.

37. *Izvestiia,* January 18, 1972, p. 2; *Pravda,* January 31, 1981, p. 3.

38. *Pravda,* May 8, 1981, p. 1.

39. *Pravda,* May 4, 1981, p. 2.

40. One of the better-known general pieces on the second economy is Gregory Grossman, "The Second Economy of the USSR," *Problems of Communism,* September–October, 1977, p. 25. The percentage-of-GNP figures cited on text pp. 55 and 98 are not, however, attributable to Gregory Grossman, as he has not published such estimates.

41. These white elephants are usually only acknowledged during a political upheaval. See *The Wall Street Journal,* June 2, 1981, p. 56.

3.

1. Ministerstvo vneshnei torgovli SSSR, *Vneshniaia torgovlia SSSR za 1918–1940 gg.* (Moscow: Vneshtorgizdat), 1960, p. 55 (hereafter VT SSSR with the appropriate years; VT SSSR 1918–1966, pp. 134–135; U.S. Bureau of the Census, *Historical Statistics of the United States,* Colonial Times to 1970, Bicentennial Edition, Part I (Washington, D.C.: U.S. Government Printing Office, 1975); Part II, p. 898; Lazar Volin, *A Century of Russian Agriculture: From Alexander II to Khrushchev* (Cambridge: Harvard University Press, 1970), p. 110.

2. VT SSSR, 1918–1966, pp. 134–135.

3. John P. Hardt and Kate S. Tomlinson, *An Assessment of the Afghanistan Sanctions: Implications for Trade and Diplomacy in the 1980's,* Subcommittee on Europe and the Middle East of the Committee on Foreign Affairs of the U.S.

House of Representatives (Washington, D.C.: U.S. Government Printing Office, April, 1981), p. 24.

4. U.S. Bureau of the Census, Statistical Abstract of the United States, 1979, 100th ed. (Washington, D.C.: U.S. Government Printing Office, 1979), pp. 416–418.

5. Pravda, December 10, 1963, p. 1.

6. Leo Tolstoy, Anna Karenina (New York: The New American Library, 1961), pp. 346–347.

7. Nar Khoz, 1976, p. 7.

8. Edward L. Kennan, p. 11.

9. Jerzy Karcz, ed. Arthur W. Wright, The Economics of Communist Agriculture: Selected Papers (Bloomington, Indiana: International Development Institution, 1979), p. 110.

10. Erlich, p. 110; Lazar Volin, A Century of Russian Agriculture (Cambridge: Harvard University Press, 1970), p. 176.

11. Karcz, pp. 34, 41.

12. Holland Hunter, "Soviet Agricultural Potential and the Surplus-Extraction Issue, 1928–1949," mimeographed, June 11, 1981, p. 9.

13. Volin, p. 177.

14. Ibid.

15. Tolstoy, p. 166.

16. Volin, p. 236.

17. Ibid.

18. David M. Schoonover. "Soviet Agricultural Policies," JEC,1979,II, 87.

19. Schoonover, p. 97.

20. Ibid.

21. Ibid., p. 96.

22. Nar Khoz, 1976, p. 44; SSSR v tsifrakh, 1980, pp. 148–150.

23. Zhurnalist, August 1981, p. 36.

24. Komsomol'skaia pravda, July 24, 1981, p. 2; Pravda, July 2, 1981, p. 6.

25. Nar Khoz, 1979, p. 370.

26. Douglas B. Diamond and W. Lee Davis, "Comparative Growth in Output and Productivity in the U.S. and U.S.S.R. Agriculture," JEC, 1979; II, 40.

27. Ibid., II, 35.

28. Ibid., II, 32.

29. Ibid., II, 41.

30. Ibid., II, 41.

31. Soviet Geography: Review and Translation, No. 6, 1968, p. 448; D. Armand, Nam i vnukam (Moscow, Mysl', 1966), p. 334.

32. P. Poletaev, "Razvitie ekonomiki i ekologiia," Planovoe khoziaistvo, December, 1979, pp. 66–67; T. Khachaturov, "Ekonomicheskie problemy ekologii," Voprosy ekonomiki, June, 1978, p. 12.

33. Izvestiia, February 4, 1982, p. 2.

34. *Pravda,* June 8, 1981, p. 3.

35. *Ekonomicheskaia gazeta,* February, 1981, No. 9, p. 23.

36. *The New York Times,* June 21, 1982, p. D-8; *Literaturnaiia gazeta,* September 16, 1981, p. 10, indicates the potato crop loss is only 25 per cent.

37. *Pravda,* November 17, 1981, p. 1–2.

38. *Nar Khoz,* 1979, p. 237, 258; V. Voronin, "Lichnye podsobnie khoziaistva i torgovlia," *Voprosy ekonomiki,* No. 6, 1980, p. 118; Diamond, "Soviet Agricultural Plans for 1981–85," *Russia at the Crossroads: The 26th Congress of the CPSU,* S. Bialer and T. Gustafson, ed. (London: Allen & Unwin, 1982), p. 117.

39. V. Vasilevskii, "Ispol'zovanie maloi tekhnika v lichnom podsobnom khoziaistve," *Voprosy ekonomiki,* No. 5, 1980, p. 132.

40. *Nar Khoz,* 1979, p. 237.

41. V. Vasilevskii, p. 67.

42. Schoonover, p. 97.

43. *Ekonomicheskaia gazeta,* September, 1980, No. 39, p. 15.

44. *Pravda,* May 25, 1982, p. 1.

4.

1. The late Alexander Gerschenkron argued that this pattern of forced growth and then stagnation has occurred numerous times in Russian history. Gerschenkron, *op. cit.,* p. 18.

2. Michael T. Florinsky, *Russia: History & an Interpretation* (New York: The MacMillan Company, 1955), II, 1425.

3. RFE-RL Radio Liberty Research, RL579 January 3, 1978, p. 1.

4. Dienes, The Soviet Union: An Energy Crunch Ahead?" *Problems of Communism* September–October, 1977, p. 59; see also Dienes and Theodore Shabad, *The Soviet Energy System: Resource Use and Policies* (Washington, D.C.: V. H. Winston & Sons, 1979), p. 42, n. 32.

5. RFE-RL Radio Liberty Research, RL 5 / 79, January 3, 1978, p. 9.

6. Murray Feshbach, "Population and the Labor Force," paper prepared for the conference on the Soviet Economy Towards the Year 2000, Airlie House, Virginia, October 24–25, 1980, p. 5–6.

7. *Lubomyr* Hajda, "Nationality and Age in Soviet Population Change," *Soviet Studies,* October, 1980, No. 4, p. 477.

8. *Ibid.,* p. 491.

9. RFE-RL, RL 316/81, August 13, 1981; *Sovetskoe gosudarstvo i pravo,* January, 1978, p. 135.

10. TSU, *Naselenie SSSR* (Moscow: Politizdat, 1980), p. 23.

11. This situation is in some ways comparable to the growing use of Spanish in the United States. However, the percentage of population affected in the United States is much smaller. Except for Puerto Rico, there is no national

policy that calls for the preservation of a language other than English as the region's main language.

12. *Literaturnaia gazeta,* March 4, 1981, p. 12; March 25, 1981, p. 12; March 3, 1982, p. 12.

13. *Literaturnaia gazeta,* September 16, 1981, p. 10; RFE-RL, *Soviet Area Audience and Opinion Research,* "Food Supply in the USSR: Evidence of Widespread Shortages," April, 1982, p. 5.

14. *Izvestiia,* September 29, 1981, p. 1.

15. *Zaria Vostoka,* November 26, 1981, p. 1.

16. *Literaturnaia gazeta,* May 6, 1981, p. 12.

17. *The International Herald Tribune,* May 5, 1982, p. 4.

18. *Pravda,* April 27, 1982, p. 3.

19. See note 40 on text p. 186.

20. Henry W. Morton, "The Soviet Quest for Better Housing: An Impossible Dream?" JEC, 1979, I, 796; *Pravda,* February 24, 1981, p. 7.

21. Toli Welihozkiy, "Automobiles and the Soviet Consumer," JEC, 1979, I, 819.

22. *Trud,* October 17, 1981, p. 2.

23. *Ibid.*

24. *Pravda,* April 8, 1981, pp. 2–3.

25. Davis and Feshbach, *Rising Infant Mortality in the USSR in the 1970s* (Washington, D.C.: U.S. Department of Commerce), Series 95, No. 74, September, 1980, p. 2.

26. Apparently in 1980, life expectancy in the U.S. and Japan also dipped slightly for the first time in decades, but in both instances this was attributed more to a flue epidemic than anything else. Moreover, the size of the drop was minor. In the U.S., it was .3 years from 74.1 years for men born in 1979 to 73.8 years for men born in 1980; *The Wall Street Journal,* April 24, 1981, p. 56. In Japan the drop was from 73.6 to 73.32; *The Japan Times,* July 26, 1981, p. 2.

27. Davis and Feshbach, p. 1; see also, *The New York Times,* June 21, 1981, p. 15.

28. Walter D. Connor, *Socialism, Politics, and Equality* (New York: Columbia University Press, 1979), p. 106; Robert C. Tucker, p. 415.

29. *Literaturnaia gazeta,* April 1, 1981, p. 12; *The New York Times,* May 7, 1978, p. 22.

30. That was one of the most emotional issues underlying the Polish workers' protests about the regime. The Secretary General of the Polish Communist Party, Edward Gierek, had set aside for himself an unusually palatial mansion.

31. Connor, p. 214.

32. *The Current Digest of the Soviet Press,* May 18, 1977, p. 18.

33. *The New York Times,* June 20, 1973, p. 19; July 5, 1974, p. 8; May 4, 1978, p. 22.

34. Hedrick Smith, *The Russians* (New York: Ballantine Books, 1977), p. 30.

35. *Pravda,* May 8, 1981, p. 2.

36. *The Current Digest of the Soviet Press,* June 10, 1981, p. 7.

37. *The New York Times,* July 12, 1981, p. E-5. For example, two dissident Soviet women reported that Viktor Boyko, the Chairman of the Communist Regional Executive Committee in the Ukraine, was an honest and helpful man.

38. RFE-RL RL267/81, July 6, 1981, p. 1.

39. Powell, *Alcohol Abuse in the Soviet Union,* forthcoming.

40. *Trud,* October 17, 1981, p. 2.

41. *The New York Times,* December 2, 1977, p. 1.

42. John C. Michael, ''The interdependent Trade Union Movement in the Soviet Union,'' RFE-RL, RL304 / 79, October 11, 1979, pp. 13–15.

43. RFE-RL, RL132 / 80 April 2, 1980; *The New York Times,* March 1, 1979, p. A-3.

44. *The New York Times,* July 24, 1980, p. A–5.

45. Mario Corti, ''Aleksei Nikitin and the Movement for Workers' Rights in the USSR,'' RFE-RL RL188 / 81, May 6, 1981; *Soviet News,* May 2, 1978, p. 149.

46. *The Washington Post,* February 1, 1981, p. 1; RL 320 / 79, October 29, 1979, p. 6; see also Kevin Klose, *Hammer and Sickle* (New York: W. W. Norton, 1983).

47. Similarly, Jacek Kuron, the intellectual force behind KOR (the Committee for Social Self-Defense) in Poland, which was the guiding force initially behind the Solidarity Union, was also a party member until he too was expelled for being too critical of the party. *The New York Times,* June 25, 1981, p. 2. Persisting in his social concerns, however, he then helped organize KOR to fight party abuses in Poland.

48. Corti, p. 4.

49. RL Research, RL484 / 76, November 29, 1976; 194 / 78 September 4, 1978; 55 / 79 February 20, 1979; 294 / 80 August 20, 1980; *The New York Times,* February 12, 1978, p. 13.

50. Mario Corti, p. 2; RFE RL October 27, 1980, 294 / 80; August 20, 1980, p. 4; 267 / 81, July 6, 1981; 59 / 79 February 20, 1979; 196 / 81, May 12, 1981, p. 3; *The Financial Times,* June 25, 1980, p. 2; *The New York Times,* October 23, 1980, p. A-8; June 24, 1980, p. A-5; February 14, 1978, p. 13; June 14, 1980, p. 1. In November 1981, officials at the Togliatti Auto Plant acknowledged openly to Western correspondents that there had been a ''labor dispute'' there and at Gorky in 1980; *The New York Times,* November 18, 1981, p. A-6; *The Financial Times,* November 24, 1981, p. 1; RFE RL December 1, 1981, p. 1.

51. RFE, RL190/81, May 7, 1981.
52. RFE, RL, RL149/81, April 7, 1981.
53. RL384/80 October 17, 1980.
54. *The Boston Globe,* November 22, 1981, p. 55.
55. *The New York Times,* July 5, 1978, p. A-7.
56. *Ibid.,* May 25, 1978, p. A-5.
57. *Ibid.,* February 20, 1981, p. A-8.
58. *The Current Digest of the Soviet Press,* March 16, 1977, p. 8; *The New York Times,* April 10, 1978, p. A-15.
59. RL44/79, February 12, 1979.
60. *Soviet News,* February 13, 1977, p. 44.
61. *The New York Times,* February 3, 1980, p. 29.
62. *Sovetskaia rossia,* January 31, 1981, p. 4.
63. *Izvestiia,* June 24, 1982, p. 6.
64. RL 190/81, RL, May 7, 1981; *Pravda,* February 24, 1981.

5.

1. The exact sequence is, "Who controls Eastern Europe controls the heartland: Who rules the heartland commands the world island: Who rules the world island commands the world." Halford J. Mackinder, "The Geographical Pivot of History," *Geographical Journal,* Vol XXII, 1904, p. 22; *Democratic Ideals and Reality,* New York, Holt, 1919, p. 50.
2. *The New York Times,* July 21, 1982, p. A5.
3. Holzman, "Is There a Soviet-U.S. Military Spending Gap?," *Challenge,* September-October 1980, p. 3; Abram Bergson, "Soviet Economic Slowdown," *Problems of Communism,* May-June, 1981, p. 33.
4. Ogarkov has subsequently become Army Chief of Staff and the Deputy Minister of Defense. John Newhouse, *Cold Dawn: The Story of SALT* (New York: Holt, Reinhart and Winston, 1973, p. 56.
5. *The New York Times,* June 21, 1981, p. E-1; April 29, 1982, p. A-4; *The Wall Street Journal,* May 28, 1982, p. 2.
6. Most observers refer to these countries as nonaligned. However, since many of them seem to spend more time criticizing the United States and the capitalist world than they do the communist world, nonaligned is probably not the proper description.
7. Frederic L. Pryor, *Communist Foreign Trade System* (Cambridge: MIT, 1963), pp. 136–137.
8. *Sovetskaia torgovlia,* February 1, 1968, p. 3; V. Goryunov, "Bourgeois Propaganda on Soviet Economic Relations with the Developing Countries," *Foreign Trade,* January 1968, p. 10; *International Affairs,* May 1963, p. 35.
9. Theodore Shabad, "Raw Material Problems of the Soviet Aluminum Industry," JEC, October, 1976, p. 661.

10. John A. Martens, ''Quantifications of Western Exports of High Technology Products to Communist Countries,'' East-West Trade Policy Staff Papers, International Trade Administration, U.S. Department of Commerce, January, 1981, p. v.

11. John P. Hardt and Kate S. Tomlinson, *An Assessment of the Afghanistan Sanctions: Implications for Trade and Diplomacy in the 1980's,* Subcommittee on Europe and the Middle East of the Committee on Foreign Affairs of the U.S. House of Representatives (Washington, D.C.: U.S. Government Printing Office, April 1981), p. 1; *The Financial Times,* November 10, 1982, p. 10.

12. ''Ekonomicheskie sviazi SSSR zarubezhnymi stranami,'' *Planovoe khoziaistvo,* October, 1980, p. 82. A controversial study released by the U.S. Department of Commerce argues that Soviet imports in 1980 amounted to as much as 20 per cent of the GNP, and exports amounted to 7 per cent. See Vladimir G. Treml and Barry L. Kostinsky, *The Domestic Value of Soviet Foreign Trade,* U.S. Bureau of the Census, Washington, D.C., Foreign Economic Report #20, April, 1982, draft.

13. *The International Herald Tribune,* August 24, 1981, p. 4.

14. Ronald Amann, Julian Cooper, and R. W. Davies, ed., *The Technological Level of Soviet Industry* (New Haven: Yale University Press, 1977), p. 64; P. Hanson, ''The Diffusion of Imported Technology in the USSR,'' *East-West Technological Cooperation,* Colloquium 1976, Brussels, NATO, Director of Economic Affairs, March 17–19, 1976, p. 143; Hanson, ''International Technology Transfer from the U.S. to the USSR,'' JEC, 1976, p. 805.

15. See also Philip Hanson and Malcolm R. Hill, ''Soviet Assimilation of Western Technology: A Survey of U.K. Exporters' Experience,'' JEC, October 10, 1979, II 596.

16. For example, see the trilogy by Anthony C. Sutton, *Western Technology and Soviet Economic Development, 1930–1945* (Stanford: Hoover Institution Press, 1971), and by the same author, *Western Technology and Soviet Economic Development, 1917–1930* (Stanford: Hoover Institution Publications, 1968); and *Western Technology and Soviet Economic Development, 1945–1965* (Stanford: Hoover Institution, 1973); Thane Gustafson, *Selling the Russians the Rope* (Santa Monica, Ca.: Rand, 1981), p. 1.

17. Amann, Cooper, and Davies, p. 65.

18. *Trud,* April 17, 1981, p. 2; *Sotsialisticheskaia industriia,* October 4, 1981, p. 2.

19. *Sotsialisticheskaia industriia,* October 4, 1981, p. 2; Philip Hanson cites other cases as well in ''The Role of Trade and Technology in the Soviet Economy,'' mimeographed.

20. Padma Desai, ''The Rate of Return on Foreign Capital Flow to the Soviet Economy,'' JEC, 1979, p. 407; Hanson, JEC, 1976, p. 799, n. 4.

21. *Pravda,* February 24, 1981, p. 5.

22. Aleksandrov, "Rech' A. P. Alexsandrov," *Vestnik, Akademii Nauk SSSR,* No. 4, 1981, p. 5; see also *Pravda,* June 2, 1981, p. 3.

23. Tsvigun, "O proiskakh imperialisticheskihk razvedok," *Kommunist,* September 10, 1981, No. 14, p. 94. Officials at Burroughs report the man was not working for them at the time of the alleged sabotage.

24. Hanson, "The End of Import-Led Growth? Some Observations on Soviet, Polish and Hungarian Experience in the 1970's," *Journal of Comparative Economics,* June, 1982, p. 130.

25. Raymond Vernon, "The Fragile Foundations of East-West Trade," *Foreign Affairs,* Summer, 1979, p. 1035.

26. Imports from the United States, Canada, Australia, and Argentina are not included, since 58 per cent of their exports to the Soviet Union consist of grain.

27. *Business Week,* May 21, 1979, p. 3.; *Soviet Weekly,* July 7, 1979, p. 7; *The Wall Street Journal,* April 2, 1981, p. 52.

28. Interview at Gosplan in Moscow, December, 1978, with N. N. Inozemtsev, Deputy Chairman of Gosplan.

29. Daniel I. Fine, "Mineral Resource, Dependency Crisis: the Soviet Union and the United States," The Resource War in 3-D—*Dependency, Diplomacy, Defense,* ed., James Arnold Miller, Daniel I. Fine, and R. Daniel McMichael (Pittsburgh: World Affairs Council of Pittsburgh), Eighteenth Worlds Affair Forum.

30. Solzhenitsyn, letter dated December 5, 1973.

31. Boris Komarov, *The Destruction of Nature* (White Plains: M. E. Sharpe, 1980), p. 126.

32. *Sotsialisticheskaia industriia,* March 24, 1978, p. 1; *Pravda,* October 12, 1974; *Pravda,* November 28, 1978, p. 1.

33. Robert Rand, "Washington, Moscow and the 'Resource War,' " RFE-RL, November 14, 1980, RL433-80.

34. *The Boston Globe,* November 15, 1981, p. 11; *The Christian Science Monitor,* November 12, 1981, p. 1.

35. Ivan Turgenev, *Fathers and Sons,* Moscow, 1861.

6.

1. Marshall I. Goldman, *Soviet Foreign Aid* (New York: Praeger Publishers, 1967), pp. 3–4.

2. See various issues of VT SSSR.

3. Mendershausen, "Terms of Trade Between the Soviet Union and Smaller Communist Countries, 1955–57," *The Review of Economics and Statistics,* May, 1959; "Mutual Price Discrimination in Soviet Bloc Trade," *The Review of Economics and Statistics,* November, 1962.

4. Holzman, "Soviet Foreign Trade Pricing and the Question of Discrimi-

nation," *Review of Economics and Statistics,* May, 1962; "More on Soviet Bloc Trade Discrimination," *Soviet Studies,* July, 1965, p. 44.

5. E. Nukhovich, "Ekonomicheskoe sotrudnichestvo SSSR s osvobodiv-shimisia stranami i burzhuaznye kritiki," *Voprosy ekonomiki,* October, 1966, p. 83, 85, 86; N. Nolkov, "Struktura vzaimoi torgovli stran sev," *Vneshniaia torgovlia,* December, 1966, pp. 10–612.

6. *The Economist,* May 22, 1982, p. 60.

7. Bronislaw Sulimierski, "Some Problems and Perspectives of Poland's Economic Relations with the West," paper prepared for conference at the Russian Research Center, Harvard University, February, 1981, p. 2.

8. Sulimierski, p. 1.

9. *The International Herald Tribune,* August 24, 1981, p. 4.

10. *The New York Times,* September 28, 1981, p. D-7.

11. Sulimierski, p. 3.

12. *The New York Times,* December 3, 1981, p. 7.

13. *The International Herald Tribune,* August 4, 1981, p. 2.

14. RFE-RL, RL163 / 81, April 16, 1981, p. 15; *The New York Times,* September 9, 1981, p. 1.

15. *The Financial Times,* November 24, 1981, p. 3.

16. *The Wall Street Journal,* September 23, 1981, p. 45; *Newsweek,* November 9, 1981, p. 55.

17. *The New York Times,* November 11, 1981, p. D-3, December 15, 1981, p. A-20.

18. *Ibid.,* November 23, 1981, p. D-4; December 15, 1981, p. A-20.

19. *The New York Times,* February 1, 1982, p. A-7.

20. Jerzy Thieme, "Economic Impass of the Military Government in Poland," January 10, 1982, p. 9, mimeographed.

21. Tibor Erdos, "Overheatedness and Efficiency of Investment in Socialist Countries," paper prepared for Fifth Japan-U.S. Forum on International Issues, Tokyo, November 27, 1981, p. 8.

22. *Ibid.*

7.

1. William Scarborough, *A Collection of Chinese Proverbs* (Shanghai: American Presbyterian Mission Press, 1875), No. 2082; suggested by Y. T. Feng.

2. *Pravda,* June 17, 1981, pp. 1–2.

3. *Nar Khoz,* 1922–1972, pp. 216–217; *Nar Khoz,* 1975, p. 318; *Nar Khoz,* 1980, p. 202.

4. Bialer, p. 66.

Bibliography

Aleksandrov, A. P. "Rech' A. P. Aleksandrov." *Vestnik, Akademii Nauk SSSR,* 1981.

Amann, Ronald, Cooper, Julian and Davies, R. W., eds. *The Technological Level of Soviet Industry.* New Haven: Yale University Press, 1977.

Armand, E. *Nam i vnukam.* Moscow: Mysl', 1966.

Beard, Charles A. and Mary R. *The Rise of American Civilization.* New York: MacMillan, 1927.

Bergson, Abram. "Toward a New Growth." *Problems of Communism,* March–April, 1973.

————. "Soviet Economic Slowdown." *Problems of Communism,* September-October, 1980.

Berliner, Joseph. *The Innovative Decision in Soviet Industry.* Cambridge: Massachusetts Institute of Technology Press, 1976.

Bialer, Seweryn. *Stalin's Successors.* Cambridge: Cambridge University Press, 1980.

Birman, Igor. "Who is Stronger and Why?" *Crossroads,* Winter–Spring, 1981.

Bobrov, Emanuel. "Applied Computer Science in the USSR: A Personal Account," papers on Soviet Science and Technology. Cambridge: Russian Research Center, Harvard University, May, 1981.

Bogomolov, O. "Ekonomicheskie sviazi SSSR zarubezhnymi stranami." *Planovoe khoziaistvo,* October, 1980.

Brzezinski, Zbigniew. *The Permanent Purge.* Cambridge: Harvard University Press, 1956.

Central Intelligence Agency. *Economic Statistics.* Washington D.C., 1980.

————. *CPSU Central Committee and Central Auditing Commission: Members Elected at the 26th Party Congress.* Washington, D.C., 1981.

Chapman, Janet. *Real Wages in Soviet Russia Since 1928.* Cambridge: Harvard University Press, 1963.

Churchill, Winston. *The Hinge of Fate.* Boston: Houghton Mifflin, 1950.

Connor, Walter. *Socialism, Politics and Equality.* New York: Columbia University Press, 1979.

Davis, Christopher and Feshbach, Murray. *Rising Infant Mortality in the USSR in the 1970s.* Washington, D.C.: U.S. Department of Commerce Series 95, 1980.

Desai, Padma. "The Rate of Return on Foreign Capital Flow to the Soviet Economy." *Soviet Economy in a Time of Change,* compendium of papers submitted to the Joint Economic Committee of the United States (hereafter referred to as Joint Economic Committee, 1979). Washington, D.C.: United States Government Printing Office, 1979.

Diamond, Douglas and Davis, W. Lee. "Comparative Growth in Output and Productivity in the US and USSR Agriculture." Joint Economic Committee, 1979.

Dienes, Leslie. "The Soviet Union: An Energy Crunch Ahead?" *Problems of Communism,* September–October, 1977.

Dienes, Leslie and Shabad, Theodore. *The Soviet Energy System: Resource Use and Policies.* Washington, D.C.: V. H. Winstopn & Sons, 1979.

Erdos, Tibor. "Overheatedness and Efficiency of Investment in Socialist Countries," paper prepared for the Fifth Japan-U.S. Forum on International Issues, Tokyo, November 27, 1981.

Erlich, Alexander. *The Soviet Industrialization Debate: 1924–1928.* Cambridge: Harvard University Press, 1960.

Feshbach, Murray. "Population and Labor Force," paper prepared for Conference on Soviet Energy Toward the Year 2000. Airlie House, Virginia, October 24, 1980.

Fine, Daniel I. "Mineral Resource, Dependency Crisis: the Soviet Union and the United States." *The Resource War in 3D—Dependency, Diplomacy, Defense.* Pittsburgh: Worlds Affair Council of Pittsburgh.

Florinsky, Michael T. *Russia, History & Interpretation.* Vol. II. New York: MacMillan, 1955.

Gerschenkron, Alexander. *Economic Backwardness in Historical Perspective.* Cambridge: The Belknap Press of the Harvard University Press, 1962.

Goldman, Marshall I. "Economic Controversy in the Soviet Union." *Foreign Affairs,* April, 1963.

———. *Soviet Foreign Aid.* New York: Praeger, 1967.

———. *The Enigma of Soviet Petroleum: Half Empty or Half Full?* Boston: George Allen & Unwin, 1980.

———. "China Rethinks the Soviet Model." *International Security,* Fall, 1980.

Goodman, Seymour. "Computers and the Development of the Soviet Economy." Joint Economic Committee, 1979.

Goryunov, V. "Bourgeois Propaganda on Soviet Economic Relations with Developing Countries." *Foreign Trade,* January, 1968.

Grossman, Gregory. "The Second Economy of the USSR." *Problems of Communism,* September–October, 1977.

Hajda, Lubomyr. "Nationality and Age in Soviet Population Change." *Soviet Studies,* October, 1980.

Hanson, Philip. "USSR Gosplan and the Matching of Production with Demand." *Radio Liberty Dispatch,* June 23, 1981.

Hardt, John, and Tomlinson, Kate. *An Assessment of the Afghanistan Sanctions: Implications for Trade and Diplomacy in the 1980s,* Subcommittee of Europe and the Middle East of the Committee on Foreign Affairs, U.S. House of Representatives. Washington, D.C.: United States Government Printing Office, April, 1981.

Hare, Paul, Radice, Hugo, and Swain, Nigel, eds. *Hungary: A Decade of Economic Reform.* London: George Allen & Unwin, 1981.

Hayes, Robert H., and Abernathy, William J. "Managing Our Way to Economic Decline." *The Harvard Business Review,* July–August, 1980.

Holzman, Franklyn. *Soviet Taxation.* Cambridge: Harvard University Press, 1955.

———. "Soviet Foreign Trade Pricing and the Question of Discrimination." *Review of Economics and Statistics,* May, 1962.

———. "More on Soviet Bloc Trade Discrimination," *Soviet Studies.* July, 1965.

———. "Is There a Soviet-U.S. Military Spending Gap? *Challenge,* September–October, 1980.

Hunter, Holland. "Soviet Agricultural Potential and the Surplus-Extraction Issue, 1928–1949." Mimeographed, June 11, 1981.

Joint Economic Committee. *Soviet Economy in a New Perspective.* Washington, D.C.: United States Government Printing Office, 1976.

———. *Soviet Economy in a Time of Change.* Washington, D.C.: United States Government Printing Office, 1979.

Kaiser, Robert. *Russia The People and the Power.* New York: Atheneum, 1976.

Karcz, Jerzy. *The Economics of Communist Agriculture: Selected Papers.* Arthur W. Wright, ed. Bloomington, Indiana: International Development Institution, 1979.

Keenan, Edward, L. "Russian Political Culture," U.S. Department of State, Contract No. 1722-4201119. Cambridge: Harvard University Press, July, 1976.

Khachaturov, T. "Prirodnye resursy i planirovanie narodnogo khoziaistva." *Voprosy ekonomiki,* August, 1973.

———. "Ekonomicheskie problemy ekologii." *Voprosy Ekonomiki,* June, 1978.

Kiser, John. "Soviet Technology: The Perception Gap." *Mechanical Engineering,* April, 1979.

198   BIBLIOGRAPHY

Konnik, I. I. ''Proportsional'nosti' v narodnom khoziaistve i denezhnoe
obrashchenie. *Dengi i kredit*, December, 1976.
Klose, Kevin. *Hammer and Sickle*. New York: W. W. Norton, 1983.
Kuznetsov, Edward. ''The Status of Soviet Political Prisoners.'' *Crossroads*,
Winter–Spring, 1981.
Mackinder, Halford, J. ''The Geographical Pivot of History.'' *Geographical
Journal*, 1904.
————. *Democratic Ideals and Reality*. New York: Holt, 1919.
Martens, John. ''Quantifications of Western Exports to High Technology Prod-
ucts to Communist Countries,'' *East-West Trade Policy Staff Papers*. Inter-
national Trade Administration, Washington, D.C., January, 1981.
Meissner, Boris. ''The 26th Party Congress and Soviet Domestic Politics.''
Problems of Communism, May–June, 1981.
Menderhausen, Horst. ''Terms of Trade Between the Soviet Union and Smaller
Communist Countries, 1955–57.'' *The Review of Economics and Statistics*,
May, 1959.
————. ''Mutual Price Discrimination in Soviet Bloc Trade.'' *The Review of
Economics and Statistics*, November, 1962.
Michael, John C. ''The Interdependent Trade Union Movement in the Soviet
Union.'' *Radio Free Europe-Radio Liberty*, 1979.
Ministerstvo vneshnei torgovli SSR. *Vneshniaia torgovlia SSSR za 1918–1940
g.* Moscow: SSSR Vneshtorgizdat, 1960.
————. *Vneshniaia torgovlia SSSR za 1918–1966*. Moscow: SSSR Vneshtor-
gizdat, 1966.
Morton, Henry W. ''The Soviet Quest for Better Housing—Impossible Dream?''
Joint Economic Committee, 1979.
Nar Khoz. Tsentral'noe statisticheskoe upravlenie. Narodnoe khoziaistvo SSSR
za 1979. Moscow, 1980.
Neuburger, Egon. *Central Planning and its Legacies*. Santa Monica, Calif.:
The Rand Corporation, December, 1966.
Newhouse, John. *Cold Dawn. The Story of SALT*. New York: Holt, Reinhart,
and Winston, 1973.
Nolkov, N. ''Struktura vzaimoi torgovli stran sev.'' *Vneshniaia torgovlia*,
December, 1966.
Nukhovich, E. ''Ekonomicheskoe sotrudnichestvo SSSR s osvobodivshimsia
stranami i burzhuarznye kritiki.'' *Voprosy ekonomiki*, October, 1966.
Nurkse, R. *Problems of Capital Formation in Underdeveloped Countries*. New
York: Oxford University Press, 1953.
Office of Technology Assessment. *Technology and Soviet Energy Availability*.
Washington Office of Technology Assessment, 1981.
Orlov, I. A. ''Nekotorye voprosy povysheniia kachestva tovarov narodnogo
potrebleniia.'' *Voprosy ekonomiki*, May, 1964.

Poletaev, P. "Razvitie ekonomiki i ekologiia." *Planovoe khoziaistvo*, December, 1979.

Powell, David. *Alcohol Abuse in the Soviet Union*, forthcoming.

Pryor, Frederic L. *Communist Foreign Trade System*. Cambridge: Massachusetts Institute of Technology Press, 1963.

Rakovskii E. "Technicheskii progress i faktor vremeni." *Planovoe khoziaistvo*, July, 1965.

Rand, Robert. "Washington, Moscow and the 'Resource War'." *Radio Free Europe-Radio Liberty*, 1980.

Rosenstein-Rodan, Paul. "Problems of Industrialization of Eastern and Southeastern Europe." *Economic Journal*, June–September, 1943.

Rostow, Walter. *Stages of Economic Growth*. Cambridge: Cambridge University Press, 1960.

Savin, A. "Tsenoobrazovanie kak ekonomicheskii rychag povysheniia effektivnosti obshchestvennogo proizvodstva." *Planovoe khoziaistvo*, November, 1979.

Schoonover, David, M. "Soviet Agricultural Policies." The Joint Economic Committee, 1979.

Shabad, Theodore. "Raw Material Problems of the Soviet Aluminum Industry, The Soviet Economy in a New Perspective," U.S. Congress. Washington D.C.: United States Government Printing Office, October, 1976.

Smith, Hedrick. *The Russians*. New York: Ballantine Books, 1977.

Solzhenitsyn, Alexandr, I. *The Gulag Archepelago*. New York: Harper and Row, 1973.

Sowell, Thomas. *Race & Economics*. New York: David McKay Co., Inc., 1975.

Sulimierski, Bronislaw. "Some Problems and Perspectives of Poland's Economic Relations with the West," paper prepared for Conference at the Russian Research Center. Harvard University, February, 1981.

Sutton, Anthony, C. *Western Technology and Soviet Economic Development, 1917–1930*. Stanford: Hoover Institution Publications, 1968.

———. *Western Technology and Soviet Economic Development 1930–1945*. Stanford: Hoover Institution Press, 1971.

Thieme, Jerzy. "Economic Impass of the Military Government in Poland." Mimeographed, New York, January 10, 1982.

Tolstoy, Leo, *Anna Karenina*. New York: The New American Library, 1961.

Tsentral'noe statisticheskoe upravlenie. *Narodnoe khoziaistvo SSSR za 1979*. Moscow, 1980. (For other years referred to as Nar Khoz an appropriate year)

Tsvigun, S. "O proiskakh imperialisticheskikh razvedok." *Kommunist*, September 10, 1981.

Tucker, Robert C. "Swollen States, Spent Society: Stalin's Legacy to Brezhnev's Russia." *Foreign Affairs*, Winter, 1981–82.

Turgenev, Ivan. *Fathers and Sons*. Moscow, 1861.

United States Bureau of the Census. *Historical Statistics of the United States, Colonial Times to 1970*, Bicentennial Edition. Washington, D.C.: United States Government Printing Office, 1975.

————. *Statistical Abstract of the United States* (100th edition). Washington, D.C.: United States Government Printing Office, 1979.

United States Communications Agency. *Soviet Perceptions of the United States, Results of a Surrogate Interview Project*. Research memorandum, June 27, 1980.

Vasilevskii, V. "Ispol'zovanie maloi tekhniki v lichnom podsobnom khoziaistve." *Voprosy ekonomiki*, No. 5, 1980.

Vernon, Raymond. "The Fragile Foundations of East-West Trade." *Foreign Affairs*, Summer, 1979.

Volin, Lazar. *A Century of Russian Agriculture: From Alexander II to Khrushchev*. Cambridge: Harvard University Press, 1970.

Voronin, V. "Lichnye podsobnie khoziaistva i torgovlia." *Voprosy ekonomiki*, November 6, 1980.

Welihozkiy, Toli. "Automobiles and the Soviet Consumer." Joint Economic Committee, 1979.

Newspapers and Journals

Boston Globe.
Business Week.
Christian Science Monitor.
Current Digest of the Soviet Press.
Ekonomicheskaia gazeta.
Financial Times.
International Herald Tribune.
Izvestiia.
Lesnaya promyslennost'.
Literaturnaia gazeta.
Naselenie SSSR.
Nash sovremennik.

New York Times.
Newsweek.
Pravda.
Sotsialisticheskaia industriia.
Sovetskaia rossia.
Sovetskaia torgovlia.
Sovetskoe gosudarstvo i pravo.
Soviet Geography: Review and Translation.
Soviet News.
Trud.
Wall Street Journal.
Washington Post.

Index